Photo-Based
3D Graphics in C++

Photo-Based
3D Graphics in C++

Compositing, Warping, Morphing, and Other Digital Special Effects

TIM WITTENBURG

JOHN WILEY & SONS, INC.

New York • Chichester • Brisbane • Toronto • Singapore

Publisher: KATHERINE SCHOWALTER
Senior Editor: DIANE D. CERRA
Managing Editor: MICHELINE FREDERICK
Text Design & Composition: NORTH MARKET STREET GRAPHICS

Designations used by companies to distinguish their products are often claimed as trademarks. In all instances where John Wiley & Sons, Inc. is aware of a claim, the product names appear in initial capital or all capital letters. Readers, however, should contact the appropriate companies for more complete information regarding trademarks and registration.

This text is printed on acid-free paper.

This publication is designed to provide accurate and authoritative information in regard to the subject matter covered. It is sold with the understanding that the publisher is not engaged in rendering legal, accounting, or other professional service. If legal advice or other expert assistance is required, the services of a competent professional person should be sought.

Library of Congress Cataloging-in-Publication Data:

Wittenburg, Tim, 1955–
    Photo-based 3D graphics in C++ : compositing, warping, morphing, and other digital special effects / Tim Wittenburg.
        p.   cm.
    Includes bibliographical references.
    ISBN 0-471-04972-7 (acid-free paper)
    1. Computer graphics.   2. Image processing—Digital techniques.
3. Three-dimensional display systems.   4. C++ (Computer program language)   I. Title.
T385.W62   1995
006.6—dc20   95-3200
                                                CIP

Printed in the United States of America

10 9 8 7 6 5 4 3 2 1

To Jackie, a woman whose grace, strength, and peaceful character I will always treasure.

P R E F A C E

Digitized images are becoming increasingly available. Collections of digitized license-free true color photos are now widely available on CD-ROM. The cost of true color scanners and video cards continues to drop. Similarly, advances in new personal computer operating systems, such as Windows 95, make it easier than ever to develop software that can handle large, memory-intensive application areas such as photo-based 3D graphics. My goal was to present this technology in such a way as to be satisfying to the technical at heart while at the same time providing a sufficient software infrastructure to make it possible to experiment with the technology and create visual effects of your own.

This book covers the fascinating topic of photo-based 3D graphics at several interest levels. In developing the software toolkit needed to support the desired capabilities, I touch upon a cross-section of subject areas:

- From a purely technological perspective, several important algorithms are covered, such as the true perspective-inverse mapping-image warp, alpha-blending, photo-based animation, and 3D graphic transformations. These techniques offer a glimpse of how digitized images can be incorporated into a traditional 3D graphical rendering system. Chapter 10 covers the highly interesting subject of alpha-blending, otherwise known as image compositing. This relatively straightforward algorithm, when combined with other techniques, has a tremendous range of applications and we try to do it justice here.

- From an object-oriented perspective, an object-oriented analysis and design is performed starting with a set of requirements. The result of the design phase is a list of classes and objects that are subsequently implemented in C++.

- From a software engineering perspective, we set about developing a photo-based graphics application by following established practices such as first defining requirements, performing a high-level design, then a detailed design, and then implementation. The level of coverage in the object-oriented design area is rather informal, considering that the size of this project is smaller than the project size for which formal design methods are intended to apply.

- From a software developer's perspective, the ICT application developed in this book operates in both Windows 3.1 and the Windows 95 32-bit environments. We therefore navigate the set of issues associated with this task. The ICT software was first developed in Win16 and Win32s. A port to the 32-bit Windows 95 environment commenced as the betas became available from Microsoft. It is interesting to note that the 16-bit code works in Windows 95 without modification.

- For those interested in exploring the graphical side of the Windows API, namely the Graphical Device Interface (GDI), we cover and use such GDI-related topics as screen and memory device contexts, the remarkable BitBlt function, off-screen animation techniques, Windows pen objects, how to handle the Windows Paint message, and many others. You will see first-hand how these fundamental building blocks contribute to the ICT application's graphical user interface.

- For those interested in possibly porting this application to another environment, such as Unix: All of the core graphics and image processing functions (for example, scene list, warp, and blend) occur in memory and do not depend on operating system–specific resources. The only arguable exception is in the cutout creation process where I used the Windows API function `polygon` to create the mask image from a hand-traced boundary. I debated whether to use an alternate standalone process, such as Bresenham's polygon rendering algorithm. I opted for the Windows API function instead primarily because it was convenient and because the Bresenham algorithm is already extensively documented in the literature [FOLE90]. The GUI is another matter. You may notice that the OWL class libraries are used as a vehicle to bring Windows messages into the application and to handle what might be called baseline Windows application behavior. Once inside the application itself, straight Windows API functions are used where needed rather than comparable OWL member functions. This approach was adopted in order to increase portability between the Borland and other C++ compilers.

Finally, although a serious and lengthy effort has been made to provide bug free software, it is, of course, a possibility that the ICT application may contain bugs. If you do in fact find a bug I would greatly appreciate hearing from you. I also welcome your suggestions and/or general comments. My CompuServe ID is [70403, 3570]. Internet users can reach me at 70403.3570@compuserve.com.

ACKNOWLEDGMENTS

My appreciation goes to George Wolberg for helpful comments related to image warping; to my good friend Joseph Lee, who drew the illustrations, helped out with the code, and consistently offered insightful and intelligent commentary; to Mike Arachtingi for his programming experience and detailed knowledge of the Windows API; to all those at Wiley who worked on this project, particularly Diane Cerra for her encouragement and patience; Tammy Boyd for her efficient handling of the paperwork needed to get the Chicago and Windows 95 betas, Micheline Frederick for keeping the process moving, and to Shelley Flannery for her professional and thorough copyediting of the manuscript.

C O N T E N T S

I. FUNDAMENTALS

II. IMAGE COMPOSITING TOOLS

13. Putting it All Together: Scene Generation   247

III.   APPLICATIONS

14. Morphing and Other Applications   283

IV.   APPENDICES

Fundamentals

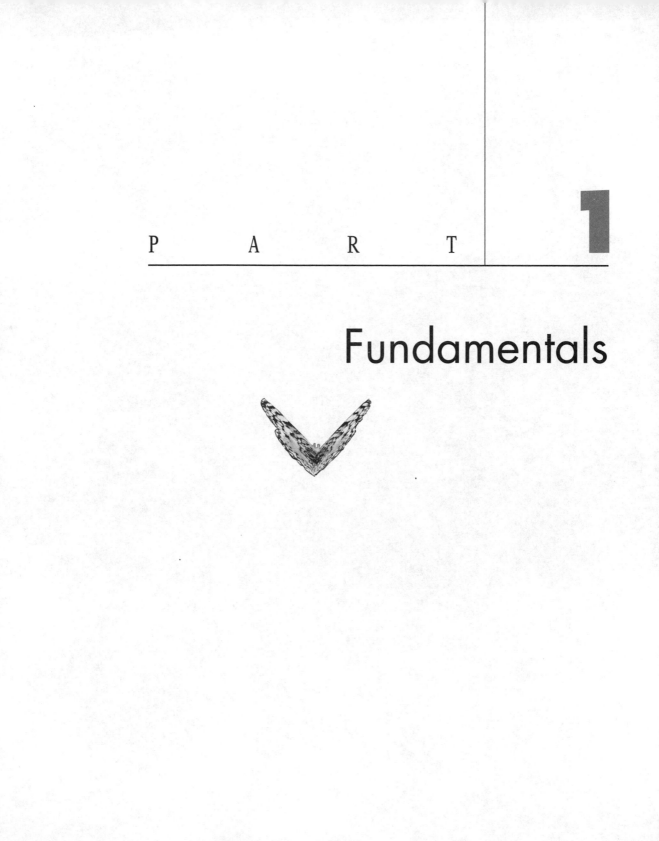

1

Introduction

1.1 What Are Photo-Based Graphics?

This book explores a number of techniques that combine traditional three-dimensional graphics technology with an amazing algorithm for manipulating digital photographs, called *alpha-blending*. The heading under which most of the techniques covered in this book can be grouped is *Digital Image Compositing*. Digital Image Compositing technology has been used for years by cinematic special effects firms to create realistic visual effects by cleverly combining several sources of imagery.

1.2 How This Book Is Organized

Part I of this book describes in detail the set of capabilities we wish to develop. With this description in hand the focus is then directed at creating a collection of fundamental services. Examples of such services are C++ class libraries that manipulate digitized photographs, three-dimensional shapes, and a 3D coordinate transformation service. In Part II our perspective shifts to that of tool maker. Having created an infrastructure of basic services in Part I, we now make use of the infrastructure to develop our most important functions: image warping, alpha-blending, and scene generation. In Part III our perspective shifts again to that of end-user/visual effects designer. Part III is an exploration of the types of visual effects that can be produced using the newly developed Image Compositing Toolkit (ICT).

1.3 Introducing ICT

During the course of this book we develop a standalone Windows 3.1– and Windows 95–compatible application called the Image Compositing Toolkit (ICT). The ICT is written in C++ and provides a set of fundamental capabilities that can be used to create unusual digital special effects and computer-generated scenes of photographic quality. The ICT includes tools for separating out the part of a photo that is of interest (called an *image cutout*) from its background. Next, a graphical preview tool is provided that enables you to set up a desired visual effect by interactively moving one or more cutouts to desired locations and orientations in a three-dimensional coordinate system. A texture mapping tool called an *image warper* is developed, which can rotate a color image in three dimensions as well as change its size. The powerful alpha-blending tool is developed. The blender (1) smoothly blends one image into another, (2) creates shadows, and (3) makes an image take on a translucent quality. Finally, a scene generator tool is provided that creates either a single image output, called a *scene,* or a sequence of images in which either the viewpoint moves or any of the cutouts in the scene can move.

1.4 Chapter Overview

In addition to describing aspects of this technology from a purely technical perspective, we develop a software toolkit with which the technology can be interactively investigated. These efforts are focused on the development of a process that has been modeled in Figure 1.1. This process model represents, at a high level, the set of capabilities developed in this book. In Chapter 2, the model shown in Figure 1.1 is expanded upon. A set of functional requirements are first created; an object-oriented analysis of the requirements is then performed. This analysis results in the definition of an object-oriented design consisting of an arrangement (architecture) of classes and functions that can be used together to satisfy the requirements. The high-level design is used as the basis for selecting the algorithms and tools that are then developed in subsequent chapters. By adopting this approach we demonstrate accepted software development practices, emulating informally the steps taken in larger development efforts. We round out Chapter 2 by developing a

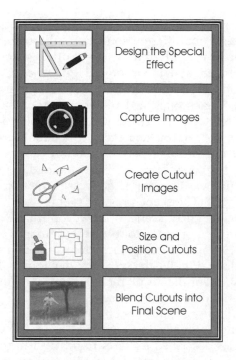

Figure 1.1 Photo-based visual effect creation process.

starter Windows application that contains all the elements of the GUI that will be used later in the program. Chapter 3 introduces a C++ **sceneList** class that manages a data structure called a *scene list,* which is a central resource containing information that describes the special effect to be produced. Chapter 4 describes the way in which color is implemented on the PC and discusses the technique used here to generate true color images. Chapter 5 describes a C++ **memImage** class that manages memory resident images. Member functions of this class provide access to popular .bmp format image files, and provide a number of other important image processing functions. Chapter 6 introduces the **tMatrix** class, which encapsulates all of the coordinate transformation functions used in this text. Chapter 7 completes Part I with a description of the C++ **shape3d** class, which manages three-dimensional shape objects (*n*-sided polygons). Part II focuses on the development of a set of photo-based graphics tools. These tools make use of the class libraries developed in Part I. Chapter 8 discusses an image cutout tool that removes objects of interest from an image file and saves these objects, called *cutouts,* in a separate image for later use. Chapter 9 describes a true perspective image warping algorithm and develops function **iWarp**, which applies a composite graphic transformation contained in a **tMatrix** object to a **memImage** object. Chapter 10 introduces a powerful algorithm known as *alpha-blending,* which is used to composite one or more images together in such a way that the human eye cannot discern that a composited image in fact is made up of images from different sources. Alpha-blending is used to smooth edges, create shadows, and for a variety of other special effects. The function **blend** is developed and incorporated into the ICT. Chapter 11 addresses the topic of hidden surface removal, a technique needed to properly render three-dimensional scenes. A depth sorting tool is developed and incorporated into ICT. Chapter 12 addresses the topic of photo-based animation and also introduces the **motionPath** class. A **motionPath** object represents an arbitrary three-dimensional path of motion that occurs within a specified length of time. The capability of ICT is expanded to include moving viewpoints and moving models. Chapter 13 addresses the two types of scene generation tools used in ICT. The scene preview tool is used to interactively position models in a special effect scene. A backdrop image can be used if desired to precisely locate and orient cutouts or other images as desired. The scene preview tool can also preview sequence effects by using a special off-screen animation technique. Finally, the scene render tool is described. The scene render tool warps and/or blends all models contained in the scene list object one by one until the desired special effect scene or sequence is complete. The scene render tool generates either 256 grayscale black-and-white images or true color images. Finally, in Chapter 14 (Part III) we apply all of the tools and technologies described in Parts I and II. A number of special effect scenes and sequences are generated, including an example of morphing. Also a number of techniques and tips are provided that will aid in the creation of more realistic and effective special effects. Appendix A provides ICT setup instructions. Appendix B is an ICT user guide. Appendix C contains notes on how to use the ICT software with the Visual C++ compiler. Appendix D is an index to all ICT software functions. Appendix E is a glossary. Appendix F is a list of references.

1.5 Assumptions

The ICT software supplied on the attached diskette was developed with the following assumptions in mind:

Floating point calculations are used instead of scaled fixed point integer calculations. The reasoning for this is primarily to take advantage of a trend in microprocessor chips, which is to have on-board floating point capability. This means that the 80x86 DX models will provide significantly better performance when operating ICT than a comparable 80x86 SX–based computer.

Because the ICT generates images in either true color (24-bit RGB) or in black and white (256 grayscale), best results are achieved by using what is called a high-color video card, which can display approximately 65 thousand colors simultaneously. The cost of these cards continues to drop. Presently, a high-color video card can be obtained for about a hundred dollars. Many personal computers are now equipped with a high-color card as part of a standard configuration.

Even though Windows 95 supports long filenames, DOS-style filenames have been used throughout to maintain compatibility with Windows 3.1.

Proficiency in the C programming language is assumed. As for C++, some of the major features of C++, particularly classes and objects, are covered in Part I. Readers not familiar with C++ may wish to pick up a good text on the subject to use as a supplement.

1.6 Setting up ICT

Appendix A contains ICT installation and setup instructions. The ICT C++ source code supplied on the accompanying diskette was developed using the Borland C++ 4.5 16- and 32-bit compilers. Appendix C describes how to use this software with the Microsoft Visual C++ 2.0 compiler.

1.7 ICT Naming Conventions

Variable and function names used in ICT conform to the following conventions. Underscores are avoided. Lowercase letters are used except in the case of compound words. In the case of compound words, the first letter of each word contained in the compound word is capitalized, but the first letter of the first word in a compound word is always lowercase.

Hungarian Notation

Hungarian notation, the practice of prefixing variable names with letters indicating the type of item stored within, are used only where necessary. If you are not familiar with this term, Table 1.1 provides several examples of hungarian notion.

Table 1.1   Hungarian Notation Examples

Prefix	Usage	Example
h	handle	hDC
sz	null-terminated string	szName
n	number	nModels

An object-oriented notation is used more prevalently in ICT to name C++ objects. Variables are prefixed with English articles such as *the* or *a* to indicate an instance of a class. Examples of this notation are: **aModelShape** or **theViewMatrix**. In this notational style, the name of the variable is carefully selected so as to provide an indication of the data type of the contents. One of the overall goals was to keep the readability of the code as high as possible. This task was particularly difficult in certain functions that interface to the Windows API functions, Borland or Visual C++ class libraries, and ICT class libraries and that therefore exhibit a plurality of standard naming conventions.

2

Designing and Building a Windows Application with Class

2.1 *Defining the Requirements*

From the field of software engineering we know that the process of developing a new software application begins by making a list of all of the functions and capabilities we wish the application to possess when it is complete. In traditional software engineering terms, this step is called defining the requirements of the application to be developed. This idea appeals to common sense; define the objective before setting out to achieve it. Once the requirements have been defined, the next step is to analyze the requirements. This step can involve identification of risk areas and exploration of alternate approaches. Approaches are selected from alternatives that will satisfy the requirements and are appropriate to the intended scope of the effort. Many times compromises are involved. The analysis phase leads quickly into a high-level design phase. Since C++

is an object-oriented development language, we use an object-oriented approach to design based on the Booch method [BOOC91]. Our design process consists of analyzing the requirements, identifying classes, and determining an arrangement (also called an architecture) of classes and functions that can be used together to satisfy the requirements and objectives outlined in the process model summary shown in Figure 1.1 in Chapter 1. Much has been written on the subject of object-oriented analysis and design. Since we proceed rather quickly through this step, those interested in more details are referred to [BOOC91] and [COAD90]. Applying these ideas to our task at hand, the following steps are taken in this chapter:

1. The functional requirements for the Image Compositing Toolkit (ICT) application are described.

2. An object-oriented analysis of the requirements is performed and a high-level design is produced consisting of an arrangement of classes and functions that interact to satisfy the requirements listed in step 1.

3. The design produced in step 2 is used as a basis for designing the major components of a Graphical User Interface (GUI) for the ICT application.

4. An ICT starter application is created using a software development tool (in this case the Borland C++ 4.5 code generator). The ICT menus and dialog box designs are then added to the starter application.

2.2   *Definition of Object-Oriented Terms*

Several useful object-oriented ideas and terms are defined here:

Object

Objects often arise from the major concepts or ideas expressed in the requirements statements described in section 2.1. Booch refers to the *Gestalts* of the problem domain as being potential sources of object definition [BOOC91]. Candidate objects are often associated with the nouns that appear in sentences describing the requirements. An object is often thought of as having a perspective. An object's associated functions can usually be delineated by taking its point of view and articulating its role in the context of the environment in which it operates.

Class

A class is a generalization that describes the set of properties and methods (functions) common to a set of like objects. In C++, the properties of a class are called *data members* and the methods are called *member functions* of the class.

Inheritance

"Inheritance is a relationship among classes, wherein one class shares the structure or behavior defined in one (single inheritance) or more (multiple inheritance) other classes. Inheritance defines a 'kind of' hierarchy among classes in which a subclass inherits from one or more superclasses; a subclass typically augments or redefines the existing structure and behavior of its superclasses" [COAD90].

Abstraction

We use abstractions every day. If we didn't we would go insane. Abstractions are a kind of shorthand that removes the complexity of the everyday world. Consider the last time you rode in a car. While moving along, did you think about what the engine, transmission, and drive train were doing as you were propelled along the road? If you are like me, definitely not! Unless you are a mechanic, the car is more or less an abstraction. It is simply a gadget I use to cruise from point A to point B.

Shaw defines an abstraction as "a simplified description or specification of a system that emphasizes some of the system's details or properties while suppressing others. A good abstraction is one that emphasizes details that are significant to the reader or user and suppresses details that are, at least for the moment, immaterial or diversionary" [SHAW84]. Some abstractions used in this text are the terms: *warp, blend,* and *scene generation*. Even though we do "get under the hood" and explore each of these tools in great detail when we switch hats in Chapter 14 and try our hand at being a special effect designer, we will tend to think of the warp, blend, and scene generation tools as abstractions.

Encapsulation

If some or all of the complexity of performing a certain function is hidden from the user, the complexity is said to have been *encapsulated*. As an example, the **sceneList** class developed in Chapter 3 encapsulates the complexity of managing a doubly linked list. The user of the **sceneList** public member functions can access the functionality the linked list provides without ever dealing with the details of managing the linked list. Here is a more formal definition of encapsulation: Encapsulation (also called Information Hiding) is a principle, used when developing an overall program structure, that each component of a program should encapsulate or hide a single design decision. The interface to each module is defined in such a way as to reveal as little as possible about its inner workings [BOOC91], [COAD90].

2.3 ICT Major Concepts and Requirements

Here is a list of concepts and desired capabilities we wish to implement in the ICT application.

The Scene

The output of the ICT is a digital image, called a *scene,* that is produced by a process of drawing or rendering a set of graphical *models* that are viewed from a known observer location called a *viewpoint.* We will need a way to describe which models should be contained in a given scene and what the viewpoint is for a given scene. The description for each scene can be captured in a data structure that stores a list of models.

Models

Each scene produced by the ICT contains a set of graphical models that represent real-world objects. A scene can contain any number of models. There are two types of models: (1) photo-based, consisting of a single-digitized photograph called an *image,* and (2) shape-based, consisting of a set of connected line segments. Each model has a name that can be referred to later during the process of defining of a scene's contents. Each model has a three-dimensional location and orientation. An individual model can be used repeatedly in the same scene or in many scenes.

The Image

Digitized photographs, or images, are stored in many file formats. In order to reduce complexity, the ICT accepts only Windows bitmap (.BMP) files. The ICT needs utilities for reading and writing Windows bitmap files.

The Sequence

An animation or *sequence* is a list of scenes. A sequence can be created in which either the viewpoint moves and/or any of the models in the scene can move.

Perspective Engine

The perspective engine contains the mathematics required to manipulate model coordinates in a three-dimensional world. The perspective engine must support any combination of three-dimensional motions.

Scene Preview

We want to preview effects that are either a single scene or a sequence. When previewing a scene, the preview mode enables each model to be interactively moved about in the scene. The preview mode also enables the scene's viewpoint to be interactively changed. When previewing a sequence, each scene in the sequence is displayed in immediate succession. Whether previewing a single scene or a sequence, the preview mode will display the name and boundary of each model in the scene.

Scene Generation

The scene generator produces the output image or images needed for the desired visual effect. The scene generator ensures that each output scene is produced in such a way that all model surfaces are properly occluded regardless of observer viewpoint. The scene generator needs to support the concept of a *backdrop image*. A backdrop image is one that is simply copied into the output image before any other model is processed.

Color

We want the software to produce either black-and-white or true color effects.

Scene and Sequence Definition

We need a process of defining in a permanent way a list of models and their three-dimensional locations and orientations. The scene generator uses this definition to create the visual effect we desire. The effect definition must handle the possibility that a model may be moving or that the viewpoint may be moving. The effect definition can then be recalled and modified at any time.

Cutouts

We want to be able to operate on a digital image in such a way as to separate a subject of interest from its surroundings. The portion of the image consisting only of the subject will be called a *cutout*. We need to be able to save the cutout image so that it can be later used as part of a model or scene definition.

Warping

We want to demonstrate a photo-based graphics technique that permits a digitized black-and-white or color photograph to be rotated, translated, and/or sized to any desired three-dimensional orientation and location.

Blending

We wish to demonstrate the ability to combine multiple images together so that the edges of overlapping images appear to combine smoothly together.

One aspect of this technique is that it can be used to make individual images or cutouts appear translucent. We wish to also show how the blending and warping techniques can be used together to create realistic looking three-dimensional shadows from any cutout image.

Morphing

We wish to demonstrate a technique called *morphing*, in which one image appears to transform itself into another image. A very simple example of this technique would be a sequence of images in which an apple turns into an orange.

2.4 Object-Oriented Design — From Requirements to Objects

The design step usually occurs after the requirements have been validated and analyzed, and the perceived level of effort has been aligned with the expectation of the project sponsors. We refer to the result of this process as the *refined requirements* list. Traditional design begins by further analyzing the refined requirements in order to identify functional dependencies. Object-oriented design in the Booch method begins by identifying classes and objects from among the refined requirements statements. As our definition of the term *object* in section 2.2 indicates, a good place to begin this process is to look at the nouns in the requirements statements. By grouping similar nouns together and by noticing recurring patterns in the requirements, candidate objects can be identified. Classes can then be arrived at by generalizing like object types into a common definition. Member functions associated with each class can be identified by looking at the verbs associated with each of the nouns that gave rise to a particular object of class definition. There is, of course, much more to the process of object-oriented design. Since we proceed directly to an application of the design process, those interested in more details are referred to [BOOC91] and [COAD90].

If ICT were being developed in a project setting, we would want to document the arrangement of classes identified during the design phase by using an appropriate object-oriented CASE tool. For our purposes, however, a diagram of the ICT class hierarchy (Figure 2.1) and the accompanying discussion in this Chapter will suffice.

Applying the class and object identification process described earlier to the list of concepts and requirements listed in section 2.3 (we assume the requirements list has already been refined), the following classes have been identified (Table 2.1).

By comparing this list of classes with the list of requirements, several major functions appear to be missing. For example, functions such as **warp**

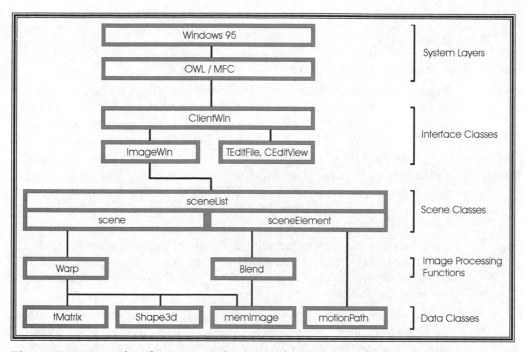

Figure 2.1   Hierarchy of major ICT classes and functions.

and **blend** do not appear in our candidate list of classes. It turns out to be appropriate to implement these functions independent of the class hierarchy since they each can be applied to sets of **memImage** objects. We will deal with these types of considerations in more detail in Chapter 9. Figure 2.1 illustrates the class and function hierarchy resulting from the high level design.

2.5   Detailed Design—The Graphical User Interface

From the requirements, it appears desirable to be able to view multiple text files and image files at the same time. The Windows Multi-Document Interface (MDI) provides this capability. We therefore decide to include the MDI as part of the ICT GUI. The other major elements of the GUI include menu items and dialog boxes. Menus provide the highest level of access to the capabilities and functions mentioned in the requirements listed in section 2.3. The ICT menus are now described.

Menu Design

Table 2.2 shows the Windows menus for the ICT application. The notation used here for menu selections is: **Menu|Menu Item**. For example, the action

Table 2.1 ICT Classes

Class	Description
imageWindow	A scrollable image window class.
memImage	A memory resident image class. These objects hold a rectangular area of picture elements (pixels) in memory that can be accessed either in random order or one row at a time. An instance of the `memImage` class can be created directly from a Windows bitmap image file. A `memImage` object can also be saved as a Windows bitmap image file.
motionPath	A class whose instance describes a three-dimensional path of motion in the Cartesian coordinate system used by ICT. This path of motion is described in a series of steps, each of which occurs within a specified number of frames in a sequence.
renderObject	A `renderObject` object encapsulates details of drawing transformed `shape3d` objects on a specific display device. These objects are used primarily to create the display generated during the scene and sequence preview operations.
sceneList	A class whose instance holds a list of models that can be previewed or rendered to produce either a single-image visual effect or a sequence.
shape3d	Instances of this class contain three-dimensional boundaries of the models used to create a scene. A `shape3d` object's vertices can be transformed by `tMatrix` objects.
tMatrix	Instances of this class perform three-dimensional coordinate transformations. Composite graphic transformations are supported as well as related matrix operations such as multiplication, transposition, and inversion.

of selecting the `Warp Image` menu item from the `Tools` menu is denoted: `Tools|Warp Image...`. The ellipsis after the menu item indicates that the act of making the selection produces a dialog box that requests additional information prior to performing the requested action.

Two additional menus appearing on the right side of the menu bar are not shown in Table 2.2: the `Windows` menu, which contains several menu items for cascading, tiling, arranging, and closing MDI child windows; and the `Help` menu, which contains an `About` menu item.

The File Menu

The File menu contains two major capabilities: (1) The selection `File|Open Scene File...` opens any text file into a text editing window. This option can be used to examine the contents of a shape file, motion path file, or the

Table 2.2 ICT Menus and Menu Items

File	*Edit*	*Search*	*Tools*	*Preview*	*Render*
New Scene	Undo	Find...	Create a Scene List...	Scene	Scene
Open Scene...	Cut	Replace...	Create Cutout	Sequence	Sequence
Close Scene	Copy	Next	Create Alpha Image...		Depth Sorting
Save Scene...	Paste		Warp Image...		
Save Scene As...	Clear		System Information		
Open Image...	Delete				
Exit					

ICT log file (ict.log). (2) The **File|Open Image...** menu item opens a .bmp image for display. Cutout images can also be prepared from images opened here, as described in Chapter 8.

The Edit Menu

The text editing options provided by this menu enable a previously opened and selected text file (such as a scene file or motion path file) to be edited.

The Search Menu

The search menu has a find and replace capability that is applied to a previously opened and selected text window.

The Tools Menu

The **Tools** menu contains a tool for opening and creating a scene list object, creating a cutout image from an image that has been previously opened, creating an alpha image, warping a test image, and obtaining a list of selected graphic capabilities of your computer system.

The Preview Menu

The **Scene** or **Sequence** menu items under this menu are activated only after a scene list has been created with the **Tools|Create a Scene List...** menu item. All models contained in the sceneList object are drawn in preview mode. Each model is represented by its boundary outline. The boundary is traced out to provide an accurate forecast of an object's appearance in the final rendered effect. The location and orientation of any model (as well as the viewpoint) can be interactively adjusted during scene preview. When scene preview is complete, the modified model locations and orientations can be saved in a new scene file.

The Render Menu

Once the contents of a scene file have been interactively previewed and adjusted, the scene is ready to be created. A scene must be previewed before it can be rendered. The rendering process follows the instructions located in the `sceneList` object and warps and/or blends each photo-based model into an output image (this image is referred to as a scene). Models can be optionally depth sorted prior to rendering by checking or unchecking the `Depth Sorting` menu item. If the depth sorting option is not checked, models are rendered in the order in which they occur in the scene file.

Dialog Box Design

In a traditional project effort, the dialog boxes (or screens) would also be designed in a manner similar to that used for the menu items before proceeding to development. In the interest of saving time, however, we proceed directly to development. The design and operation of the dialog boxes are described in section 2.9.

2.6   *Borland C++ 4.5 Application Development*

We are now ready to begin development of the ICT application. The Borland C++ 4.5 Interactive Development Environment (IDE) and Resource Workshop are used to create the ICT menus and dialog boxes. A similar process can be followed using the Visual C++ compiler. Appendix C contains more details.

We first need to generate a C++ application that can operate properly in the Windows environment. The process of developing a C++ Windows application of any complexity from scratch can be challenging and time consuming. Since we wish to remain focused on the subject of photo-based graphics, we need a fairly direct route to obtaining this C++ Windows "starter" application. Fortunately, both Borland and Visual C++ development environments contain tools that are able to generate such a Windows starter application for us. Therefore, our approach to developing the ICT application will be to first generate the Windows starter application using the available C++ development tools. The necessary menu items and dialog boxes will then be added to the starter application. Each of these steps will be covered in this chapter. The resulting starter application will feature all the GUI elements we have designed so far. The specific photo-based graphics tools and functions that are executed in response to various menu selections are added in subsequent chapters. This approach enables us to deal with a majority of the Windows-specific implementation issues in this chapter, thereby allowing us to focus more completely in later chapters on the platform-independent photo-based graphics techniques themselves.

The code generators in either the Borland C++ or Visual C++ development environment will actually create most of the Windows-specific application source code for us. We use the following steps to create the ICT starter application:

1. Generate the Windows application source code using the code generator supplied with either Borland or Visual C++ development environments.

2. Create the ICT menu resources.

3. Create the ICT dialog box resources.

In the last section of this chapter we show how a user's interaction with the newly created ICT starter application (for example, a menu item selection or button click) causes one or more Windows messages to be produced. Each Windows message passes through the starter application and is mapped to a specific function in the ICT application. These functions are called *response functions* because they respond to an incoming windows message. The response functions are defined in the ICT starter application, but are essentially empty. Later, the specialized photo-based graphics tools and functions will be added to these response functions.

2.7 *Creating the ICT Starter Application*

The Borland Application Expert and Resource Editor are used to create C++ source code and resources for the ICT starter application. The initial source code for the ICT starter application is generated by first opening the Borland C++ application and selecting the **Project|New Project...** menu item and entering the name of a new project file. We used the name ict.ide. After being returned to the main menu, select the **Project|App Expert** menu item. The screen shown in Figure 2.2 is displayed. Each of the topics listed under the topics section (on the left side of Figure 2.2) can be expanded by clicking on the "plus" (+) symbols. The application name is specified in the **Application|Basic Options** screen; the name for the main window class and corresponding source code filename is specified under the **Main Window|Basic Options** screen. Similarly, names for the MDI client window source code file and child window source code file must be supplied under the **MDI Child/View|Basic Options** screen. Finally, the Multi-Document Interface and Status line check boxes were checked as shown on the right-hand side of Figure 2.2.

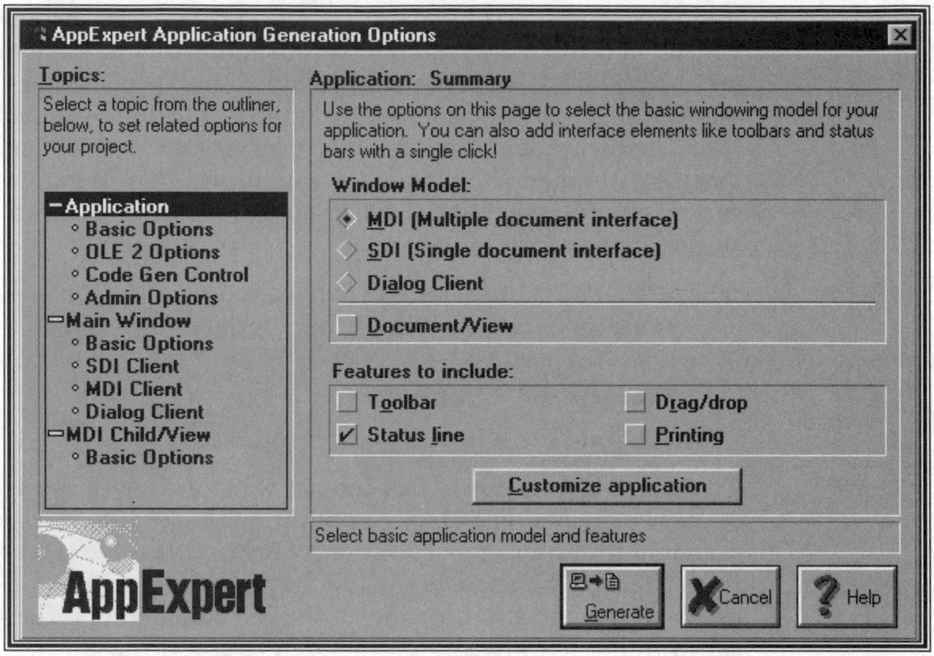

Figure 2.2 AppExpert options.

Now the magical moment arrives: The source code is generated by pressing the **Generate** button located on the bottom of the screen illustrated in Figure 2.2. At this point, several files are added to the project. These files can be viewed by selecting the **Project** menu item from the Borland C++ **View** menu. There are two important files we should mention: ClientWn.cpp contains the response function source code for processing ICT menu item selections. ChildWn.cpp contains source code for the editable text windows that can be opened by selecting the ICT **File|Open Scene File...** menu item.

Several additions are now made to the original source code generated by the C++ compiler. The first major addition is a scrollable image window class called **imageWindow**, which has been implemented as an MDI child window. The source code for this class is found in the file imageWn.cpp. We do not describe the details of this particular class since most of the capability is provided using Object Windows Library (OWL) functions.

2.8 Creating Menus

We begin creating menu resources by opening the Borland C++ compiler and opening the starter application (ict.ide) using the **Project|Open Proj**-

ect menu item. Now we open the Resource Manager by selecting the **Tools|Resource Manager** menu item. The resource workshop screen appears. We use the **Project|Open** menu item to open the file ictapp.rc. A screen similar to that shown in Figure 2.3 appears. We actually want to edit the menu resource created by the code generator in the previous step.

We scroll down to the MENU topic located on the left side of the screen illustrated in Figure 2.3 and double click the entry labeled: MDI_MENU(100). The menu editor screen now appears as shown in Figure 2.4. The procedure is to select the menu or menu item on the right side of the screen as a starting point. To obtain a new menu item, select an existing menu item and press the **insert** key. The new menu item appears in the tool menu that appears at the lower right-hand of the screen. The name **Item** has been supplied as a default; you may change the name as needed. The horizontal lines between menu items are called *separators;* a menu separator can be added by selecting **Menu|New Separator**. We continue adding menu items and menus in this manner until all of the menus shown in Table 2.2 have been created. Now let's take a closer look at one of the menu items. Select the menu item **Create Alpha Image...**; the screen shown in Figure 2.4 should appear.

This screen shows the menu item text on the upper-left portion of the screen. Immediately below, located in a text box labeled Item Help, is the message box text that will appear when the menu item is selected. Below that is another text box labeled Item ID. The constant named in this text box is

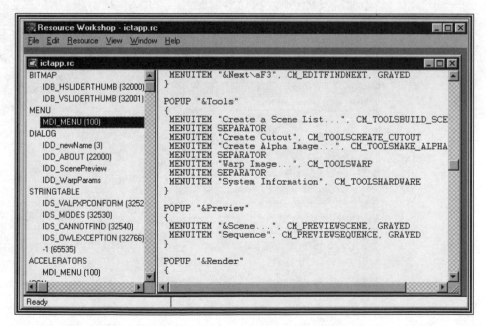

Figure 2.3 Resource workshop: resource selection.

the resource ID. The resource ID is a link between the action of selecting this menu item and the corresponding message that is received by the ICT application. These resource ID definitions are saved in the ictapp.rh file. Figure 2.5 illustrates the relationship between the resource file, the resource header file, and C++ source files that make reference to the resource IDs as needed.

Upon selecting **File|Exit**, the resource workshop presents a dialog box asking if you wish to save the changes; select **Yes**. The ICT menus are saved in the file ict.rc. At this point you should be able to rebuild the ICT starter application and verify that the new menus are present.

2.9   *Creating Dialog Boxes*

We use the resource editor now to create dialog boxes for the interactive warping tool and the scene preview tool. We will describe this process here for the image warping tool dialog box. A similar process is used to create the scene preview dialog box. The dialog box we wish to create is shown in Figure 2.6.

We open the resource editor and again open the ictapp.rc file. The screen illustrated in Figure 2.3 appears. Now select the resource labeled

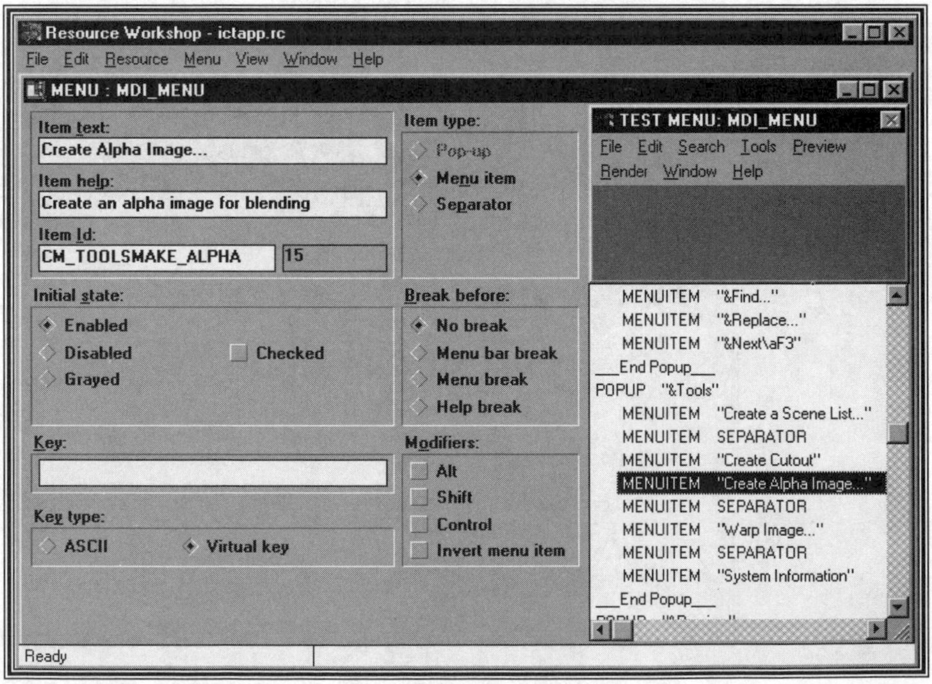

Figure 2.4   Resource workshop: menu creation.

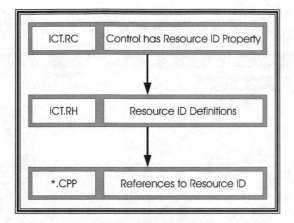

ICT.RC | Control has Resource ID Property

ICT.RH | Resource ID Definitions

*.CPP | References to Resource ID

Figure 2.5 Resource ID relationships.

DIALOG from the list box on the left side of the screen. Now select the **Resource|New** menu item. The dialog editor now appears, similar to that shown in Figure 2.6. The dialog box editor tools appear on the right side of the screen. Dialog box controls are added to the empty dialog box by selecting them from the button bars on the right side of the screen and dropping them onto the dialog box on the left side of the screen. (For more information see the Borland on-line documentation.) Figure 2.6 shows the completed warp tool dialog box on the left side of the screen as it appears in the dialog box editor. Now let's look at a text box resource ID. Select the text box labeled X Axis:. The screen shown in Figure 2.7 appears. In the text box marked **Control ID** is the resource ID for the X Axis rotation text box. The connection between this resource ID and a C++ source file that references this control follows the same pattern as that shown for the menu items in Figure 2.5.

2.10 *Running the ICT Starter Application*

The completed source code for the ICT starter application including the **imageWindow** class software, menu items, and dialog boxes is located in the x:\ict\starter directory. Try running the application by opening the ict.ide project file in this directory and pressing the lightning bolt button on the Borland tool bar to compile and execute the application. When the build is complete, the ICT MDI client window appears in a maximized state. Notice that the menus and menu items defined in Table 2.1 appear. Notice also that text files can be opened and edited using the **File|Open Scene File...** menu item. Expressions can be searched for and replaced using the **Find** Menu and its menu items. Windows Bitmap images can be displayed using

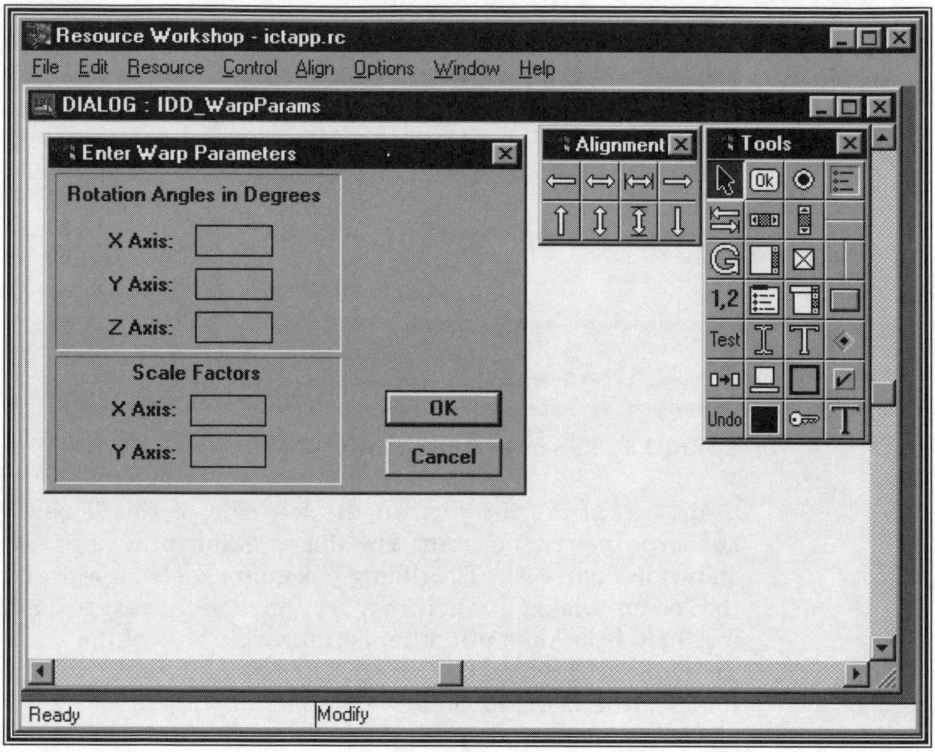

Figure 2.6 Resource workshop: dialog box creation.

the **File|Open Image...** menu item. This option can be tested now by displaying the ICT test image ericglas.bmp, which is located in the x:\ict\gallery directory. Figure 2.8 is a sample screen showing the ICT client (also called the MDI parent) window after opening two images and a scene file. Figure 2.8 is also an example of the MDI interface in action.

The **About...** dialog box, created by the code generator, can be selected and displayed as well. Now try selecting **Preview|Scene** or **Preview|Sequence** menu items. Both of these menu selections display a "To be Installed" message box. Let's explore what is happening here in more detail. If you are familiar with Windows messaging you may wish to skip to the next section.

2.11 Windows Messages

The action of selecting an ICT menu item causes the windows operating system to send a Windows message to the ICT starter application. A device

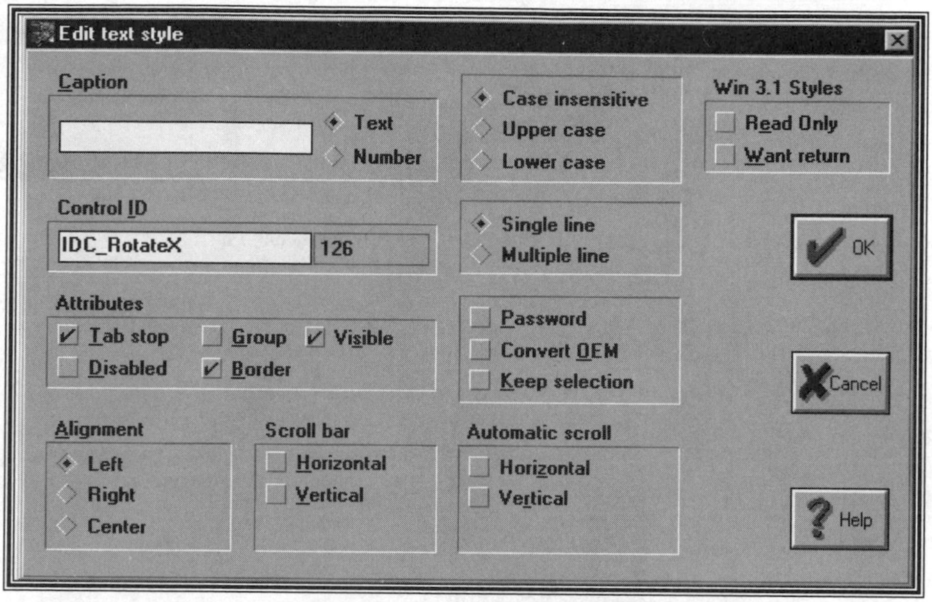

Figure 2.7 Resource workshop: resource ID definition.

called a *response table* in Borland source code, and alternately a *message map* in Visual C++ source code, is used to route the Windows message to an appropriate response function within the application. All we need to do is fill in the response table with event names and the appropriate functions to call. What could be simpler! The starter application we have developed so far contains the graphical user interface and all related response functions needed to support the ICT as designed. Now let's look at the response table in more detail.

How OWL Handles Windows Messages

The response table transfers messages passed in from Windows to our application. Implemented as a set of C++ macros, the response table indicates which function in our application is to be called when a particular Windows message is received. The response table for the ICT starter application is described in this section. A response table must first be declared before it is defined. The clientWn.h file contains the following statement:

```
DECLARE_RESPONSE_TABLE(ictMDIClient);
```

This macro call effectively declares that a response table for the **ictMDI-Client** window class exists. The clientWn.cpp file contains the following code fragment:

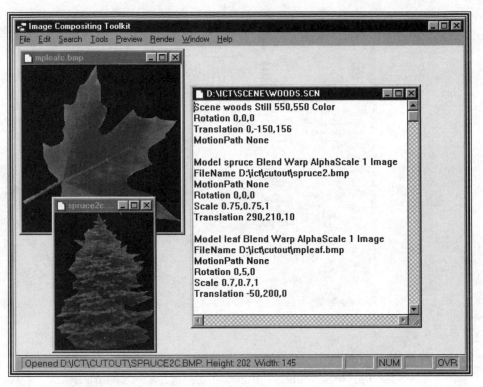

Figure 2.8 The ICT multi-document interface.

```
DEFINE_RESPONSE_TABLE1(ictMDIClient, TMDIClient)
EV_COMMAND(CM_MDIFILEOPEN, evFileOpen),
EV_COMMAND(CM_FILEOPEN_IMAGE, evOpenImage),
EV_COMMAND(CM_TOOLSBUILD_SCENE_LIST, evBuildSceneList),
EV_COMMAND(CM_TOOLSCREATE_CUTOUT, evCreateCutout),
EV_COMMAND(CM_TOOLSHARDWARE, evHardware),
EV_COMMAND(CM_TOOLSMAKE_ALPHA, evMakeAlpha),
EV_COMMAND(CM_TOOLSWARP, evWarpParams),
EV_COMMAND(CM_PREVIEWSCENE, evPreviewScene),
EV_COMMAND(CM_PREVIEWSEQUENCE, evPreviewSequence),
EV_COMMAND(CM_RENDERSCENE, evRenderScene),
EV_COMMAND(CM_RENDERSEQUENCE, evRenderSequence),
EV_COMMAND(CM_RENDERDEPTH_SORTING, evDepthSorting),
EV_COMMAND_ENABLE(CM_TOOLSCREATE_CUTOUT, ceCreateCutout),
EV_COMMAND_ENABLE(CM_PREVIEWSCENE, cePreviewScene),
EV_COMMAND_ENABLE(CM_PREVIEWSEQUENCE, cePreviewSequence),
EV_COMMAND_ENABLE(CM_RENDERSCENE, ceRenderScene),
EV_COMMAND_ENABLE(CM_RENDERSEQUENCE, ceRenderSequence),
EV_COMMAND_ENABLE(CM_RENDERDEPTH_SORTING, ceDepthSorting),
END_RESPONSE_TABLE;
```

The first statement in the response table definition:

```
DEFINE_RESPONSE_TABLE1(ictMDIClient, TMDIClient)
```

indicates the beginning of the response table and that the class **IctMDI-Client** associated with this response table is a descendant of the Borland OWL class **TMDIClient**, which, if you didn't know it, is a descendant of the base class **TWindow**. Knowledge of a class's location in a class hierarchy is an important part of understanding the behavior and the information available to us. We know that the ICT **IctMDIClient** class inherits all of the public and protected data members as well as the member functions of its parents in the class hierarchy. A specific example of what this means is that we now know that an **IctMDIClient** window has a handle already defined, called **HWindow**. We know this is true because the base class **TWindow** has such a data member. Making the most efficient use of classes derived from either Borland's OWL or Microsoft's MFC depends on the development of a working knowledge of what data members and functions are automatically inherited from the parent classes.

The second statement in the response table declaration is an entry that maps a GUI event to a function in our application. This entry contains three parts:

```
EV_COMMAND(CM_MDIFILENEW, evFileNew),
```

EV_COMMAND is an OWL macro that is called in response to a menu item selection event. **CM_MDIFILENEW** is the Resource ID created in the Resource Workshop when we first created the menus and menu items. As indicated earlier, these constants and their definitions appear in the header file ict.rh, which is maintained automatically by the resource workshop. Finally, **evFileNew** is the name of the function called in response to the ICT application's receipt of a message from Windows that the **File|New** menu item has been selected. Looking now at the remaining entries in the response table example, it becomes clear that there is an entry in the response table for each menu item selection. That is, each menu item selection event will cause a particular function to be called in response.

We notice a number of additional entries in the response table of which the following is an example:

```
EV_COMMAND_ENABLE(CM_TOOLSCREATE_CUTOUT, ceCreateCutout),
```

Entries beginning with the macro **EV_COMMAND_ENABLE** specify a function to be called that determines whether the menu item is to be enabled or disabled. More information about these types of response table entries can be found by looking up OWL class **TCommandEnabler** in the OWL Reference Manual. In this case, we indicate that we will provide a function **ceCreate-**

Cutout that will be called when the menu corresponding to the **Tools|Create Cutout** (**CM_TOOLSCREATE_CUTOUT**) menu item is selected. Notice that this function is called when the appropriate menu is selected, not the menu item. A moment of reflection causes us to realize that the proper time to determine the appearance of each menu item occurs *after* the menu has been selected and *before* all the menu items in the selected menu are displayed on the screen. It is at this moment that the function **ceCreateCutout** is called. The response table definition is concluded by the following statement:

```
END_RESPONSE_TABLE;
```

It should now be apparent that the response table will need our attention in any situation where specific Windows events, such as clicking on a control or selecting a menu item, need to be related to corresponding functions in our application. In these situations we will need to add entries to an appropriate response table. Response tables can be associated with any class derived from the **TWindow** base class. In Chapter 8 we will add entries to the **imageWindow** class response table so that we can use mouse events to trace an outline around the portion of an image we want to include later in a visual effects scene.

2.12   *The Process Log*

The graphical user interface of most Windows applications is based on the assumption that the program will respond immediately to any user-initiated event. Most of the time the ICT GUI is interactive in this sense. However, there are cases, for example, when a scene is being rendered, where the computer's response may not be immediate. When a scene is rendered by selecting the **Render|Scene** menu item, the computer may not respond with the completed scene until many minutes have passed, particularly if color images are being produced. Because the process of rendering a scene is not necessarily an interactive one, we need a way of recording the progress of ICT as it operates. Consequently, ICT maintains a log file. The log file can be used to get an indication of ICT's progress in completing the requested tasks. The process log is a text file named ict.log, which is created each time ICT is started. If the ict.log file already exists from a previous session, it is overwritten. In this way, log files do not build up unnecessarily. Messages are posted to the process log using a globally defined function **Status-Print**. The **StatusPrint** function has a single argument that points to a message to be logged. The message argument passed to function **Status-Print** is also displayed on the status bar, which is located on the bottom-left area of the ICT client window. If any message is reported to the status bar, a record of that message can also be found in the process log. If, for example,

ICT attempts to open an image file that does not exist, detailed messages are displayed in the status bar and also reported to the process log. Since the status bar displays only the last message, the process log often contains additional information.

2.13   The Preference Object

ICT reads and writes several types of files. A set of default directories and pathnames are used by ICT in order to place files in consistent locations. For example, the location of the process log file and directories for output images, input images, and other types of files all need to be supplied to ICT. Hardwiring these pathnames into the code is definitely not desirable in the event that any of these locations should need to be changed. We have therefore encapsulated definitions for all of these directories and pathnames in a C++ class called: **preference**. One instance of the **preference** class, called **ictPreference**, is created each time ICT is invoked. The **ictPreference** object serves as a central location for the default directories and pathnames used by ICT. The directories and pathnames themselves are protected data members. Two public member functions, **getPath** and **setPath**, are provided to get and set respectively any of the **ictPreference** directories and pathnames. ICT consistently uses the **ictPreference** object to determine where it should either find certain files or write output files. In the event that you need to change any of these locations, it is a simple matter to change them, either dynamically, using additional code and the function **setPath**, or by simply editing the **ictPreference** object's default pathname definitions. The **preference** class definition and member function source code is located in the file childWn.cpp.

2.14   ICT Starter Application Listing

A complete listing of the ICT starter application is included here. The ICT starter application is a standalone project that exists on the accompanying diskette in its own directory: x:\ict\starter. You may wish to build this application and become familiar with the general layout of the software. The following listing consists of five files whose contents are summarized in Table 2.3:

Here are the ICT Starter Application Listings:

```
// ClientWn.cpp
//
DEFINE_RESPONSE_TABLE1(ictMDIClient, TMDIClient)
 EV_COMMAND(CM_MDIFILEOPEN, evFileOpen),
 EV_COMMAND(CM_FILEOPEN_IMAGE, evOpenImage),
```

```
EV_COMMAND(CM_TOOLSBUILD_SCENE_LIST, evBuildSceneList),
EV_COMMAND(CM_TOOLSCREATE_CUTOUT, evCreateCutout),
EV_COMMAND(CM_TOOLSHARDWARE, evHardware),
EV_COMMAND(CM_TOOLSMAKE_MASK, makeMask),
EV_COMMAND(CM_TOOLSWARP, warpParams),
EV_COMMAND(CM_PREVIEWSCENE, evPreviewScene),
EV_COMMAND(CM_PREVIEWSEQUENCE, evPreviewSequence),
EV_COMMAND(CM_RENDERSCENE, evRenderScene),
EV_COMMAND(CM_RENDERSEQUENCE, evRenderSequence),
EV_COMMAND(CM_RENDERDEPTH_SORTING, evDepthSorting),
EV_COMMAND_ENABLE(CM_TOOLSCREATE_CUTOUT, ceCreateCutout),
EV_COMMAND_ENABLE(CM_PREVIEWSCENE, cePreviewScene),
EV_COMMAND_ENABLE(CM_PREVIEWSEQUENCE, cePreviewSequence),
EV_COMMAND_ENABLE(CM_RENDERSCENE, ceRenderScene),
EV_COMMAND_ENABLE(CM_RENDERSEQUENCE, ceRenderSequence),
EV_COMMAND_ENABLE(CM_RENDERDEPTH_SORTING, ceDepthSorting),
//{{ictMDIClientRSP_TBL_END}}
END_RESPONSE_TABLE;

ictMDIClient::ictMDIClient () : TMDIClient (){
 // Change the window's background color
 SetBkgndColor(RGB(0xf8, 0xfc, 0xf8));
 ChildCount = 0;
 Attr.Style |=WS_MAXIMIZE;
}

ictMDIClient::~ictMDIClient (){
 delete ictPreference;
 Destroy();
}
```

Table 2.3 ICT Starter Application Files

Filename	*Description*
clientWn.cpp	Contains the MDI client window class and placeholders for all options that can be selected from the ICT menu.
childWn.cpp	Contains several support window classes generated by the AppExpert. The ICT **preference** class library is also defined in this file.
myDialog.cpp	Contains ICT specific dialog box classes, the warp parameter dialog box member functions, and the scene preview dialog box member functions.
ictApp.cpp	Contains the application's entry point.
imageWn.cpp	Contains the class library for a scrollable image window class. Also contains placeholders for mouse event response functions, which will enable cutout images to be prepared.

```
void ictMDIClient::SetupWindow (){
 // Default SetUpWindow processing.
 TMDIClient::SetupWindow ();
 warpRotateX = 0.0; warpRotateY = 0.0; warpRotateZ = 0.0;
 warpTranslateX = 0.0; warpTranslateY = 0.0; warpTranslateZ = 0.0;
 warpScaleX = 1.0; warpScaleY = 1.0; warpScaleZ = 1.0;
 viewRotateX = 0.0; viewRotateY = 0.0; viewRotateZ = 0.0;
 viewTranslateX = 0.0; viewTranslateY = 0.0; viewTranslateZ = 0.0;
 isDirty = 0;
 cutoutEnabled = 0;
 previewSceneEnabled = 0;
 previewSequenceEnabled = 0;
 renderSceneEnabled = 0;
 renderSequenceEnabled = 0;
 depthSortingEnabled = 1;
 previewing = FALSE;
 outputRows = 250; // Set these in case a sceneList is not read in
 outputColumns = 250;
 changeViewPoint = FALSE;
}
void ictMDIClient::Paint(TDC& dc, BOOL, TRect&){
}


void ictMDIClient::OpenFile (const char *fileName){
 if (fileName) lstrcpy(FileData.FileName, fileName);
 //
 // Create a MDIChild window whose client is TEditFile.
 ictMDIChild* child = new ictMDIChild(*this, "",
 new TEditFile(0, 0, 0, 0, 0, 0, 0, FileData.FileName));
 //
 // Associate ICON w/ this child window.
 child->SetIcon(GetApplication(), IDI_DOC);
 //
 // If the current active MDI child is maximized then this one should be
 // also.
 ictMDIChild *curChild = (ictMDIChild *)GetActiveMDIChild();
 if (curChild && (curChild->GetWindowLong(GWL_STYLE) & WS_MAXIMIZE))
 child->Attr.Style |= WS_MAXIMIZE;
 child->Create();
}


void ictMDIClient::OpenImageFile (const char *fileName){
 if (fileName) lstrcpy(FileData.FileName, fileName);
 ictMDIChild* child = new ictMDIChild(*this,"", new imageWindow (this));
 child->SetIcon(GetApplication(),IDI_DOC);
 child->Create();
 //
 // The window is created. Load the image file into the window
 imageWindow *client = TYPESAFE_DOWNCAST(child->GetClientWindow(),
   imageWindow);
```

```
    if (client){
     client->CmFileRead(fileName);
     imageDC = client->theDC(); // Save this dc in the client object
     }
    }
    void ictMDIClient::evFileOpen (){
     //
     // Display standard Open dialog box to select a filename.
     FileData.Flags =
       OFN_FILEMUSTEXIST | OFN_HIDEREADONLY | OFN_OVERWRITEPROMPT;
     FileData.SetFilter("All Files (*.scn)|*.scn|");
     *FileData.FileName = 0;
     if (TFileOpenDialog(this, FileData).Execute() == IDOK) OpenFile();
    }


    void ictMDIClient::evOpenImage (){
     //
     // Display standard Open dialog box to select a filename.
     FileData.Flags =
       OFN_FILEMUSTEXIST | OFN_HIDEREADONLY | OFN_OVERWRITEPROMPT;
     FileData.SetFilter("All Files (*.bmp)|*.bmp|");
     *FileData.FileName = 0;
     if (TFileOpenDialog(this, FileData).Execute() == IDOK)
      OpenImageFile(FileData.FileName);
    }


    void ictMDIClient::evBuildSceneList (){
    }


    void ictMDIClient::evPreviewScene (){
     previewing = TRUE;
     // Execute a modal dialog
     if (GetModule()->ExecDialog(
      new scenePreviewDialog(this,"IDD_ScenePreview", 0, this)) == IDOK){
      renderSceneEnabled = 1;
     }
     previewing = FALSE;
     isDirty = 1;
    }
    void ictMDIClient::evPreviewSequence (){
     previewing = TRUE;
     if (GetModule()->ExecDialog(
      new scenePreviewDialog(this,"IDD_ScenePreview", 0, this)) == IDOK){
      renderSequenceEnabled = 1;
     }
     previewing = FALSE;
     isDirty = 1;
    }
```

```
void ictMDIClient::evRenderScene (){
}

void ictMDIClient::evRenderSequence (){
}

void ictMDIClient::evCreateCutout (){
 cutoutEnabled = 1 - cutoutEnabled;
}

void ictMDIClient::evDepthSorting (){
 depthSortingEnabled = 1 - depthSortingEnabled;
}

void ictMDIClient::ceCreateCutout (TCommandEnabler& ce){
 if(cutoutEnabled)
 // Checked,Unchecked are OWL enumerated constants
 ce.SetCheck(ce.Checked);
 else
  ce.SetCheck(ce.Unchecked);
}

void ictMDIClient::cePreviewScene (TCommandEnabler& ce){
 ce.Enable(previewSceneEnabled);
}

void ictMDIClient::cePreviewSequence (TCommandEnabler& ce){
 ce.Enable(previewSequenceEnabled);
}

void ictMDIClient::ceRenderScene (TCommandEnabler& ce){
 ce.Enable(renderSceneEnabled);
}

void ictMDIClient::ceRenderSequence (TCommandEnabler& ce){
 ce.Enable(renderSequenceEnabled);
}

void ictMDIClient::ceDepthSorting (TCommandEnabler& ce){
 if(depthSortingEnabled)
 // Checked,Unchecked are OWL enumerated constants
 ce.SetCheck(ce.Checked);
 else
  ce.SetCheck(ce.Unchecked);
}

void ictMDIClient::evHardware (){
```

```
}
void ictMDIClient::warpParams (){ // Execute a modal dialog.
 if(isDirty){      // If the client window has been drawn on, erase it.
  isDirty = 0;
  Invalidate(TRUE);
 }


 if (GetModule()->ExecDialog(
  new warpDialog(this,"IDD_WARPPARAMS", 0, this)) == IDOK){
  WarpImage();
 }
}


void ictMDIClient::makeMask (){
}


void ictMDIClient::WarpImage (){
}
  // ChildWn.cpp


  //
ictMDIChild::ictMDIChild (TMDIClient &parent, const char far *title,
TWindow *clientWnd, BOOL shrinkToClient, TModule *module)
  : TMDIChild (parent, title, clientWnd == 0 ? new
TEditFile(0, 0, 0)
  : clientWnd, shrinkToClient, module)
{
}


ictMDIChild::~ictMDIChild ()
{
  Destroy();
}


preference::preference(){
 strcpy(processLogPath, "c:\\ict\\scene\\ict.log");
 strcpy(shapeFileDir, "c:\\ict\\shape\\");
 strcpy(sequenceFileDir, "c:\\ict\\shape\\");
 strcpy(outputImageDir, "c:\\ict\\output\\");
 strcpy(inputImageDir, "c:\\ict\\cutout\\");
 strcpy(maskDir, "c:\\ict\\cutout\\");
}


char *preference::getPath(short pathIndicator){
  switch(pathIndicator){
  case ProcessLog:
   return processLogPath;
```

```
        case ShapeFileDirectory:
        return shapeFileDir;

        case SequenceFileDirectory:
        return sequenceFileDir;

        case OutputImageDirectory:
        return outputImageDir;

        case InputImageDirectory:
        return inputImageDir;

        case MaskImageDirectory:
        return maskDir;

        default:
           char msgText[MAXPATH];
           sprintf(msgText, "getPath: unknown option. %d", pathIndicator);
           StatusPrint(msgText);
           return (char *)0;
        }
}

void preference::setPath(short pathIndicator, char *thePath){
    switch(pathIndicator){
      case ProcessLog:
      strcpy(processLogPath, thePath);
      return;

      case ShapeFileDirectory:
      strcpy(shapeFileDir, thePath);
      return;

      case SequenceFileDirectory:
      strcpy(sequenceFileDir, thePath);
      return;

      case OutputImageDirectory:
      strcpy(outputImageDir, thePath);
      return;

      case InputImageDirectory:
      strcpy(inputImageDir, thePath);
      return;

      case MaskImageDirectory:
      strcpy(maskDir, thePath);
      return;
```

```
     default:
      char msgText[MAXPATH];
      sprintf(msgText, "setPath: unknown option. %d", pathIndicator);
      StatusPrint(msgText);
      return;
      }
}

preference::~preference() {}
//
// myDialog.cpp

class ProjectRCVersion {
public:
  ProjectRCVersion (TModule *module);
  virtual ~ProjectRCVersion ();

  BOOL GetProductName (LPSTR &prodName);
  BOOL GetProductVersion (LPSTR &prodVersion);
  BOOL GetCopyright (LPSTR &copyright);
  BOOL GetDebug (LPSTR &debug);

protected:
  LPBYTE   TransBlock;
  void FAR   *FVData;

private:
  // Don't allow this object to be copied.
  ProjectRCVersion (const ProjectRCVersion &);
  ProjectRCVersion & operator =(const ProjectRCVersion &);
};

ProjectRCVersion::ProjectRCVersion (TModule *module)
{
  char   appFName[255];
  DWORD  fvHandle;
  UINT   vSize;

  FVData = 0;

  module->GetModuleFileName(appFName, sizeof(appFName));
  DWORD dwSize = GetFileVersionInfoSize(appFName, &fvHandle);
  if (dwSize) {
   FVData = (void FAR *)new char[(UINT)dwSize];
   if (GetFileVersionInfo(appFName, fvHandle, dwSize, FVData))
      if (!VerQueryValue(FVData, "\\VarFileInfo\\Translation",
        (void FAR* FAR*)&TransBlock, &vSize)) {
```

```
          delete FVData;
          FVData = 0;
        }
    }
}


ProjectRCVersion::~ProjectRCVersion ()
{
  if (FVData)
    delete FVData;
}


BOOL ProjectRCVersion::GetProductName (LPSTR &prodName)
{
  UINT  vSize;
  char  subBlockName[255];
  wsprintf(subBlockName, "\\StringFileInfo\\%081x\\%s",
     *(DWORD *)TransBlock, (LPSTR)"ProductName");
  return FVData ? VerQueryValue(FVData, subBlockName,
     (void FAR* FAR*) &prodName, &vSize) : FALSE;
}


BOOL ProjectRCVersion::GetProductVersion (LPSTR &prodVersion)
{
  UINT  vSize;
  char  subBlockName[255];

  wsprintf(subBlockName, "\\StringFileInfo\\%081x\\%s",
     *(DWORD *)TransBlock, (LPSTR)"ProductVersion");
  return FVData ? VerQueryValue(FVData, subBlockName,
     (void FAR* FAR*)&prodVersion, &vSize) : FALSE;
}


BOOL ProjectRCVersion::GetCopyright (LPSTR &copyright)
{
  UINT  vSize;
  char  subBlockName[255];

  wsprintf(subBlockName, "\\StringFileInfo\\%081x\\%s",
     *(DWORD *)TransBlock, (LPSTR)"LegalCopyright");
  return FVData ? VerQueryValue(FVData, subBlockName,
     (void FAR* FAR*)&copyright, &vSize) : FALSE;
}


BOOL ProjectRCVersion::GetDebug (LPSTR &debug)
{
  UINT  vSize;
  char  subBlockName[255];
```

```
    wsprintf(subBlockName, "\\StringFileInfo\\%081x\\%s",
      *(DWORD *)TransBlock, (LPSTR)"SpecialBuild");
    return FVData ? VerQueryValue(FVData, subBlockName,
      (void FAR* FAR*)&debug, &vSize) : FALSE;
}


ictAboutDlg::ictAboutDlg (TWindow *parent, TResId resId, TModule *module)
  : TDialog(parent, resId, module)
{
}


ictAboutDlg::~ictAboutDlg ()
{
  Destroy();


}


void ictAboutDlg::SetupWindow ()
{
  LPSTR prodName, prodVersion, copyright, debug;
  // Get the static text whose value is based on VERSIONINFO.
  TStatic *versionCtrl = new TStatic(this, IDC_VERSION, 255);
  TStatic *copyrightCtrl = new TStatic(this, IDC_COPYRIGHT, 255);
  TStatic *debugCtrl = new TStatic(this, IDC_DEBUG, 255);


  TDialog::SetupWindow();


  // Process the VERSIONINFO.
  ProjectRCVersion applVersion(GetModule());


  // Get the product name, product version, and legal copyright strings.
  applVersion.GetProductName(prodName);
  applVersion.GetProductVersion(prodVersion);
  applVersion.GetCopyright(copyright);
  // IDC_VERSION is the product name and version number, the initial value
  // of IDC_VERSION is the word Version (in whatever language) product name
  // VERSION product version.
  char  buffer[255];
  char  versionName[128];
  versionCtrl->GetText(versionName, sizeof(versionName));
  wsprintf(buffer, "%s %s %s", prodName, versionName, prodVersion);
  versionCtrl->SetText(buffer);


  copyrightCtrl->SetText(copyright);


  // Get the SpecialBuild text only if the VERSIONINFO resource is there.
  if (applVersion.GetDebug(debug))
    debugCtrl->SetText(debug);
```

```
}
//
// Warp Dialog
warpDialog::warpDialog (TWindow *parent, TResId resId, TModule *module,
            ictMDIClient *client)
    : TDialog(parent, resId, module)
{
theClient = client;
editXAngle = new TEdit(this, IDC_XAngle, 10,0);
editYAngle = new TEdit(this, IDC_YAngle, 10,0);
editZAngle = new TEdit(this, IDC_ZAngle, 10,0);
editXScale = new TEdit(this, IDC_XScale, 10,0);
editYScale = new TEdit(this, IDC_YScale, 10,0);
}

DEFINE_RESPONSE_TABLE1(warpDialog, TDialog)
 EV_COMMAND(IDOK, clickFinish),
END_RESPONSE_TABLE;

warpDialog::~warpDialog ()
{
   delete editXAngle;
   delete editYAngle;
   delete editZAngle;
   delete editXScale;
   delete editYScale;
}

void warpDialog::SetupWindow ()
{
char theBuffer[32];
TDialog::SetupWindow();
theClient->warpRotateX = 0.0; theClient->warpRotateY = 0.0;
theClient->warpRotateZ = 0.0;
theClient->warpScaleX = 1.0; theClient->warpScaleY = 1.0;
theClient->warpScaleZ = 1.0;
sprintf(theBuffer,"%6.2f",theClient->warpRotateX);
editXAngle->SetText(theBuffer);
sprintf(theBuffer,"%6.2f",theClient->warpRotateY);
editYAngle->SetText(theBuffer);
sprintf(theBuffer,"%6.2f",theClient->warpRotateZ);
editZAngle->SetText(theBuffer);
sprintf(theBuffer,"%6.2f",theClient->warpScaleX);
editXScale->SetText(theBuffer);
sprintf(theBuffer,"%6.2f",theClient->warpScaleY);
editYScale->SetText(theBuffer);
}

void warpDialog::clickFinish ()
{
```

```
char theBuffer[16];
editXAngle->GetText(theBuffer,10);
theClient->warpRotateX = atof(theBuffer);
editYAngle->GetText(theBuffer,10);
theClient->warpRotateY = atof(theBuffer);
editZAngle->GetText(theBuffer,10);
theClient->warpRotateZ = atof(theBuffer);
editXScale->GetText(theBuffer,10);
theClient->warpScaleX = atof(theBuffer);
editYScale->GetText(theBuffer,10);
theClient->warpScaleY = atof(theBuffer);
CmOk();
}
//
// scenePreview Dialog
scenePreviewDialog::scenePreviewDialog (TWindow *parent, TResId resId,
  TModule *module, ictMDIClient *client): TDialog(parent, resId, module)
{
theHWND = parent->HWindow; // handle to the window to contain the wireframe
                           // drawing
theClient = client;
ckbTranslateZ = new TCheckBox(this,IDC_CKBTranslateZ, 0, 0);
ckbTranslateY = new TCheckBox(this,IDC_CKBTranslateY, 0, 0);
ckbTranslateX = new TCheckBox(this,IDC_CKBTranslateX, 0, 0);
ckbRotateZ = new TCheckBox(this,IDC_CKBRotateZ, 0, 0);
ckbRotateY = new TCheckBox(this,IDC_CKBRotateY, 0, 0);
ckbRotateX = new TCheckBox(this,IDC_CKBRotateX, 0, 0);
ckbScaleY = new TCheckBox(this,IDC_CKBScaleY, 0, 0);
ckbScaleX = new TCheckBox(this,IDC_CKBScaleX, 0, 0);
ckbScaleZ = new TCheckBox(this,IDC_CKBScaleZ, 0, 0);
ckbMoveViewPoint = new TCheckBox(this,IDC_ViewPoint, 0,0);

cmbModels = new TComboBox(this, IDC_COMBOBOXModels,32,0);

btnOK = new TButton(this, IDC_ButtonOK,0);
btnMinus = new TButton(this, IDC_BUTTONMinus,0);
btnPlus = new TButton(this, IDC_BUTTONPlus,0);
btnReset = new TButton(this, IDC_BUTTONReset,0);
btnCancel = new TButton(this, IDC_ButtonCancel,0);

edtX = new TEdit(this, IDC_EDITX, 10,0);
edtY = new TEdit(this, IDC_EDITY, 10,0);
edtZ = new TEdit(this, IDC_EDITZ, 10,0);
edtRotateX = new TEdit(this, IDC_RotateX, 8, 0);
edtRotateY = new TEdit(this, IDC_RotateY, 8, 0);
edtRotateZ = new TEdit(this, IDC_RotateZ, 8, 0);
edtScaleX = new TEdit(this, IDC_ScaleX, 8, 0);
edtScaleY = new TEdit(this, IDC_ScaleY, 8, 0);
```

```
edtScaleZ = new TEdit(this, IDC_ScaleZ, 8, 0);
edtTranslateX = new TEdit(this, IDC_TranslateX, 8, 0);
edtTranslateY = new TEdit(this, IDC_TranslateY, 8, 0);
edtTranslateZ = new TEdit(this, IDC_TranslateZ, 8, 0);


}


DEFINE_RESPONSE_TABLE1(scenePreviewDialog, TDialog)
 EV_COMMAND(IDC_ButtonOK, clickFinish),
 EV_LBN_SELCHANGE(IDC_COMBOBOXModels, chooseModel),
 EV_COMMAND(IDC_BUTTONMinus, decrement),
 EV_COMMAND(IDC_BUTTONPlus, increment),
 EV_COMMAND(IDC_BUTTONReset, reset),
 EV_COMMAND(IDC_BUTTONCancel, cancel),
 EV_COMMAND(IDC_ViewPoint, setViewPoint),
END_RESPONSE_TABLE;


scenePreviewDialog::~scenePreviewDialog ()
{
delete edtX;
delete edtY;
delete edtZ;
delete ckbTranslateZ;
delete ckbTranslateY;
delete ckbTranslateX;
delete ckbRotateZ;
delete ckbRotateY;
delete ckbRotateX;
delete ckbScaleY;
delete ckbScaleX;
delete ckbScaleZ;
delete cmbModels;
delete btnOK;
delete btnMinus;
delete btnPlus;
delete btnReset;
delete btnCancel;
delete ckbMoveViewPoint;
delete edtRotateX;
delete edtRotateY;
delete edtRotateZ;
delete edtScaleX;
delete edtScaleY;
delete edtScaleZ;
delete edtTranslateX;
delete edtTranslateY;
delete edtTranslateZ;
}
```

```
void scenePreviewDialog::SetupWindow ()
{
    TDialog::SetupWindow();
    TRect clientRect=GetClientRect();
    // Adjust the dialog box size and position
    TRect windowRect=GetWindowRect();
    int dialogLeft = 50;
    int dialogWidth = windowRect.right-windowRect.left+1;
    int dialogHeight = windowRect.bottom-windowRect.top+1;
    int dialogTop = 320;
    MoveWindow(dialogLeft, dialogTop, dialogWidth, dialogHeight, TRUE);
}


void scenePreviewDialog::clickFinish (){
 CmOk();
}


void scenePreviewDialog::cancel (){
 CmCancel();
}


void scenePreviewDialog::chooseModel (){
}


void scenePreviewDialog::setViewPoint ()
{
}
void scenePreviewDialog::reset ()
{
  if(theClient->changeViewPoint == FALSE){ //if manipulating a model...
    theClient->warpTranslateX = 0.0;
    theClient->warpTranslateY = 0.0;
    theClient->warpTranslateZ = 0.0;

    theClient->warpScaleX = 1.0;
    theClient->warpScaleY = 1.0;
    theClient->warpScaleZ = 1.0;

    theClient->warpRotateX = 0.0;
    theClient->warpRotateY = 0.0;
    theClient->warpRotateZ = 0.0;

  }
  else                 //if manipulating the viewPoint...
  {
    theClient->viewTranslateX = 0.0;
    theClient->viewTranslateY = 0.0;
    theClient->viewTranslateZ = 0.0;
```

```
    theClient->viewRotateX = 0.0;
    theClient->viewRotateY = 0.0;
    theClient->viewRotateZ = 0.0;


 }
}

void scenePreviewDialog::decrement ()
{
}

void scenePreviewDialog::increment ()
{
}


float fPolar(float angle){
 if(angle > 0.){
   while(angle >= 360.)
   angle -= 360.;
 }
 else{
   while(angle <= 0.)
   angle += 360.;
 }
 if(angle == 360.) angle = 0.;
 return angle;
}


//
// name Dialog
nameDialog::nameDialog (TWindow *parent, TResId resId, TModule *module,
   char *theName)
   : TDialog(parent, resId, module){
theFileName = theName;
editNewName = new TEdit(this, IDC_nameInput, 9, 0);
}

DEFINE_RESPONSE_TABLE1(nameDialog, TDialog)
 EV_COMMAND(IDOK, clickFinish),
END_RESPONSE_TABLE;

nameDialog::~nameDialog (){
   delete editNewName;
}

void nameDialog::SetupWindow (){
 char theBuffer[16];
 TDialog::SetupWindow();
 sprintf(theBuffer,"");
```

```
   editNewName->SetText(theBuffer);
  }


  void nameDialog::clickFinish () {
   char theBuffer[16];
   editNewName->GetText(theBuffer,16);
   strcpy(theFileName, theBuffer);
   CmOk();
  }


  //  ictapp.cpp
  //
  ictApp App;
  TStatusBar *StatusText;       // Declare a global status bar.
  void StatusPrint(char *aMessage);
  preference* ictPreference;     // Declare a global preference object.


  void StatusPrint(char *aMessage)
  {
  // Optionally write the message to a processing log.
   short myDebug = TRUE; // short myDebug = FALSE;
   if (myDebug == TRUE){
    char msgText[128];
    char *theString;
    theString = msgText;
    FILE *log;
    if ((log = fopen(ictPreference->getPath(ProcessLog), "a+")) == NULL){
     StatusText->SetText("StatusPrint: Unable to open Process.log");
     App.PumpWaitingMessages();
    }
    strcpy(theString, aMessage);
    int myLength = strlen(theString);
    *(theString + myLength) = '\n';
    *(theString + myLength + 1) = '\0';
    fwrite(theString, strlen(theString), 1, log);
    fclose(log);
   }
  //
  // Now display the message on the status bar.
   StatusText->SetText(aMessage);
   App.PumpWaitingMessages(); //Flush the message queue.
  }


  //{{ictApp Implementation}}
  //
  // Build a response table for all messages/commands handled.
  // by the application.
  //
  DEFINE_RESPONSE_TABLE1(ictApp, TApplication)
  //{{ictAppRSP_TBL_BEGIN}}
```

```
        EV_COMMAND(CM_HELPABOUT, CmHelpAbout),
         //{{ictAppRSP_TBL_END}}
    END_RESPONSE_TABLE;


    ictApp::ictApp () : TApplication("Image Compositing Toolkit"){}


    ictApp::~ictApp (){}


    void ictApp::InitMainWindow (){
        EnableBWCC(); // Load bwcc.dll
        TDecoratedMDIFrame* frame = new TDecoratedMDIFrame(Name, MDI_MENU,
          *(new ictMDIClient), TRUE);


      nCmdShow = SW_SHOWMAXIMIZED;
      frame->SetIcon(this, IDI_MDIAPPLICATION);
      frame->AssignMenu(MDI_MENU);
      frame->Attr.AccelTable = MDI_MENU;
      sb = new TStatusBar(frame, TGadget::Recessed,
        TStatusBar::CapsLock    |
        TStatusBar::NumLock     |
        TStatusBar::ScrollLock  |
        TStatusBar::Overtype);
      frame->Insert(*sb, TDecoratedFrame::Bottom);
      StatusText = sb;
      MainWindow = frame;
      ictPreference = new preference();
    //
    // Initialize the process log
      remove(ictPreference->getPath(ProcessLog));
      time_t theTime;
      time(&theTime);
      char msgText[64];
      sprintf(msgText,"ICT Process Log. %s", ctime(&theTime));
      msgText[43] = ' '; // Remove the carriage return.
      StatusPrint(msgText);
    }


    void ictApp::CmHelpAbout ()
    {
      //
      // Show the modal dialog.
      //
      ictAboutDlg(MainWindow).Execute();
    }


    int OwlMain (int, char* [])
    {
      int result;
      ictApp App;
```

```
    result = App.Run();
  return result;
}
// ImageWn.cpp
//


DEFINE RESPONSE TABLE1(imageWindow, TWindow)
  EV WM SIZE,
  EV WM PALETTECHANGED,
  EV WM SETFOCUS,
  EV WM LBUTTONDOWN,
  EV WM RBUTTONDOWN,
  EV WM LBUTTONUP,
  EV WM LBUTTONDBLCLK,
END RESPONSE TABLE;

imageWindow::imageWindow(ictMDIClient *aClient, short
  imHeight, short imWidth):
  TWindow(0, 0, 0){
  Attr.Style |= WS VSCROLL | WS HSCROLL | CS DBLCLKS;
  BkgndBrush = new TBrush(::GetSysColor(COLOR WINDOW));
  Scroller = new TScroller(this, 1, 1, 200, 200);
  SetCaption(0);
  theClient = aClient;
  firstPress = FALSE;
  hBitmap = NULL;
  anImage = NULL;
}

imageWindow::~imageWindow(){
  DeleteObject(hBitmap);
  delete BkgndBrush;
  delete anImage;
  anImage = NULL;
}

void imageWindow::SetCaption(char* name){
  char caption[MAXPATH + MAXAPPNAME + 2 + 1];
  strcpy(theFileName, name ? name : "(Untitled)");
  strcpy(caption, theFileName);
  if (Parent)
    Parent->SetCaption(caption);
}

void imageWindow::CmFileRead(char *fileName){
  char msgText[MAXPATH];
  char fileTitle[MAXPATH];
  int imHeight, imWidth;
  TOpenSaveDialog::GetFileTitle(fileName, fileTitle, MAXPATH);
```

```
    strcpy(theFileName, fileTitle);
    loadBMP(theFileName);
    SetCaption(strlwr(theFileName));
    imHeight = anImage->getHeight();
    imWidth = anImage->getWidth();
    sprintf(msgText,"Opened %s. Height: %d Width: %d", fileName,imHeight,
      imWidth);
    StatusPrint(msgText);
}


void imageWindow::adjustScroller(){
  TRect clientRect = GetClientRect();
  TPoint Range(Max(PixelWidth-clientRect.Width(), 0),
  Max(PixelHeight-clientRect.Height(), 0));
  Scroller->SetRange(Range.x, Range.y);
  Scroller->ScrollTo(0, 0);
  if (!GetUpdateRect(clientRect, FALSE)) Invalidate(FALSE);
}


void imageWindow::EvSize(UINT SizeType, TSize& Size){
  TWindow::EvSize(SizeType, Size);
  if (SizeType != SIZEICONIC) adjustScroller();
}


void imageWindow::EvSetFocus(HWND){
  Invalidate(FALSE);
}


void imageWindow::Paint(TDC& gdc, BOOL, TRect&){
  HBITMAP holdBitmap;
  if(!hBitmap){
  // StatusPrint("imageWindow::Paint hBitmap not defined");
     return;
  }
  HDC dc = GetDC(HWindow);
  TRect clientRect = GetClientRect();

  HDC memDC = CreateCompatibleDC(dc);
  // select the bitmap into the memory DC
  holdBitmap = (HBITMAP)SelectObject(memDC, hBitmap);
  SetStretchBltMode(memDC, COLORONCOLOR);
  SelectObject(memDC, *BkgndBrush);
  RECT imageRect;
  imageRect.left = 0; imageRect.top = 0;
  imageRect.right = PixelWidth; imageRect.bottom = PixelHeight;
    clientRect.left += (int)Scroller->XPos;
    clientRect.right += (int)Scroller->XPos;
    clientRect.top += (int)Scroller->YPos;
    clientRect.bottom += (int)Scroller->YPos;
```

```
      BitBlt(dc, imageRect.left, imageRect.top,
        imageRect.right - imageRect.left,
        imageRect.bottom - imageRect.top,
        memDC, imageRect.left + (int)Scroller->XPos,
        imageRect.top + (int)Scroller->YPos, SRCCOPY);

      PatBlt(dc, PixelWidth, 0,
        clientRect.right - PixelWidth, clientRect.bottom, PATCOPY);
      PatBlt(dc, 0,PixelHeight,
        clientRect.right, clientRect.bottom - PixelHeight, PATCOPY);
    SelectObject(memDC,holdBitmap);
    DeleteDC(memDC);
    DeleteDC(dc);
}


BOOL imageWindow::associateMemImage(memImage *theImage){
  if(anImage != NULL) {
    StatusPrint("associateMemImage: image already associated with this window");
    return FALSE;
  }
  anImage = theImage;
  getBitmap();
  Invalidate(FALSE);
  return TRUE;
}


void imageWindow::getBitmap(){
  HDC dc;
  HANDLE hloc;
  PBITMAPINFO pbmi;
  HBITMAP hbm;
  RGBQUAD pal[256];
  dc = GetDC(HWindow);
  hloc = LocalAlloc(LMEM ZEROINIT | LMEM MOVEABLE,
    sizeof(BITMAPINFOHEADER) + (sizeof(RGBQUAD) * 256));
  pbmi = (PBITMAPINFO) LocalLock(hloc);

  for(short a = 0; a < 256; a++){
    pal[a].rgbRed=a;
    pal[a].rgbGreen=a;
    pal[a].rgbBlue=a;
    pal[a].rgbReserved=0;
  }

  pbmi->bmiHeader.biSize = sizeof(BITMAPINFOHEADER);
  pbmi->bmiHeader.biWidth = anImage->getWidth();
  pbmi->bmiHeader.biHeight = anImage->getHeight();
  pbmi->bmiHeader.biPlanes = 1;
```

```
    pbmi->bmiHeader.biBitCount = anImage->getBitsPerPixel();
    pbmi->bmiHeader.biCompression = BI_RGB;

    memcpy(pbmi->bmiColors, pal, sizeof(RGBQUAD) * 256);
    //create a bitmap data structure containing the memImage bits
    hBitmap = CreateDIBitmap(dc, (BITMAPINFOHEADER FAR*) pbmi,
      CBM_INIT, anImage->getBytes(), pbmi, DIB_RGB_COLORS);
    LocalFree(hloc);
    PixelWidth = anImage->getWidth();
    PixelHeight = anImage->getHeight();
    adjustScroller();
    ReleaseDC(HWindow, dc);
}


BOOL imageWindow::loadBMP(char* name){
  char msgText[MAXPATH];
    anImage = new memImage(name, 0, 0, RANDOM, 'R', 0);
   if( !anImage->isValid()){
     sprintf(msgText, "Cannot open bitmap file: %s", name);
     StatusPrint(msgText);
     return FALSE;
   }
   lstrcpy(theFileName, name);
   getBitmap();
   return TRUE;
}


void    imageWindow::EvLButtonDown(UINT, TPoint& point){
  if(theClient->cutoutEnabled){
    if (firstPress == FALSE) {
      firstPress = TRUE;
      aShape = new shape3d(MAXVERTICES);
  // MAXVERTICES defined in shape3d.h
      StatusPrint("LButtonDown event: Created shape object");
    }
  }
}


void    imageWindow::EvLButtonUp(UINT, TPoint& point){
  if(theClient->cutoutEnabled){
  char msgText[MAXPATH];
  if(firstPress == FALSE) return;
  sprintf(msgText, "Adding point %d: (%d, %d)", aShape->getNumVertices(),
    point.x, point.y);
  StatusPrint(msgText);
  short myStatus;
  myStatus = aShape->addWorldVertex(point.x, point.y, 0);
  // z = 0 at the screen
  HPEN hpen;
```

```
    HDC theDC = GetDC(HWindow);
    hpen = CreatePen(PS SOLID, 1, RGB(255, 255, 255));
    SelectObject(theDC, hpen);
    int x, y, z;
    myStatus = aShape->getPreviousWorldVertex(&x, &y, &z);
    if (myStatus == 0){
      MoveToEx(theDC, x, y, 0L);
      LineTo(theDC, point.x, point.y);
    }
    else {
      MoveToEx(theDC, point.x, point.y, 0L); // draw a single point
      LineTo(theDC, point.x+1, point.y+1);
    }
      ReleaseDC(HWindow, theDC);
      DeleteObject(hpen);
    }
}


void    imageWindow::EvLButtonDblClk(UINT, TPoint& point){
char msgText[MAXPATH], newName[MAXPATH],
cutoutName[MAXPATH];
char imageFileName[MAXPATH];
if(theClient->cutoutEnabled){
  sprintf(msgText, "Save, Exit");
  StatusPrint(msgText);
  // Remove the vertex added by the first click in the double-click
  aShape->deleteLastWorldVertex();
  if (GetModule()->ExecDialog(
    new nameDialog((TWindow *)this, IDD newName, 0, newName)) == IDOK){
    strcpy(imageFileName, theFileName);
    sprintf(msgText, "Creating alpha image");
    StatusPrint(msgText);
    sprintf(cutoutName,"%s",newName);
    StatusPrint(cutoutName);

    short myStatus = prepareCutout(aShape, HWindow,
    imageFileName, cutoutName, PixelWidth, PixelHeight);
    if(myStatus != 0) {
      sprintf(msgText, "Unable to Create Cutout. %d", myStatus);
      StatusPrint(msgText);
      delete aShape;
      theClient->cutoutEnabled = FALSE;
      firstPress = FALSE;
      return;
    }
    delete aShape;
    theClient->cutoutEnabled = FALSE;
    sprintf(msgText, "Cutout Created Successfully");
    StatusPrint(msgText);
```

```
          firstPress = FALSE;
      }
   }
}
void    imageWindow::EvRButtonDown(UINT, TPoint& point){
   if(theClient->cutoutEnabled){
      char msgText[MAXPATH];
      sprintf(msgText, "Deleting: (%d, %d)",point.x, point.y);
      StatusPrint(msgText);
      HPEN hpen;
      HDC theDC = GetDC(HWindow);

      hpen = CreatePen(PS_SOLID, 1, RGB(0, 0, 0));
      SelectObject(theDC, hpen);
      short theStatus;
      int x, y, z, px, py, pz;
      aShape->getLastWorldVertex(&x, &y, &z);
      aShape->getPreviousWorldVertex(&px, &py, &pz);
      MoveToEx(theDC, px, py, 0L);
      LineTo(theDC, x, y);
      theStatus = aShape->deleteLastWorldVertex();
      if (theStatus == -1){}
      ReleaseDC(HWindow, theDC);
      DeleteObject(hpen);
   }
}
```

3

Making a Scene

This chapter introduces a C++ class library that manages a scene list data structure that contains all the information needed to preview or create a special effects scene or sequence. The scene list is really the backbone of the ICT program. All of the other classes developed in this text essentially support the process of previewing and creating special effects images. All of the information about the visual effect to be produced comes together in a **sceneList** object.

3.1   Why Do We Need a Scene List?

Most Windows applications are built around an entirely interactive graphical user interface. When the user pushes a button or clicks on a control, the computer performs the desired action very quickly, usually in seconds. As we shall see, warping and blending images is quite computationally expensive, and can therefore be time consuming—just how time consuming depends on factors such as the number and sizes of the images being processed and the speed of the processor chip in your computer. Depending on the situation, many minutes may be required to produce the desired effect scene or sequence. Because of the potentially lengthy scene creation times, it would be inappropriate to create a graphical user interface that effectively requires that the scene be created interactively, warping or blending one image at a time. We therefore need to prepare a single set of instructions ahead of time for creating the desired effect in its entirety. In this way, we can "push the start button" and then step back and let ICT render all the models in the scene in one uninterrupted step. The **sceneList** class contains all the needed capabilities to support this method of operation. Descriptions of all the models we want to be involved in the effect scene are placed into the **sceneList** object. The **sceneList** member function **preview** enables all of the models in an effect scene to be viewed and interactively positioned on the screen. The **sceneList** member function **render** then renders each model in the scene list until the effect is complete. These two functions make use of, directly or indirectly, all of the other classes and functions developed in this text.

Only one **sceneList** object is created while the ICT application is running. The **sceneList** object encapsulates a linked list data structure where each member of the list is a description of an individual model in the scene. This linked list is illustrated in Figure 3.1. The first node in the list represents information about the scene itself, such as the size of the output image, and whether the image will be rendered in color or in black and white.

Each model is represented as an instance of the **sceneElement** class, a class whose data members describe model attributes. The model description includes the location and orientation, whether the model is image-based or shape-based, whether it is moving, and so forth. The scene list object is created during setup of the ICT MDI client window and is destroyed as part of the ICT termination procedure.

Models are placed into the **sceneList** object by reading them from a text file called a *scene file*. Selecting the **Tools|Create Scene List...** option

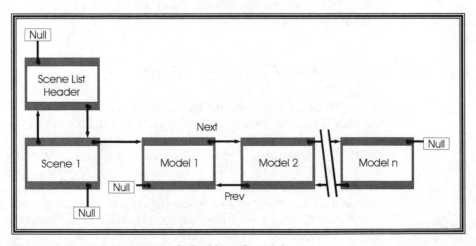

Figure 3.1 A **sceneList** is a linked list of models.

will open a file browser that enables a scene file to be opened. Any existing models are cleared from the scene list and it is repopulated with the models from the selected scene file.

3.2   Scene File Format

The scene file format is described in detail in this section. Most of the terms used here should be familiar since they were discussed in the requirements section of Chapter 2. If there are terms in this section you do not recognize, be assured that these terms will be described in more detail in later chapters.

The generic scene file format is as follows:

```
scene sceneName [Sequence|Still] outHeight, outWidth [Color|Monochrome]
Rotation Rx,Ry,Rz
Translation Tx,Ty,Tz
MotionPath [None|PathName]
Model modelName [Blend|NoBlend] [Warp|NoWarp] AlphaScale
alpha [Image|Shape]
FileName pathName
MotionPath [None|pathName]
AlphaImagePath [Default|pathName] (optional)
Rotation rx,ry,rz
Scale sx,sy,sz
Translation tx,ty,tz
```

where [a|b] indicates that either *a* or *b* is required and '//' indicates a comment that can be used at the beginning of any line. Continuation lines are not supported. The really wonderful news about scene files is that a scene file maker utility program has been provided on the accompanying diskette in the x:\ict\sfm directory. This utility has an intuitive graphical user interface and it will create correctly formatted scene files based on your selections and entries. The scene file maker utility is described in more detail in the ICT user guide located in Appendix B.

Here is a sample scene file that contains two models:

```
scene house Still 512,480 Color
Rotation 0,0,0
Translation -4,106,512
MotionPath None

Model house NoBlend NoWarp AlphaScale 1 Image
FileName c:\ict\gallery\HOUSE1.BMP
MotionPath None
Rotation 0,0,0
Scale 1,1,1
Translation 0,0,0
```

```
Model tree1 Blend Warp AlphaScale 1 Image
FileName c:\ict\CUTOUT\SPRUCEC.BMP
MotionPath None
Rotation 0,0,0
Scale 1,1,1
Translation 40,0,-120
```

The scene file contents will be described in detail in the following sections.

The first four lines of a scene file describe overall features of the special effect scene to be produced. The first line begins with the word **scene** and is followed by a single word that names the scene:

```
scene house Still 512,480 Color
```

Scenes and Sequences

A single output image called a *still* image is produced by ICT when the keyword STILL is used. To indicate that the intended special effect is a sequence of images, the keyword SEQUENCE is used. If the special effect is a sequence then the scene definition must include a motion path file, even if the viewpoint does not move. The reason for this is that the number of frames in the sequence is determined by reading the motion path file associated with the scene node in the scene list. This topic is discussed further in Chapter 12.

Output Image Size (outHeight, outWidth)

The size of the output image is indicated by the height in pixels followed by a comma and then by the width in pixels. If a backdrop image is used in the special effect, the output image size should be set to the size of the backdrop image. If the size of the backdrop image is not immediately known, the outHeight, outWidth parameters can both be set to zero. If the first model in the scene list is a backdrop image then ICT will open the image and set the size of the output image to equal the size of the backdrop image.

Color or Monochrome

Specifying COLOR will produce output in true color. Specifying MONOCHROME will produce a black-and-white (256-grayscale) output image. If the input images are true color format, and a monochrome output is being produced, the Green color plane of the true color image is used.

Scene and Model Transformations

The keywords ROTATION, SCALE, and TRANSFORMATION can be applied either to a scene or model (with one exception: SCALE cannot be applied to the viewpoint). The TRANSLATION and ROTATION keywords included in the scene definition indicate that the output scene or scenes will appear from the point of view of an observer located at the indicated translation and rotation. Graphic transformations specified in the scene file are applied to a model by the scene preview and scene render tools. Each of these graphic transformations is described briefly in the following.

A three-dimensional rotation is indicated by the ROTATION keyword:

```
Rotation Rx,Ry,Rz.
```

The angles Rx, Ry, and Rz are specified in degrees and indicate the amount by which the model is to be rotated about the X, Y, and Z axes respectively.

A scaling or sizing transformation is indicated by the keyword SCALE:

```
Scale Sx,Sy,Sz.
```

where Sx, Sy, and Sz are scale factor applied to X, Y, and Z axis coordinates respectively. Each scale factor must be greater than zero. A scale factor of zero will cause the model to disappear from the scene. A scale factor of 1.0 indicates no scaling will occur. Scale factors greater than one will cause the model to be enlarged. Scale factors less than one will cause the model to shrink.

Finally, a translation is indicated by the keyword TRANSLATION:

```
Translation Tx,Ty,Tz
```

where Tx, Ty, and Tz are the number of units to move the model along the X, Y, and Z axes respectively.

Note that the transformations indicated in the scene file are applied to either the model or the viewpoint default position and orientation. In other words, the transformations indicated are relative in the sense that they indicate how a model or viewpoint is to be changed relative to its current location and orientation.

Models

Each model included in a visual effect is described in a scene file using the terms listed below. A model's description begins with the following:

```
Model house NoBlend NoWarp AlphaScale 1 Image
```

To Blend or Not to Blend

After each model is transformed to the proper size and orientation, it must be composited into the result image. Two settings control how the compositing operations take place. The first method, indicated by the keyword BLEND, uses the alpha-blending process discussed in Chapter 10. The

NOBLEND keyword is used if the model is simply to be copied into the result image.

To Warp or Not to Warp

Use the WARP keyword to cause the image to be warped with the indicated Rotation, Scale, and Translation transformations described previously. If the image is not to be warped, use the NOWARP keyword. If NOWARP is specified and the image to be copied into the final scene is larger than the output image size, the lower leftmost rectangular portion of the image is copied into the output image.

The Alpha Scale Factor

The Alpha Scale factor is a number between −1 and 1. The Alpha Scale factor alters the translucency of the image being composited into the result image. A value of one indicates a completely opaque object, values increasingly less than one indicate an object that is increasingly transparent. An Alpha Scale factor of exactly zero will cause a matt object to be generated as described in Chapter 10. Negative alpha image values are used to generate dark translucent objects such as shadows. The effect of a negative Alpha Scale factor is to subtract the image being composited from the corresponding intensities in the result image. This process is described further in Chapter 10.

Photo-Based Models vs. Shape-Based Models

The last keyword in the first line of the model description has two possible values: IMAGE or SHAPE. If the model is photo-based, the IMAGE keyword is used. If the model is shape-based, then the SHAPE keyword is used. The second line of a model description begins with the keyword FILENAME. If the model is photo-based, the pathname following the FILENAME keyword must point to a .bmp format image file. If the model is shape-based, the pathname following the FILENAME keyword must point to a shape file.

Specifying an Alpha Image

Any image can be used as an alpha image. A separate line containing the keyword ALPHAIMAGEPATH and a pathname can be supplied when an alpha image other than the default image created during the cutout image creation process is to be used. Use of this keyword is optional.

Sequences and Motion Paths

Finally, if the special effect to be produced is a sequence, and the model moves during the sequence, then a line whose first word is the keyword MOTIONPATH must be added along with a pathname to a .pth file that specifies the location and orientation of this model in each frame of the sequence. If the special effect is a single image then the MOTIONPATH keyword is still used and a motion path of NONE is supplied as shown in the scene file example on the bottom of page 55. Motion path files are described in detail in Chapter 12.

3.3   *Classes: sceneList, scene, and sceneElement*

Now that we have described the format of the scene file in detail you should be getting an overall idea of the capabilities of the ICT. Now let's look at the three **sceneList**-related C++ classes in more detail. Since this is the first C++ class presented, we will spend more time introducing and describing relevant aspects of the C++ language. A great way to get a quick look at a class and size up its features and capabilities is to look at its header file. If you can get an idea of what the data members and member functions are doing, the header file can serve as a preview of the class itself.

Because a visual effect scene can contain a variable number of models, a linked list data structure offers clear advantages over a fixed type of data structure such as an array. The scene list data structure is illustrated in Figure 3.1.

An alternative approach (and certainly a tempting one) to using a linked list would be to use a PC-compatible relational database to store and retrieve scene and model information as needed. The linked list approach taken here is a bit more time consuming to develop but has the major advantage that ICT's capability to manage scene and model information is self-contained and therefore does not require additional commercial software.

The scene list actually consists of three tightly coupled classes: A class aptly named **sceneList** manages a linked list consisting of a single scene node that is an instance of a class named **scene**. The single scene list node is then linked to one or more nodes that are instances of class **sceneElement**. There is one **sceneElement** node in the linked list for each model in the scene. Figure 3.1 illustrates a scene list object and its related objects. Each **sceneElement** node stores all information needed to preview or render a single model. We begin our discussion of these classes by looking at the header file sceneLst.h in more detail. This file actually contains definitions for classes **scene**, **sceneList**, and **sceneElement**.

The first statements in the header file declare a new datatype. We need a data type that can be used to store together the *x*, *y*, and *z* rotation angles, for example. The **fpoint** data type also comes in handy for storing three-dimensional coordinates. We define the **fpoint** type as follows:

```
struct fpoint
{float x,y,z;};
```

It is worth mentioning that C++ treats structure declarations like declarations of new data types. This means that instances of this structure can now be declared in the same way as simple variables are declared:

```
fpoint aCoordinate;
```

An **fpoint** structure has three elements: an *x, y,* and *z* floating point coordinate. When referring to these elements in a C++ program we must include the structure to which they belong. For example, the proper notation to set *x* to zero using our example is: **aCoordinate.x = 0**. One last point before we move on: Suppose we declare **aCoordinate** to be a pointer to a fpoint like this:

```
fpoint *aCoordinate;
```

In this case we must refer to the element *x* in a slightly different manner. To set the *x* element of the **aCoordinate** structure now we would use: **aCoordinate->x = 0**. The arrow simply indicates to the compiler that **aCoordinate** is a pointer to the structure.

Next we define the **sceneElement** class used to represent individual models. Note that the variables used in a C++ class definition are called *data members*. The functions listed inside the class definition are called *member functions*:

```
class sceneElement {
private:
    char *modelName;            // Name of the Model
    char *modelMotionPath;    ·  // Motion file for the model
    motionPath *modelMotion;    // Contains motion path if moving model
    short modelType;            // 1 = image. 2 = graphic (class shape3d)
    char *fileName;             // File Name of image
    short statusIndicator;      // 1 indicates bad file name ==> object
                                // ignored
    renderObject *screenObject; // pointer to screen renderable
                                // representation
    short blendIndicator;       // 1 = use alpha blending, 0 = no alpha
                                // blending
    short warpIndicator;        // 1 = warp image, 0 = do not warp image
    float alphaScale;           // Default = 1.0 (used for shadows)
    fpoint *rotation;           // Angles
    fpoint *scale;              // < 1 = contraction. > 1 = expansion.
    fpoint *translation;        // Pixels
    char *alphaPath;            // Optional. Alpha image pathname
    short sortLayer;            // Optional. Used for depth sorting
    short valid;                // 1 if constructor successful
    sceneElement *preventry;    // Point to previous Scene element
    sceneElement *nextentry;    // Point to next Scene element
```

```
   friend class sceneList;
public:
sceneElement(char *mName, char * fName, short blendI, short theType,
   short warpI, float aScale, fpoint *rt, fpoint *sc, fpoint *tr,
   char *motionPath, char *alphaPath, short sortLayer);
   ~sceneElement();
   void fshowlist();
   void writeFile(ofstream *fileout);
   short isValid(void);
};
```

Each model has a name stored in the **sceneElement** data member **model-Name**. The filename describing how the model moves through a sequence is stored in data member **modelMotionPath**. If the special effect is a single scene, then the **modelMotionPath** is set to "None." The variable **next** is a pointer to a **motionPath** object. This object simply stores the contents of the file indicated by **modelMotionPath** data member. If the model is not moving, **modelMotion** is set to zero. The data member **Type** contains the model type and is set to a value of one if the model is image based, and to a value of two if the model is based on a shape file. If the model is image based, the **fileName** data member is set to the image filename; if the model is shape based, the **fileName** data member is set to the shape filename.

The **statusIndicator** provides the status of the **sceneElement** object. Recall that C++ constructors are not permitted a return value. Since we are creating **sceneElement** objects by reading either an image file or a shape file, the **sceneElement** constructor needs a way to indicate whether it was able to successfully open the desired file and create the **sceneElement** object. Toward this end the **statusIndicator** data member is zero if the object was successfully created. If the file could not be found, or some other error occurred during creation of the **sceneElement** object, the **statusIndicator** is set to one.

The **screenObject** data member is a pointer to a **renderObject**. The **renderObject** encapsulates device-specific information for drawing the model on a Windows screen during scene preview. These **renderObject** objects are created the first time a scene is previewed. The **blendIndicator** is set to one if the model is to be blended into the background image; if not, **blendIndicator** is set to zero. The **warpIndicator** is set to one if the model is to be warped. The **alphaScale** data member is a scale factor used during blending and can be used to make shadows. The **alphaScale** factor is described in more detail in Chapter 10.

Next come the three transformations: rotation, scale, and translation, which indicate a model's position and orientation relative to the origin of the world coordinate system. Finally, there are two pointers, **nextentry** and **preventry**, which point to the next and previous models in the scene list. The value of **nextentry** is zero if the model is the last one on the list. The value of **preventry** is Null if the model is first on the list.

Next, the following statement appears:

```
friend class sceneList;
```

The **friend** keyword indicates that class **sceneElement** can access and modify the private data members of class **SceneList**. Class **sceneElement** is made a friend of class **sceneList** because the **sceneElement** member functions update the **sceneList** data member **currentModel**. This subject is discussed further later in this chapter. Next, notice the **public:** statement. The **PUBLIC** keyword indicates that all following member functions and data members can be accessed directly from other parts of the program. The **PRIVATE** keyword indicates that these data members can be accessed only by **friend** classes (more on this shortly). That is, **private** data members cannot be accessed by simply referencing them in a C++ program. If not specifically declared, the **private** keyword is implicit in every class declaration. We do this to protect the data members from arbitrarily being accessed by any other part of the program. Instead of declaring these data members **public**, we make them private and then provide **public** member functions that access the **private** data members. This is one of the major ways in which encapsulation is implemented in C++. Each class definition, in effect, becomes an interface that we then write to as the application is built.

Now let's turn our attention to the public member functions of **sceneElement**. The first function after the **public** keyword has the same name as the class name: **sceneElement**. This function is called a *constructor* and it is used to create an instance of the class, that is, a **sceneElement** object. To create a **sceneElement** object we use the C++ **new** keyword like this:

```
sceneElement *aModel = new sceneElement(mName,
fName,...,motionPath);
```

You will see this type of statement often in C++—the declaration and initialization of a variable in a single line of code. The fragment **sceneElement *aModel** declares that **aModel** is a pointer to a **sceneElement** object. The pointer's value is supplied by the **new** keyword, which calls the constructor, which allocates the necessary memory. The **new** keyword, operating in concert with the constructor, then returns a pointer to the new **sceneElement** object: **aModel**. This is the reason why constructor functions are not allowed to return values of their own: Constructors are always used to return a pointer to the newly created object.

As an aside, you will notice that some classes introduced in this book will have several constructor functions. In the C programming language it would be an error to declare multiple functions with the same name. However in C++, the name of a function includes its list of arguments (the list of arguments is called the function's signature). Thus it is generally true that

C++ functions can share a common name, as long as each function signature is unique.

Getting back to the **sceneElement** class, the function **~sceneElement()** is called a *destructor*; it must be called when the **sceneElement** object is to be destroyed in order to deallocate any memory that may have been set aside when the **sceneElement** object was created or to perform other cleanup duties. Once again this action is initiated by a C++ keyword: **delete**. To delete the **sceneElement** object created previously we would use the statement:

```
delete aModel;
```

The member function **fShowList** can be used to print the contents of a **sceneElement** object on the screen. Member function **writeFile** saves the model information to a file and is used as part of the procedure to save a scene file.

Class Scene

Moving along in the header file, we come to the definition of the **scene** class:

```
class scene {
private:
  char *sceneName;                        // Name of the Scene
  char *sensorPath;                       // Viewpoint Path file for a sequence
  motionPath *sensorMotion;               // Has motion path if moving view
                                          // point
  short sequenceType;                     // 1 = nonSequence, 2 = sequence
  short colorMode;                        // 1 = Black and White, 2 = RGB Color
  int outputRows;                         // Number of rows (y) in output image
  int outputColumns;                      // Number of columns(X) in output
                                          // image
  fpoint *rotation;                       // viewPoint Angles
  fpoint *translation;                    // viewPoint location relative to
                                          // (0,0,0)
  sceneElement *tail;                     // point to last Scene element
  sceneElement *head;                     // point to first Scene element
  sceneElement *currentSceneElement;      // current scene element
  scene *prevEntry;
  scene *nextEntry;
  short valid;                            // 1 if constructor successful
  friend class sceneList;
public:
  scen(char *, short, short, short, short, fpoint *,fpoint *, char *);
  ~scene();
  void writeFile(ofstream *fileout);
  short isValid(void);
};
```

All of the data members of the **scene** class are declared **private**. Data member **sceneName** is the name of the **scene**. Only one **scene** node is allowed per **sceneList** object. Data member **sensorPath** is the name of a motion path file used to describe how the viewpoint moves when the special effect is a sequence. Data member **sensorMotion** is a pointer to a **motionPath** object that contains the **motionPath** information stored in the file indicated by data member **sensorPath**. Data member **sequenceType** is set to one for a single image output, and two for a sequence. The **colorMode** is one for black-and-white output, two for color output. Data members **outputRows** and **outputColumns** define the size of the output image(s) to be produced by ICT. Data member **outputRows** indicates the number of horizontal lines or rows in the output image. The number of output rows corresponds to the height (the Y dimension) of the image in pixels. Data member **outputColumns** is equal to the number of pixels in each row. The number of columns corresponds to the width (the X dimension) of the image in pixels.

The next two data members, **rotation** and **translation**, are used only if the ICT output special effect is a single scene. Data members **rotation** and **translation** together define what is called the *observer viewpoint*. They define the orientation and location respectively of the observer. This means that the scene produced by ICT will correspond to what would be seen by an observer located at the indicated viewpoint in the world coordinate system. These terms will be described in greater detail in Chapter 6.

A scene has an associated list of models. A pointer to the first model in the list of models is saved in the data member **head**. Similarly, a pointer to the last model in the list of models is saved in the data member **tail**. Because **head** and **tail** are maintained by **sceneList** member functions, class **scene** is also a friend of class **sceneList**. A pointer to the last referenced model is also maintained in the data member **currentSceneElement**. Use of this pointer permits "a current model" to be efficiently accessed by separate member functions. Use of the **currentSceneElement** pointer avoids the computationally expensive situation in which different member functions requiring access to the current model would have to search the entire model list to find the current model before operating on it.

Finally, **prevEntry** points back to the header node of the **sceneList**. Data member **nextEntry** is always set to zero. The **nextEntry** pointer is used by the **sceneList** member functions to traverse the scene list. For this reason class **scene** is also a friend of class **sceneList**.

Turning our attention now to the public member functions of class **scene** we see that there are a constructor and destructor function, as well as a function **writeFile**, which is used to save the scene-related information in a scene file.

Class sceneList

A lengthy class definition for the scene list itself can be found in sceneLst.h:

```cpp
class sceneList{
public:
  scene *sceneListHead;      // Points to the head of the list
  scene *currentScene;       // Points to the current Scene
  memImage *backdropImage;   // An optional backdrop image
  sceneList();
  ~sceneList();
  void display();
  short readList(char *errorText, char *pathName);
  short writeList(char *errorText, char *pathName);
  sceneElement *setCurrentModel(char *desiredModel);
  void setCurrentModelTransform(float rx, float ry, float rz,
    float sx, float sy, float sz, float tx, float ty, float tz);
  void getCurrentModelTransform(float *rx, float *ry, float *rz,
    float *sx, float *sy, float *sz, float *tx, float *ty, float *tz);
  short addScene (char *theSceneName, short theSequence, short
    outImageCols, short outImageRows, short theColorMode, fpoint *rt,
    fpoint *tr, char *theMotionPath);
  short addSceneElement(char *mdName, char *fName, short blendI, short
    theType, short warpI, float aScale, fpoint *rt, fpoint *sc, fpoint *tr,
    char *motionPath, char *alphaPath, short sortLayer);
  void showModels(TComboBox *theCombo);
  short getSceneElements(char *);
  short getSceneInfo(char *name, short *type,
    short *cMode, int *outRows, int *outCols);
  short setSceneOutImageSize(int outRows, int outCols);
  short getViewPoint(float *viewX, float *viewY, float *viewZ,
    float *rotateX, float *rotateY, float *rotateZ);
  short setViewPoint(float viewX, float viewY, float viewZ,
    float rotateX, float rotateY, float rotateZ);
  int listLength();
  void clear();
  short previewSequence(HWND displayWindow, tMatrix *modelMatrix,
    tMatrix *viewMatrix);
  short previewStill(HWND displayWindow, tMatrix *modelMatrix,
    tMatrix *viewMatrix);
  short render (HWND displayWindow, tMatrix *viewMatrix,
    short depthSortingEnabled);
  short depthSort(sceneElement *Models[], float distances[], short
    *numModels, short depthSortingEnabled);
  void copyTransforms(short effectType, sceneElement *theModel,
    motionNode *aMotion, bundle *xfrm);
  void sceneList::getViewMatrix(
    tMatrix *viewMatrix, int frameCounter, scene *theScene);
```

```
   friend class scene;
   friend class sceneElement;
};
```

Notice that the **sceneList** class has no private data members, and only one member function is declared **private**. In contrast to the previous two classes we have discussed, whose data members and member functions are predominantly private, most of the interface to the **sceneList** class is declared **public**. The scene list has a public interface because ICT interacts with the **sceneList** object, not its related **scene** and list of **sceneElement** objects. The **sceneElement** and **scene** classes are used only by the **sceneList** member functions. By arranging the classes **sceneList**, **scene**, and **sceneElement** in this way, the details of accessing and managing the linked list of models we have described are completely hidden. The user simply calls the appropriate public **sceneList** member function to perform the desired task.

Now let's look at the **sceneList** data members in more detail. The **sceneList** object has a header node whose location is contained in the data member **sceneListHead**. An output scene can contain a backdrop image. The backdrop image is one that is simply copied into the output scene as a first step. The image-based models located in the **sceneList** object are then optionally warped and/or blended into the backdrop image. A backdrop image is defined to exist if the first model in a scene file is not warped or blended. In this case the **backdropImage** data member will point to a **memImage** object. Instances of class **memImage** are described in detail in Chapter 5.

Here is a listing of the header file sceneLst.h:

```
#define MAXMODELS 256   //size of model array for depth sorting
                        //increase if > MAXMODELS are to be used in a scene
//{{SceneList}}
void StatusPrint(char *);

struct fpoint{
  float x,y,z;
};

struct bundle{
  float rx, ry, rz;
  float sx, sy, sz;
  float tx, ty, tz;
  float alpha;
};

class sceneElement {
private:
  char *modelName;              // Name of the Model
  char *modelMotionPath;        // Motion file for the model
```

```
        motionPath *modelMotion;      // Contains motion path if moving model
        short modelType;              // 1 = image. 2 = graphic (class shape3d)
        char *fileName;               // File Name of image
        short statusIndicator;        // 1 indicates bad file name ==> object
                                      // ignored
        renderObject *screenObject;   // Pointer to screen renderable
                                      // representation
        short blendIndicator;         // 1 = use alpha blending, 0 = no alpha
                                      // blending
        short warpIndicator;          // 1 = warp image, 0 = do not warp image
        float alphaScale;             // Default = 1.0 (used for shadows)
        fpoint *rotation;             // Angles
        fpoint *scale;                // < 1 = contraction. > 1 = expansion.
        fpoint *translation;          // Pixels
        char *alphaPath;              // Optional. Alpha image pathname
        short sortLayer;              // Optional. Used for depth sorting
        short valid;                  // 1 if constructor successful
        sceneElement *preventry;      // Point to previous Scene element
        sceneElement *nextentry;      // Point to next Scene element
        friend class sceneList;
    public:
    sceneElement(char *mName, char * fName, short blendI, short theType,
        short warpI, float aScale, fpoint *rt, fpoint *sc, fpoint *tr,
        char *motionPath, char *alphaPath, short sortLayer);
        ~sceneElement();
        void fshowlist();
        void writeFile(ofstream *fileout);
        short isValid(void);
    };


    class scene {
    private:
        char *sceneName;                   // Name of the Scene
        char *sensorPath;                  // ViewPoint Path file for a sequence
        motionPath *sensorMotion;          // Has motion path if moving view
                                           // point
        short sequenceType;                // 1 = nonSequence, 2 = sequence
        short colorMode;                   // 1 = Black and White, 2 = RGB Color
        int outputRows;                    // Number of rows (y) in output image
        int outputColumns;                 // Number of columns(X) in output
                                           // image
        fpoint *rotation;                  // ViewPoint Angles
        fpoint *translation;               // ViewPoint location relative to
                                           // (0,0,0)
        sceneElement *tail;                // Point to last Scene element
        sceneElement *head;                // Point to first Scene element
        sceneElement *currentSceneElement; // Point to current scene element
        scene *prevEntry;
        scene *nextEntry;
        short valid;                       // 1 if constructor successful
```

```
      friend class sceneList;
public:
   scene(char *, short, short, short, short, fpoint *,fpoint *, char *);
   ~scene();
   void writeFile(ofstream *fileout);
   short isValid(void);
};


class sceneList{
public:
   scene *sceneListHead;        // Points to the head of the list
   scene *currentScene;         // Points to the current Scene
   memImage *backdropImage;     // An optional backdrop image
   sceneList();
   ~sceneList();
   void display();
   short readList(char *errorText, char *pathName);
   short writeList(char *errorText, char *pathName);
   sceneElement *setCurrentModel(char *desiredModel);
   void setCurrentModelTransform(float rx, float ry, float rz,
   float sx, float sy, float sz, float tx, float ty, float tz);
   void getCurrentModelTransform(float *rx, float *ry, float *rz,
   float *sx, float *sy, float *sz, float *tx, float *ty, float *tz);
   short addScene (char *theSceneName, short theSequence,
      short outImageCols, short outImageRows, short theColorMode, fpoint *rt,
      fpoint *tr, char *theMotionPath);
   short addSceneElement(char *mdName, char *fName, short blendI,
      short theType, short warpI, float aScale,fpoint *rt,fpoint *sc, fpoint
      *tr, char *motionPath, char *alphaPath, short sortLayer);
   void showModels(TComboBox *theCombo);
   short getSceneElements(char *);
   short getSceneInfo(char *name, short *type,
      short *cMode, int *outRows, int *outCols);
   short setSceneOutImageSize(int outRows, int outCols);
   short getViewPoint(float *viewX, float *viewY, float *viewZ,
   float *rotateX, float *rotateY, float *rotateZ);
   short setViewPoint(float viewX, float viewY, float viewZ,
      float rotateX, float rotateY, float rotateZ);
   int listLength();
   void clear();
   short previewSequence(HWND displayWindow, tMatrix *modelMatrix,
      tMatrix *viewMatrix);
   short previewStill(HWND displayWindow, tMatrix *modelMatrix,
      tMatrix *viewMatrix);
   short render (HWND displayWindow, tMatrix *viewMatrix,
      short depthSortingEnabled);
   short depthSort(sceneElement *Models[], float distances[],
      short *numModels, short depthSortingEnabled);
   void copyTransforms(short effectType, sceneElement *theModel,
      motionNode *aMotion, bundle *xfrm);
```

```
void sceneList::getViewMatrix(
  tMatrix *viewMatrix, int frameCounter, scene *theScene);
friend class scene;
friend class sceneElement;
};
```

Now the **sceneList** member functions are described. Because of the large number of functions, each are summarized here:

- The list of member functions begins with a constructor and destructor function: **sceneList()** and **~sceneList()**.

- Member function **readList** reads a scene file of the format described in section 3.2 and populates the scene list. Member function **writeList** saves the content of the scene list object to a scene file.

- Member function **setCurrentModel** sets the **currentModel** data member of a scene list's scene object to the model whose name is passed in as the function's only argument.

- Member function **setCurrentModelTransform** sets the rotation, scale, and translation transformations of the current model using the nine arguments supplied.

- Member function **getCurrentModelTransform** returns the rotation, scale, and translation transformations of the current model in the nine function arguments.

- Member function **addScene** adds a **scene** object node to the **sceneList** object and sets its data members using the supplied arguments. This member function may be called only once per **sceneList** object.

- Member function **addSceneElement** adds a model to the scene list and sets its data members using the supplied arguments. This member function may be called only after **addScene** has been called.

- Member function **showModels** places a list of all the model names contained in a scene list into the OWL **TComboBox** object whose pointer is supplied.

- Member function **getSceneInfo** returns the scene name, special effect type (scene or sequence), color mode (color or monochrome), and the output image size.

- Member function **setSceneOutputImageSize** sets the height and width of the output image.

- Member function **getViewPoint** returns the viewer location and orientation in the six supplied arguments.

- Member function **setViewPoint** sets the viewer location and orientation using the six supplied arguments.

- Member function **listLength** returns as its value the one relative number of models in the scene list object. If the scene list has no models, **listLength** returns zero.

- Member function **clear** removes all models from the scene list as well as the scene node.

- Member function **previewStill** previews a single-image visual effect by traversing the list of models in the scene list and displaying on the screen the name and boundary line segments of each model.

- Member function **previewSequence** previews a sequence visual effect by traversing the list of models in the scene list and displaying on the screen the name and boundary line segments of each model using an off-screen animation technique.

- Member function **render** traverses the list of models in the scene list, appropriately rendering each photo-based model and placing it into the output image.

- Member function **depthSort** is called by the **render** member function to determine the order in which the models are to be rendered. Function **depthSort** calculates the distance from the center of each model to the viewpoint, and then sorts the distances and causes the models that are farthest away from the viewpoint to be rendered first. The **depthSort** function assumes the total number of models in the scene list will not exceed the constant MAXMODELS defined in the sceneLst.h header file.

Finally, we notice that the **sceneList** class is a friend of both class **scene** and class **sceneElement**. Since the **sceneList** member functions alter data members of both the **scene** object and **sceneElement** objects, it is made a friend of both classes. The source code for most of the member functions of classes **scene**, **sceneElement**, and **sceneList** is listed below. Functions not listed here are covered in later chapters. The source code for these functions is contained in two files: sceneLst.cpp and model.cpp.

```
sceneList::sceneList(){
  fpoint *rt = new fpoint();
  fpoint *sc = new fpoint();
  sceneListHead = new scene("sceneList", 0, 0, 0, 0, rt, sc, " ");
  backdropImage = 0;
  currentScene = NULL;
  delete rt;
  delete sc;
}

sceneList::~sceneList(){
  clear(); //clear the list of models
```

```
      if(backdropImage != NULL) delete backdropImage;
      delete sceneListHead;
}

sceneElement *sceneList::setCurrentModel(char *desiredModel){
    scene *theScene = sceneListHead;
    sceneElement *aModel;
    theScene = theScene->nextEntry; // Point to the scene Node
    aModel = theScene->head;
    while (aModel != NULL){
        if(strcmp(aModel->modelName, desiredModel) == 0){
            theScene->currentSceneElement = aModel;  // Indicate scene's current
                                                      // model
            return(aModel);
        }
        aModel = aModel->nextentry;  // Point to the next model
    }
    return 0;  //Model not found
}

void sceneList::setCurrentModelTransform(float rx, float ry, float rz,
    float sx, float sy, float sz, float tx, float ty, float tz){
    scene *theScene = sceneListHead;
    sceneElement *currentModel;
    theScene = theScene->nextEntry; // Point to the scene Node
    currentModel = theScene->currentSceneElement;
    currentModel->rotation->x = rx;
    currentModel->rotation->y = ry;
    currentModel->rotation->z = rz;
    currentModel->scale->x = sx;
    currentModel->scale->y = sy;
    currentModel->scale->z = sz;
    currentModel->translation->x = tx;
    currentModel->translation->y = ty;
    currentModel->translation->z = tz;
}

void sceneList::getCurrentModelTransform(float *rx, float *ry, float *rz,
float *sx, float *sy, float *sz, float *tx, float *ty, float *tz){
    scene *theScene = sceneListHead;
    sceneElement *currentModel;
    theScene = theScene->nextEntry; // Point to the scene Node
    currentModel = theScene->currentSceneElement;
    *rx = currentModel->rotation->x;
    *ry = currentModel->rotation->y;
    *rz = currentModel->rotation->z;
    *sx = currentModel->scale->x;
    *sy = currentModel->scale->y;
    *sz = currentModel->scale->z;
    *tx = currentModel->translation->x;
```

```
      *ty = currentModel->translation->y;
      *tz = currentModel->translation->z;
    }

    short sceneList::readList(char *errorText, char *pathName){
      char TheText[128], *TheKeyWord;
      char theModelName[64], theFileName[MAXPATH], theMotionPath[MAXPATH];
      char theSceneName[MAXPATH], theAlphaPath[MAXPATH];
      int lineCounter, numScenes, outImageCols, outImageRows;
      short notFound, theBlend, theWarp, theSequence, theColorMode, theType,
        getOutImageSizeFlag, theSortLayer;
      float theAlpha;
      fpoint *rt, *sc, *tr;
      short myStatus, minLineSize = 4;
#define BLANK " "
#define DUPLICATESCENE 3
#define IMAGE 1
#define SHAPE 2

      ifstream filein;
      filein.open(pathName);
      if (filein.fail()){
        sprintf(errorText,"Unable to open file: %s",pathName);
        return -1;
      }
      filein >> ws;        // Turn off linefeeds
      strcpy(theMotionPath, "None");
      strcpy(theAlphaPath, "Default");
      lineCounter = 0; numScenes = 0, theSortLayer = 0;
      rt = new fpoint();
      sc = new fpoint();
      tr = new fpoint();
      sprintf(errorText, "Scene file read successfully");

      while(TRUE){  // Get the scene components
      while(strcmpi(TheKeyWord = getNextLine((char *)TheText, &lineCounter,
        &filein, minLineSize), "MODEL") != 0){

        char *aBase,*aSceneName,*effectType, *aColorMode;
        char *tempImageSize;
        notFound = TRUE;

        if (strcmpi (TheKeyWord, "SCENE") == 0){
          notFound = FALSE;
          aBase = TheText + 6;

          aSceneName = strtok(aBase,BLANK);
          if(aSceneName != NULL)
```

```
      strcpy(theSceneName, aSceneName);
    else {
      sprintf(errorText,"Missing value or term on Line %d", lineCounter);
      delete rt; delete sc; delete tr;
      filein.close();
      return -1;
    }


    effectType = strtok(NULL,BLANK);
    theSequence = 1;
    if(effectType != NULL){
      if(strcmpi(effectType,"SEQUENCE") == 0) theSequence = 2;
    }
    else {
      sprintf(errorText,"Missing value or term on Line %d", lineCounter);
      delete rt; delete sc; delete tr;
      filein.close();
      return -1;
    }


    tempImageSize = strtok(NULL,BLANK);
    aColorMode = strtok(NULL,BLANK);
    theColorMode = MONOCHROME;
    if(aColorMode != NULL){
      if(strcmpi(aColorMode,"COLOR") == 0) theColorMode = COLOR;
    }
    else {
      sprintf(errorText,"Missing value or term on Line %d", lineCounter);
      delete rt; delete sc; delete tr;
      filein.close();
      return -1;
    }


    if(tempImageSize != NULL){ // Output Image Height,Width
      outImageRows = atoi(strtok(tempImageSize, ","));
      outImageCols = atoi(strtok(NULL,BLANK));
      getOutImageSizeFlag = FALSE;
      if(outImageCols == 0 || outImageRows == 0)
        getOutImageSizeFlag = TRUE;
    }
    else {
      sprintf(errorText,"Missing value or term on Line %d", lineCounter);
      delete rt; delete sc; delete tr;
      filein.close();
      return -1;
    }
} // end scene processing
if(strcmpi (TheKeyWord, "MOTIONPATH") == 0){
strcpy(theMotionPath,(char *)TheText + 11);
```

```
        if(strlen(theMotionPath) == 0){
          sprintf(errorText,"MotionPath file missing on Line %d", lineCounter);
          delete rt; delete sc; delete tr;
          filein.close();
          return -1;
        }
        notFound = FALSE;
      }


      if(strcmpi (TheKeyWord, "ROTATION") == 0) {
        char *theRt, localRt[64];
        theRt = strtok((char *)TheText + 9, BLANK);
        strcpy(localRt, theRt);
        rt->x = atof(strtok(localRt, ","));
        rt->y = atof(strtok(NULL, ","));
        rt->z = atof(strtok(NULL, ","));
        notFound = FALSE;
      }


      if(strcmpi (TheKeyWord, "TRANSLATION") == 0) {
        char *theTr, localTr[64];
        theTr = strtok((char *)TheText + 12, BLANK);
        strcpy(localTr,theTr);
        tr->x = atof(strtok(localTr, ","));
        tr->y = atof(strtok(NULL, ","));
        tr->z = atof(strtok(NULL, ","));
        notFound = FALSE;
      }


      if (strcmpi (TheKeyWord, "EOF") == 0) {
        sprintf(errorText,"sceneFile may be corrupted or has no models");
        delete rt; delete sc; delete tr;
        filein.close();
        return -1;
      }


      if (notFound) {
        sprintf(errorText,"Unknown Keyword: %s. Line %d", TheKeyWord,lineCounter);
        delete rt; delete sc; delete tr;
        filein.close();
        return -1;
      }
    }  // loop until a model is detected


// Add the scene to the sceneList and read its elements.
    numScenes++;
    if (numScenes > 1){
      sprintf(errorText,"Only 1 scene definition permitted per scene file",
```

```
        lineCounter);
      delete rt; delete sc; delete tr;
      filein.close();
      return -1;
    }
  myStatus = addScene (theSceneName, theSequence, outImageCols,
    outImageRows, theColorMode, rt, tr, theMotionPath);
  if(myStatus != 0) {
    sprintf(errorText,"Could not add Scene to Scene List. Line %d",
      lineCounter);
    delete rt; delete sc; delete tr;
    filein.close();
    return -1;
  }

  theType = IMAGE;
  strcpy(theMotionPath,"");
  strcpy(theFileName,"");
  short nModels = 0;
  char *aModelName, *aBlend, *aWarp, *aScale, *aScaleValue, *aType;
  theBlend = 1;,theWarp = 1;,theAlpha = 1.0;

  while(strcmpi(TheKeyWord, "SCENE") != 0){
    notFound = TRUE;
    //
    // We Expect MODEL, ROTATION, SCALE, TRANSLATION, or MOTIONPATH
    if (strcmpi (TheKeyWord, "MODEL") == 0) {
      nModels++;
      if (nModels > 1){
        myStatus = addSceneElement(theModelName, theFileName, theBlend,
          theType, theWarp, theAlpha, rt, sc, tr, theMotionPath,
            theAlphaPath, theSortLayer);
        if(myStatus != 0){
          sprintf(errorText,"Could not add model to scene list. Line %d",
            lineCounter);
          delete rt; delete sc; delete tr;
          filein.close();
          return -1;
        }
        theBlend = 1; theWarp = 1;theAlpha = 1;theType = IMAGE;
        strcpy(theMotionPath,"");
        strcpy(theFileName,"");
      }
      aModelName = strtok((char *)TheText+6,BLANK);
      strcpy(theModelName,aModelName);
      aBlend = strtok(NULL,BLANK);
      aWarp = strtok(NULL,BLANK);
      aScale = strtok(NULL,BLANK);
      aScaleValue = strtok(NULL,BLANK);
      aType = strtok(NULL,BLANK);
```

```
      theBlend = 1;
      if(aBlend != NULL){
        if(strcmpi(aBlend,"NOBLEND")==0) theBlend = 0;
      }
      else {
        sprintf(errorText,"Missing value or term on Line %d", lineCounter);
        delete rt;delete sc;delete tr;
        filein.close();
        return -1;
      }

      theWarp = 1;
      if(aWarp != NULL){
        if(strcmpi(aWarp,"NOWARP")==0) theWarp = 0;
      }
      else {
        sprintf(errorText,"Missing value or term on Line %d", lineCounter);
        delete rt; delete sc; delete tr;
        filein.close();
        return -1;
      }

      theAlpha = 1.0;
      if(aScale != NULL){
      if(strcmpi(aScale,"ALPHASCALE")==0) {
        theAlpha = atof(aScaleValue);
      }
    }
    else {
      sprintf(errorText,"Missing value or term on Line %d", lineCounter);
      delete rt; delete sc; delete tr;
      filein.close();
      return -1;
    }

    theType = IMAGE;
    if(aType != NULL){
      if(strcmpi(aType,"SHAPE") == 0) theType = SHAPE;
    }
    else {
      sprintf(errorText,"Missing value or term on Line %d", lineCounter);
      delete rt;delete sc;delete tr;
      filein.close();
      return -1;
    }

    notFound = FALSE;
  }

  if(strcmpi (TheKeyWord, "ROTATION") == 0) {
    char *theRt;
```

```
    char localRt[64];
    theRt = strtok((char *)TheText + 9, BLANK);
    strcpy(localRt,theRt);
    rt->x = atof(strtok(localRt, ","));
    rt->y = atof(strtok(NULL, ","));
    rt->z = atof(strtok(NULL, ","));
    notFound = FALSE;
}


if(strcmpi (TheKeyWord, "SCALE") == 0) {
 char *theSc, localSc[64];
    theSc = strtok((char *)TheText + 6, BLANK);
    strcpy(localSc,theSc);
    sc->x = atof(strtok(localSc, ","));
    sc->y = atof(strtok(NULL, ","));
    sc->z = atof(strtok(NULL, ","));
    notFound = FALSE;
}


if(strcmpi (TheKeyWord, "TRANSLATION") == 0) {
    char *theTr, localTr[64];
    theTr = strtok((char *)TheText + 12, BLANK);
    strcpy(localTr,theTr);
    tr->x = atof(strtok(localTr, ","));
    tr->y = atof(strtok(NULL, ","));
    tr->z = atof(strtok(NULL, ","));
    notFound = FALSE;
}


if(strcmpi (TheKeyWord, "MOTIONPATH") == 0) {
    strcpy(theMotionPath,(char *)TheText + 11);
    if(strlen(theMotionPath) == 0){
        sprintf(errorText,"MotionPath file missing on Line %d", lineCounter);
        delete rt; delete sc; delete tr;
        filein.close();
        return -1;
    }
    notFound = FALSE;
}
if(strcmpi (TheKeyWord, "ALPHAIMAGEPATH") == 0) {
    strcpy(theAlphaPath,(char *)TheText + 15);
    if(strlen(theAlphaPath) == 0){
        sprintf(errorText,"Alpha Image Path file missing. Line %d", lineCounter);
        delete rt;delete sc;delete tr;
        filein.close();
        return -1;
    }
    notFound = FALSE;
}
```

```
    if(strcmpi (TheKeyWord, "FILENAME") == 0) {
      strcpy(theFileName,(char *)TheText + 9);
        if(getOutImageSizeFlag == TRUE){
          short bpp, bmpStatus;
          bmpStatus = readBMPHeader(theFileName, &outImageRows,
            &outImageCols, &bpp);
          if(bmpStatus != 0) {
            sprintf(errorText,"File name not valid. Line %d",
              lineCounter);
            delete rt; delete sc; delete tr;
            filein.close();
            return -1;
          }
          setSceneOutImageSize(outImageRows, outImageCols);
          getOutImageSizeFlag = FALSE;
        }
      notFound = FALSE;
    }


    if (strcmpi (TheKeyWord, "EOF") == 0 ){
    // Save the last model
    myStatus = addSceneElement(theModelName, theFileName, theBlend,
      theType, theWarp, theAlpha, rt, sc, tr, theMotionPath,
        theAlphaPath, theSortLayer);
      if(myStatus != 0){
        sprintf(errorText,"Could not add a model to scene list. Line %d",
        lineCounter);
        delete rt; delete sc; delete tr;
        filein.close();
        return -1;
      }
      delete rt; delete sc; delete tr;
      filein.close();
      return 0;
    }

    if (notFound){
      sprintf(errorText,"Unknown Keyword: %s Line %d",TheKeyWord,
        lineCounter);
      StatusPrint(errorText);
      delete rt; delete sc; delete tr;
      filein.close();
      return -1;
    }
    TheKeyWord = getNextLine((char *)TheText, &lineCounter, &filein,
      minLineSize);
    }
  }
}
```

```
void sceneList::showModels(TComboBox *theCombo){
  scene *theScene = sceneListHead;
  theScene = theScene->nextEntry;  //Skip over the list header
  theCombo->ClearList();
  sceneElement *theModel = theScene->head;
  while (theModel != NULL){
    theCombo->AddString(theModel->modelName);
    theModel = theModel->nextentry;
  }
}

int sceneList::listLength(){
  scene *theScene = sceneListHead;
  theScene = theScene->nextEntry;  //Skip over the list header
  if(theScene == NULL) return(0);
  int theLength = 0;
  sceneElement *theModel = theScene->head;
  while (theModel != NULL){
    theLength++;
    theModel = theModel->nextentry;
  }
  return(theLength);
}

short sceneList::getSceneInfo(char *name, short *type,
  short *cMode, int *outRows, int *outCols){
  scene *theScene = sceneListHead;
  theScene = theScene->nextEntry;  //Skip over the list header
  if (theScene == NULL) return -1;
  strcpy(name, theScene->sceneName);
  *type = theScene->sequenceType;
  *cMode = theScene->colorMode;
  *outRows = theScene->outputRows;
  *outCols = theScene->outputColumns;
  return 0;
}

short sceneList::setSceneOutImageSize(int outRows, int
outCols){
  scene *theScene = sceneListHead;
  theScene = theScene->nextEntry; //Skip over the list header
  if (theScene == NULL) return -1;
  theScene->outputRows = outRows;
  theScene->outputColumns = outCols;
  return 0;
}

short sceneList::getViewPoint(float *viewX, float *viewY,
float *viewZ, float *rotateX, float *rotateY, float *rotateZ){
```

```
  scene *theScene = sceneListHead;
  theScene = theScene->nextEntry; //Skip over the list header
  if (theScene == NULL) return -1;
  *viewX = theScene->translation->x;
  *viewY = theScene->translation->y;
  *viewZ = theScene->translation->z;
  *rotateX = theScene->rotation->x;
  *rotateY = theScene->rotation->y;
  *rotateZ = theScene->rotation->z;
  return 0;
}


short sceneList::setViewPoint(float viewX, float viewY,
float viewZ, float rotateX, float rotateY, float rotateZ){
  scene *theScene = sceneListHead;
  theScene = theScene->nextEntry;  //Skip over the list header
  if (theScene == NULL) return -1;
  theScene->translation->x = viewX;
  theScene->translation->y = viewY;
  theScene->translation->z = viewZ;
  theScene->rotation->x = rotateX;
  theScene->rotation->y = rotateY;
  theScene->rotation->z = rotateZ;
  return 0;
}


short sceneList::writeList(char *errorText, char *fileName){
  scene *theScene = sceneListHead;
  theScene = theScene->nextEntry;  // Skip over the list header

  ofstream fileOut(fileName);
  if (fileOut.fail()){
    sprintf(errorText,"Unable to open file: %s",fileName);
    return -1;
  }
  theScene->writeFile(&fileOut); // Write out the scene description
  sceneElement *theModel = theScene->head;
  while (theModel != NULL) {
    theModel->writeFile(&fileOut); // Write out each model description
    theModel = theModel->nextentry;
  }
  fileOut.close();
  return 0;
}


void getFileName(char *outputFileName, char *prefix, short
counter,
  short theColor){
  char colorChar;
```

```
    if (theColor == RED)colorChar = 'r';
    if (theColor == GREEN)colorChar = 'g';
    if (theColor == BLUE)colorChar = 'b';
    if (theColor == 0)colorChar = 'c';
    sprintf(outputFileName, "%.4s%#03d%c.bmp\0", prefix, counter, colorChar);
}


void appendFileName(char *outputFileName, char *prefix,char *suffix){
    sprintf(outputFileName, "%.7s%s.bmp\0", prefix, suffix);
}


void getAlphaName(char *inputName, char *alphaName){
    char drive[MAXDRIVE], dir[MAXDIR], file[MAXFILE], ext[MAXEXT];
    fnsplit(inputName,drive,dir,file,ext);
    short theLength = strlen(file);
    if(theLength > 0) *(file+theLength-1) = 'a';  // Substitute an 'a'
    fnmerge(alphaName,drive,dir,file,ext);
}


void sceneList::copyTransforms(short effectType,
    sceneElement *theModel, motionNode *aMotion, bundle *xfrm){
    if(effectType == SEQUENCE && theModel->modelMotion > NULL){
        xfrm->rx = aMotion->rx;
        xfrm->ry = aMotion->ry;
        xfrm->rz = aMotion->rz;
        xfrm->sx = aMotion->sx;
        xfrm->sy = aMotion->sy;
        xfrm->sz = aMotion->sz;
        xfrm->tx = aMotion->tx;
        xfrm->ty = aMotion->ty;
        xfrm->tz = aMotion->tz;
        xfrm->alpha = aMotion->alpha;
    }
    else {
        xfrm->rx = theModel->rotation->x;
        xfrm->ry = theModel->rotation->y;
        xfrm->rz = theModel->rotation->z;


        xfrm->sx = theModel->scale->x;
        xfrm->sy = theModel->scale->y;
        xfrm->sz = theModel->scale->z;


        xfrm->tx = theModel->translation->x;
        xfrm->ty = theModel->translation->y;
        xfrm->tz = theModel->translation->z;
        xfrm->alpha = theModel->alphaScale;
    }
}
```

```
void sceneList::getViewMatrix(
  tMatrix *viewMatrix, int frameCounter, scene *theScene){
  motionNode *aMotion = new motionNode;
  viewMatrix->setIdentity();
  const float DTR = 3.1415926 / 180.0;
  float xRadians, yRadians, zRadians;
  if(theScene->sensorMotion > NULL){
    theScene->sensorMotion->getNode(frameCounter, aMotion);
    xRadians = aMotion->rx * DTR;
    yRadians = aMotion->ry * DTR;
    zRadians = aMotion->rz * DTR;
  }
  else {
    xRadians = theScene->rotation->x * DTR;
    yRadians = theScene->rotation->y * DTR;
    zRadians = theScene->rotation->z * DTR;
  }

  viewMatrix->rotate(-xRadians, -yRadians, -zRadians);
  if(theScene->sensorMotion > NULL)
    viewMatrix->translate(-aMotion->tx, -aMotion->ty, -aMotion->tz);
  else {
    viewMatrix->translate(
    -theScene->translation->x,
    -theScene->translation->y,
    -theScene->translation->z);
  }
  delete aMotion;
}
```

Here is a listing of the member functions in model.cpp

```
short sceneElement::isValid(){
  if (valid)
    return 1;
  else
    return 0;
}


short scene::isValid(){
  if (valid)
    return 1;
  else
    return 0;
}


sceneElement::sceneElement(char *mName, char * fName, short blendI,
  short theType, short warpI, float aScale, fpoint *rt,
```

```
    fpoint *sc, fpoint *tr, char *theMotionPath, char *theAlphaPath,
    short theSortLayer){

    statusIndicator = NULL;
    modelName = new char[strlen(mName) + 1];
    strcpy(modelName, mName);
    fileName = new char[strlen(fName) + 1];
    strcpy(fileName, fName);
    blendIndicator = blendI;
    modelType = theType;
    warpIndicator = warpI;
    alphaScale = aScale;
    rotation = new fpoint();
    rotation->x = rt->x;
    rotation->y = rt->y;
    rotation->z = rt->z;

    scale = new fpoint();
    scale->x = sc->x;
    scale->y = sc->y;
    scale->z = sc->z;

    translation = new fpoint();
    translation->x = tr->x;
    translation->y = tr->y;
    translation->z = tr->z;
    screenObject = NULL;
    //
    // Handle moving models
    valid = 1;
    modelMotionPath = new char[strlen(theMotionPath) + 1];
    strcpy(modelMotionPath, theMotionPath);
    modelMotion = NULL;
    if(strlen(modelMotionPath) > 1 && strcmpi(modelMotionPath, "NONE") != 0)
{
        //
        // The model is moving
        modelMotion = new motionPath();
        int myStatus = modelMotion->readMotion(modelMotionPath);
        if (myStatus != 0){  // if the motion file could not be read,
          StatusPrint("SceneList.ReadList: Moving Model has invalid motion file");
          delete modelMotion;
          modelMotion = NULL;
          valid = 0;
        }
    }

    alphaPath = new char[strlen(theAlphaPath) + 1];
    strcpy(alphaPath, theAlphaPath);
```

```
    sortLayer = theSortLayer;
    preventry = NULL;
    nextentry = NULL;
}


void sceneElement::fshowlist(){  // Display scene's elements traversing
    sceneElement *next = this;        // the list in the forward direction.
    while (next != NULL){
      next->display();
      next = next->nextentry;
    }
}


sceneElement::~sceneElement(){
    delete modelName;
    delete fileName;
    delete rotation;
    delete scale;
    delete translation;
    delete modelMotionPath;
    delete alphaPath;
    if(screenObject != NULL) delete screenObject;
    if(modelMotion != NULL) delete modelMotion;
}


scene::~scene(){
    delete sceneName;
    delete sensorPath;
    delete rotation;
    delete translation;
    if(sensorMotion != NULL) delete sensorMotion;
}


void sceneElement::writeFile(ofstream *fileout){
    char blendArray[16], warpArray[16],modelArray[16];
    strcpy (blendArray, "Blend");
    strcpy(warpArray,"Warp");
    strcpy(modelArray,"Image");
    if(blendIndicator == 0) strcpy(blendArray,"NoBlend");
    if(warpIndicator == 0) strcpy(warpArray,"NoWarp");
    if(modelType == 2) strcpy(modelArray,"Shape");
    *fileout << "Model " << modelName << " " << blendArray << " "
    << warpArray << " AlphaScale " << alphaScale << " " << modelArray << '\n'
    << "FileName "<< fileName << '\n' <<  "MotionPath " << modelMotionPath
    <<'\n' << "AlphaImagePath " << alphaPath <<'\n' << "Rotation "
    << rotation->x <<"," << rotation->y <<"," << rotation->z <<'\n'
    << "Scale " << scale->x <<"," << scale->y <<"," << scale->z <<'\n'
    << "Translation " << translation->x <<"," << translation->y <<","
```

```cpp
        << translation->z << "\n\n";
}


void scene::writeFile(ofstream *fileout){
  char sequenceArray[16], colorArray[16];
  strcpy (sequenceArray, "Sequence");
  strcpy(colorArray, "Color");
  if(sequenceType == 1) strcpy(sequenceArray, "Still");
  if(colorMode == 1) strcpy(colorArray, "Monochrome");


  *fileout << "scene " << sceneName << " " << sequenceArray << " "
  << outputRows << "," << outputColumns << " " << colorArray << '\n'
  << "Rotation " << rotation->x <<"," << rotation->y <<"," << rotation->z
  <<'\n' << "Translation " << translation->x <<"," << translation->y
  <<"," << translation->z << "\n" << "MotionPath " << sensorPath << "\n\n";
}

scene::scene(char *sName, short seqType, short numOutCols,
short numOutRows,
  short aColorMode, fpoint *rt, fpoint *tr, char *sensorpth){
  sceneName = new char[strlen(sName)+1];
  strcpy(sceneName, sName);
  sequenceType = seqType;
  outputColumns = numOutCols;
  outputRows = numOutRows;
  colorMode = aColorMode;

  rotation = new fpoint();
  rotation->x = rt->x;
  rotation->y = rt->y;
  rotation->z = rt->z;

  translation = new fpoint();
  translation->x = tr->x;
  translation->y = tr->y;
  translation->z = tr->z;

  sensorPath = new char[strlen(sensorpth)+1];
  strcpy(sensorPath, sensorpth);
  sensorMotion = NULL;
  if(strlen(sensorPath) > 1 && strcmpi(sensorPath, "NONE") != 0) {
    //
    // The view point is moving
    valid = 1;
    sensorMotion = new motionPath();
    int myStatus = sensorMotion->readMotion(sensorPath);
    if (myStatus != 0){ // if the motion file could not be read,
      StatusPrint("Scene: Moving ViewPoint has invalid motion file");
```

```
        delete sensorMotion;
        sensorMotion = NULL;
        valid = 0;
     }
   }
   currentSceneElement = NULL;
   tail = NULL;
   head = NULL;
   prevEntry = NULL;
   nextEntry = NULL;
}


short sceneList::addScene(char *theSceneName,short theType,
short outImCols,
short outImRows, short theColorMode, fpoint *rt, fpoint
*tr, char *thePath){
  short status = 0;
  scene *newScene = new scene (theSceneName, theType, outImCols, outImRows,
  theColorMode, rt, tr, thePath);
  if (!newScene->isValid()) status = 1;
  sceneListHead->nextEntry = newScene;
  newScene->prevEntry = sceneListHead;
  currentScene = newScene; //Make the new scene the Current scene
  return status;
}
short sceneList::addSceneElement(char *mdName, char * fName, short blendI,
  short theType, short warpI, float aScale,fpoint *rt,
  fpoint *sc, fpoint *tr, char *motionPath, char *theAlphaPath,
  short theSortLayer){
  scene *aScene = currentScene;  //Add an element to the current scene
  sceneElement *aModel;
  aModel = aScene->head;
  short myStatus = 0;
  sceneElement *theModel = new sceneElement(mdName, fName, blendI, theType,
    warpI, aScale, rt, sc, tr, motionPath, theAlphaPath, theSortLayer);
  if(!theModel->isValid())return 1;


  if(aScene->head == NULL){
    aScene->head = theModel;
    theModel->preventry = NULL;
    theModel->nextentry = NULL;
  }
  else{
    aModel = aScene->head;  // Find the last element
    while (aModel->nextentry != NULL)
      aModel = aModel->nextentry;
    aModel->nextentry = theModel;
    theModel->preventry = aModel;
  }
```

```
    aScene->tail = theModel;
    return myStatus;
}


void sceneList::display(){
  scene *aScene = sceneListHead;
  scene *currentScene;
  sceneElement *model;
  currentScene = aScene->nextEntry;
  while (currentScene != NULL){
    currentScene->display(); // Scene Display
    model = currentScene->head;
    model->display();  // Model Display
    currentScene = currentScene->nextEntry;
  }
}


void sceneList::clear(){
  scene *aScene = sceneListHead;
  sceneElement *theModel, *nextModel;

  if(aScene->nextEntry == 0) return; // Don't clear an empty list
  aScene = aScene->nextEntry;
  theModel = aScene->head;
  while (theModel != NULL){
    nextModel = theModel->nextentry; // Get the pointer to next model
    delete theModel;  // Before deleting current model
    theModel = nextModel;
  }
  delete aScene;
  aScene = sceneListHead;
  aScene->nextEntry = 0;
  backdropImage = 0;
}
```

3.4   *Adding a Scene List to ICT*

The **sceneList** object is created when the ICT MDI client window is created. The function **ictMDIClient::Setup** contains among other things the statement:

```
sceneList *aSceneList = new sceneList();
```

which creates a new scene list. This scene list is populated with instructions for creating a visual effect when the **Tools|Create Scene List...** menu item is selected and a scene file is specified.

3.5   *Reading a Scene File*

Selecting the **Tools | Create Scene List...** option brings up a file browser that enables the selection of a scene file (or any other text file). After the **OK** button is pressed, the scene list is cleared if necessary and the function **readSceneList** is used to read the indicated scene file and repopulate the scene list.

3.6   *Editing a Scene File*

Scene files can be opened and edited using the **File|Open Scene...** menu item. The scene file is opened into a text editing window. The **File|Open Scene...** option can also be used, by the way, to edit motion path files or view the ICT process log file. The clipboard functions **cut**, **copy**, and **paste** can be used under the **Edit** menu. Expressions can also be searched for and replaced using the **Search** menu options.

CHAPTER 4

Color

This chapter describes in general how color is implemented on a personal computer and how ICT creates color special effects. Little or no prior knowledge of this topic is assumed. Those who are familiar with this subject may wish to skip to the next chapter.

Before getting started, we need to make a distinction between the terms *color table* and *palette*. In a functional sense, both terms refer to an equivalent mechanism of mapping between a set of color index values and a corresponding set of RGB colors. The distinction usually found in the literature is that the *color table* is a reference to the color mapping (an array of RGB colors) stored in an image file or used directly in a software program. The term *palette* tends to refer to a set of hardware registers located in the computer's video card which contain the equivalent array of RGB colors. These terms are often used interchangeably. If this paragraph meant nothing to you, read on and hopefully all will be made clear.

Most color image file formats popular on the personal computer today implement color using a color table. Figure 4.1 illustrates a 16-color image and its color table. In order to investigate further, we need to review a bit of computer science: Any digital image is stored in the computer as an array of numbers. Each number is called a *pixel*, which is short for "picture element." The total number of colors displayable in a given color image

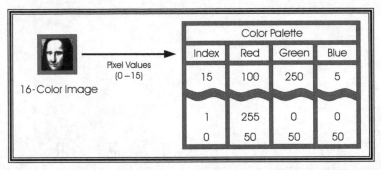

Figure 4.1 The VGA color palette.

depends on how many bits deep each pixel is. Since each bit is, in fact, a digit in the binary number system, the depth of a pixel in bits is the number of powers of two that can be represented in each pixel. The depth of a pixel in bits is called its resolution. For example, if one bit is stored for each pixel in the image, then each pixel can have only two possible values: on or off (one or zero). If 2 bits are stored for each pixel, then each pixel can have one of 2^2 or four possible values. A pixel's value shall be referred to as its *intensity*. For example, if an image has 16 colors, we reason that each pixel must be 4 bits deep since 16 is 2^4. In fact, each of the pixels in our example image is stored in the .bmp file as a number between 0 and 15. This may seem strange at first, but it's much more efficient than storing the colors themselves. To understand why, let's look at the color table itself.

4.1 The Color Table and True Color

The color table is used to convert the pixel intensities to numbers that express an actual color that can be displayed by the video card in your computer. These colors are expressed in the RGB color system. There are several formal systems used to describe the colors themselves; we discuss only the RGB system here, because it is relevant to both Windows and the .bmp file format. This system represents any individual color as a combination of red, green, and blue color components, hence the name RGB! If the red, green, and blue components are considered as X, Y, and Z axes respectively in a three-dimensional coordinate system, each color could be plotted at its proper coordinates. For example, a pure blue color could be represented in the RGB color coordinate system as (0,0,255). This color coordinate system is often called the RGB color space. Sources such as [FOLE90] describe the RGB and other color systems in more detail.

Each red, green, and blue color component in the color table is 8 bits deep so each component has a total possible number of 2^8 or 256 intensities.

This means that the RGB system can express all the colors resulting from a combination of 256 shades of red with 256 shades of green with 256 shades of blue. How many colors is that? That would be 256 × 256 × 256 or 16,777,216! Thus each color in the RGB color system is actually a 24-bit number because it contains 8 bits of red, 8 bits of green, and 8 bits of blue. We could save the 24-bit colors for each pixel in a true color image file; however, this would require prohibitively large amounts of disk space. A much more efficient way of storing colors was needed in the early days of computing, so the palette system was developed. What is stored for each pixel is actually the index into the color palette. Thus, for a 4-bit image, only 2^4 or 16 entries are needed in the color table. In this case, the palette contains 16 RGB colors occupying positions 0–15 in the color table as shown in Figure 4.1. Each pixel in this type of image having a value between 0 and 15 will be translated by the VGA card and the corresponding RGB color will be displayed. The numbers 0–15 are called *indexes* because they actually refer to positions in the color table, rather than to actual RGB colors.

The genius of the palette system is that a color image can be stored in a fraction of the space that would otherwise be required to store the RGB color value for each pixel. In addition, the range of colors that can be expressed by the color table is equal to the entire range of the RGB color system, which is over 16.7 million colors. This system is ideal for saving icons and drawings that do not require more than 16 colors to be displayed simultaneously. But what if we want to simultaneously display all the colors in a digitized photograph? No problem, just enlarge the number of bits per pixel and lengthen the corresponding color table. Many color photographs are digitized at a resolution of eight bits per pixel, using a color table of 2^8 or 256 entries. This level of resolution is quite adequate for some types of images. The average color image captured from a video source or flat bed scanner, however, contains far more than 256 colors. We deal with this reality shortly.

The whole purpose of this discussion so far has been to illuminate some of the issues involved when considering the task of compositing many color images together. We want to be able to combine two or more color images together to form a single result color image. If each of these color images uses a color table that represents different subsets of the total RGB color space, then many more than 256 colors must be processed during the image compositing process. Since the image compositing process combines colors from many different images together, new colors will be created during processing. If we convert all the colors from all the color images to be composited together in a given effect into a single color space before processing begins, the new colors created during processing will have no meaning because they will in fact be derived from color indices that are not required to have any consistent relationship with the RGB colors to which they map.

A better approach to this color problem involves more processing steps; however, it provides a superb result regardless of the number of images to be composited or their range of colors. This approach is used by most movie special effects companies; it is, essentially, not to use color tables. The first step is to convert all color images that use a color table into a true color format. This step substitutes the color indices with their corresponding RGB color values. (Many commercial image editing tools feature such a conversion capability.) The .bmp color table is not used in this format. All needed processing then occurs using true colors; the resulting images will consequently be produced in a true color format as well.

Once the images have been produced, they need to be displayed. It turns out that, unless your application demands it, a true color video card is not required to display a true color image! A so-called *high color* card will suffice in almost all cases. The term high-color has been used by manufacturers to describe video cards that can display between 32,767 and 65,535 RGB colors simultaneously. The 65,535-color variety of card is recommended. The price of such cards is around $100.

4.2   *How the ICT Handles Color*

The Image Compositing Toolkit operates in two color modes: monochrome and RGB. Monochrome mode accepts and processes eight-bit monochrome (256 shade grayscale) images. The result is an 8-bit monochrome image. This color mode is great for testing out a concept in a relatively short time. The second mode is RGB mode, which accepts and processes 24-bit true color images. The result is also a 24-bit true color image.

Now a word about the method used by ICT to process 24-bit color images. It would be possible to accept 24-bit .bmp images as input; however, the 24-bit .bmp format packs the three color values for each pixel together into consecutive storage locations. As observed in later chapters, the warping and compositing processes require that each component color image be processed separately. Consequently, it is more efficient for the ICT to accept and process a 24-bit color image that exists in the form of three separate 8-bit .bmp files. For this reason, software has been provided as part of the ICT that can open a standard true color .bmp image file and then read the desired component color image into memory. Thus, in RGB mode, all warping and compositing operations are simply performed three times, once for each red, green, and blue color component image. When the effect scene has been generated, the resulting image exists in the form of three separate 8-bit monochrome .bmp images, which are then converted into a single 24-bit .bmp image, ready for viewing.

5

Handling Images

Images might be considered the coin of the realm in the ICT application, since most of the major functions utilize or produce images in some manner. We therefore need to develop an infrastructure for handling images. More specifically, we need to provide compatibility with a commonly used image file format. Once the image has been opened we need to be able to access any information that has been stored with the image that describes its attributes, for example, the image size and pixel depth. More importantly, we need to be able to conveniently access the pixels in the image. These methods also need to support both color and monochrome images. All these capabilities are supported in a C++ class library, developed in this chapter, called **memImage**.

Along with the ability to access images stored in the popular Windows .bmp file format, the **memImage** member functions support two well-known concepts: An image can be opened for either sequential or random access.

5.1 *Random Access*

There are situations when we wish to read the entire image into memory and then perform some process on the image whereby every memory location in the image is assumed to be immediately available. The price paid for this convenience is that large amounts of memory can be consumed depending on the size of the images or the number of images being operated on at any given time.

An image opened for random access can be thought of as a rectangular array of pixels. Figure 5.1 shows that the origin of the memory resident image is in the lower-left corner. Coordinates in the **memImage** coordinate system are one relative. Two **memImage** member functions, **getMPixel** and **setMPixel**, will retrieve or set respectively the pixel at an indicated *x,y* location using the coordinate system shown in Figure 5.1.

The function prototypes for **getMPixel** and **setMPixel** are:

```
BYTE getMPixel(long x, long y);
short setMPixel (long x, long y, BYTE value);
```

As indicated by the definition above, **getMPixel** returns the pixel at location *x,y* in a variable of type BYTE. The BYTE data type is defined in windows.h and is equivalent to unsigned char. "Ah, wait!" you may be thinking, "this means that the largest pixel that can be retrieved will have a value of 255." After the discussion in the previous chapter about color, it appears that there is not enough pixel resolution to handle true color images that have a color depth of 24 bits. How right you are! Most of the **memImage** class functions are designed to handle true color images as if they were in fact three 256 grayscale component images: an 8-bit red image, an 8-bit green image, and an 8-bit blue image. Consequently, when pixels are retrieved from a true color image, a red, green, or blue component color must be specified. A variation of **getMPixel** is defined for this purpose:

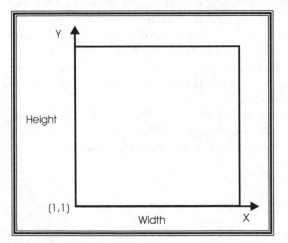

Figure 5.1 Image coordinates.

```
BYTE getMPixel(long x, long y, char aColor);
```

where **aColor** is either 'R', 'G', or 'B' depending on whether the red, green, or blue image is being processed.

Image Clipping

It is important to realize that member functions **getMPixel** and **setMPixel** contain built-in image clipping functions. If either **getMPixel** or **setMPixel** are called with coordinates located outside the bounds of the associated image array, no action is taken.

5.2   Sequential Access

There are situations where it is advantageous to open and process a .bmp formatted image file one line at a time. The primary advantage of this approach is that considerably less memory is required because only one line of the image needs to reside in the computer at any one time. The disadvantage of this approach is that it cannot be used for operations that require access to random locations in the image.

Two **memImage** member functions are defined to read and write the lines in an image sequentially:

```
short readNextRow();
short writeNextRow();
```

Each of these functions returns a status of zero if the operation was successful; if the next row of the image could not be accessed, a status of −1 is returned.

5.3   The Memory Resident Image Class (memImage)

Now let's take a closer look at the **memImage** class definition itself, which can be found in the file memImage.h:

```
class memImage {
protected:
FILE *fp;
char fileName[80];
short imageHeight;
short imageWidth;
short bitsPerPixel;
short paddedWidth;
```

```
        short pads;
        short accessMode;
        short theColorSpec;
        short valid;
        BYTE HUGE *bytes;
        void allocate(short, short);
        public:
          memImage (short height, short width);
          memImage (memImage *);
          memImage (char *fileName, short imLength, short imWidth,
              short imAccessMode, char rw, short colorSpec);
          short readNextRow();
          short writeNextRow();
          void clear();
          void display(HDC dc);
          void close();
          HBITMAP getBmp(HDC);
          short getHeight();
          short getWidth();
          BYTE HUGE * getBytes();
          short isValid();
          void smoothX3NN();
          void smoothY3NN();
          void createMask(memImage *outImage);
          void copy(memImage *outImage, short xoffset, short yoffset);
          short drawMask(
          HDC dc, POINT far *thePoints, int numVertices);
          short unPack(memImage *unpackedImage);
          short memImage::maskCopy(
          memImage *originalImage, char *imagePrefix, shape3d *aShape);
          BYTE getMPixel(long x, long y);
          BYTE getMPixel(long x, long y, char aColor);
          short setMPixel(long x, long y, BYTE value);
          short writeBMP(char *fileName);
          short readBMP(char *fileName, short theColor);
          virtual ~memImage();
        };
```

Let's look at the protected **memImage** data members, as shown in Table 5.1. The use of many of these data members is self-explanatory. Several others bear further explanation. First, let's look at the concept of a color specification.

The Color Specification

A color specification specifies the color properties of the associated image object. The private data member **theColorSpec** contains the color specification that can be assigned any of the following constant values, defined in memImage.h:

Table 5.1 Class **memImage** Protected Data Members

Data Member	Usage
fp	A pointer to FILE. FILE is a standard C file type. When the image file is open, this pointer has a valid value.
fileName	The full pathname of the .bmp image file.
imageHeight	The number of rows in the image. Can also be considered the *Y* dimension of the image in pixels.
imageWidth	The number of columns in the image. Can also be considered the *X* dimension of the image in pixels.
bitsPerPixel	The pixel depth of this image. Values of 1, 8, or 24 are supported.
paddedWidth	The smallest multiple of 4 bytes that can contain **imageWidth** pixels.
pads	The number of bytes difference between **paddedWidth** and **imageWidth**.
accessMode	One of two possible values: RANDOM or SEQUENTIAL.
theColorSpec	Specifies the type of image that is expected (see text for details).
valid	Indicates whether the **memImage** constructor was successful; 1 if successful; else valid is set to 0.
bytes	Pointer to the pixels in the image file.

```
#define REDCOLOR            1
#define GREENCOLOR          2
#define BLUECOLOR           3
#define EIGHTBITMONOCHROME  2
#define RGBCOLOR            7
#define ONEBITMONOCHROME    8
```

A color specification of REDCOLOR, GREENCOLOR, or BLUECOLOR is used when accessing true color images: **theColorSpec** is assigned the appropriate value indicating which of the three component images is being processed. A color specification of EIGHTBITMONOCHROME is used when an 8-bit black-and-white image is to be used. From the values assigned to the color specification constants, one can observe that the color specification EIGHTBITMONOCHROME is effectively equivalent to the color specification GREENCOLOR. A color specification of RGBCOLOR is used if a 24-bit color image is to be created. A color specification of ONEBITMONO-CHROME is used in the process of creating a cutout image and its corresponding mask image (more on this in Chapter 8). The color specification is primarily used to indicate how much memory is to be allocated, and in the case of accessing a true color image, which component image to retrieve.

The Validity Indicator

The **memImage** data member **valid** is used to indicate whether the constructor was successful or not. Recall that because a C++ constructor returns a pointer to the object it has created it is not permitted to return an application specific value. In the case of setting up the image in memory, there are many things that can go wrong. For example, the file pathname may not be valid, or there may not be sufficient memory for the image itself. If these or other operations are not completed successfully, an informative message is posted to the process log and the **valid** data member is set to zero. The public member function **isValid** can be used to determine whether the **memImage** object was successfully created.

Where Are the Pixels?

The data member **bytes** is a pointer to the pixels contained in the **memImage** image defined in the **memImage** header file as **BYTE HUGE *bytes**. This statement declares the data member **bytes** to be a HUGE pointer to a set of unsigned characters. One might observe that the HUGE designation is no longer necessary now that Windows 95 has a flat memory model. Despite this fact, we have retained the traditional definition in order to maintain compatibility with Windows 3.x.

Memory Allocation

There is only one protected member function in the **memImage** class: the memory allocation function **allocate**. Each of the **memImage** constructors call function **allocate** to obtain memory from the system in which to store the image. Function **allocate** calculates the amount of memory needed based on the values of **theColorspec**, **imageWidth**, and whether the data member **accessMode** is SEQUENTIAL or RANDOM. Function **allocate** also accommodates a requirement of the .bmp file format that specifies that the amount of memory used to contain a single row of the image be a multiple of 4 bytes. In other words, the length of an image row must be DWORD aligned. Function **allocate** calculates the smallest multiple of 4 bytes that can contain **imageWidth** pixels. This calculated width is stored in the private data member **paddedWidth**. In addition, the number of bytes needed to pad each row to satisfy the 4-byte multiple requirement is saved in the data member **pads**.

Creating a memImage Object

There are three **memImage** constructors:

```
memImage (short height, short width);
memImage (memImage *);
memImage (char *fileName, short imHeight, short imWidth,
short imAccessMode, char rw, short colorSpec);
```

The constructor:

```
memImage (char *fileName, short imHeight, short imWidth,
short imAccessMode, char rw, short colorSpec);
```

is capable of opening an image for all the situations we have described so far. The argument **fileName** is needed only if the image is opened for read access. A filename can be specified later if needed when using the member function **writeBMP**. Neither the image height **imHeight** nor the image width **imWidth** are required if the image is opened for read access. If both these arguments are set to zero, then the image will be opened in its entirety. The image access mode **imAccessMode** has two possible values: RANDOM or SEQUENTIAL. The argument **rw** has a value of either 'R' or 'W' based on whether the image is being opened for read or write access. Finally, the argument **theColorSpec** contains a color specification, which was described earlier.

Copying a memImage

The constructor shown below essentially copies a **memImage** object, using its sole calling parameter, a pointer to the **memImage** object to be copied.

```
memImage (memImage *);
```

The constructor:

```
memImage (short height, short width);
```

best represents the concept behind this entire class: the memory resident image object. This constructor creates a memory resident image, 8 bits per pixel of the size indicated by its two calling parameters: **height** and **width**. The memory resident image created by this constructor can later be saved in the .bmp image file format using the member function **writeBMP**.

5.4   *Handling Windows Bitmap Images*

The memImage class contains two member functions that access Windows bitmap images: **readBMP**, and **writeBMP**. A related function (not a member of the **memImage** class) named **readBMPHeader** reads the information header of a .bmp image file and returns the image size and the number of bits per pixel.

The .bmp file format was selected because bitmaps were designed to be used with the Windows operating system and can therefore be drawn on the screen with relative speed. The .bmp image file format actually is a family of formats. We are primarily interested in 8-bit monochrome or 24-bit (true color) .bmp image files of the uncompressed variety.

5.5   *The Windows Bitmap File Format*

The .bmp file format consists essentially of four parts or data structures that are listed here in order as follows: a file header, an information header, a color table, and finally, the image pixels themselves. We will now examine these four components of a .bmp file in more detail.

The bitmap file header is quite short and is defined in windows.h as follows:

```
typedef struct tabBITMAPINFOHEADER {
  UINT bfType;
  DWORD bfSize;
  UINT bfReserved1;
  UINT bfReserved2;
  DWORD bfOffBits;
} BITMAPINFOHEADER;
```

The **bfType** field should always contain the letters **BM** (short for bitmap of course!), which indicate to all concerned that the file is a windows bitmap (.bmp) file. The **bfType** field holds the file size. Fields **bfReserved1** and **bfReserved2** are not presently used. It's a good idea to leave these fields alone in the event that Microsoft decides to use them in the future. The field **bfOffbits** contains the number of bytes that must be skipped over in order to arrive at the location of the image pixels.

The bitmap information header contains basic information about the characteristics of the image and is also defined in windows.h:

```
typedef struct tabBITMAPINFOHEADER{
  DWORD biSize;
  LONG biWidth;
  LONG biHeight;
```

```
    WORD  biPlanes;
    WORD  biBitCount;
    DWORD biCompression;
    DWORD biSizeImage;
    LONG  biXPelsPerMeter;
    LONG  biYPelsPerMeter;
    DWORD biClrUsed;
    DWORD biClrImportant;
} BITMAPINFOHEADER;
```

The field **biSize** holds the length of the header in bytes; **biWidth** and **biHeight** indicate the width and height of the image respectively. The field **biBitCount** indicates the number of bits per pixel in the image. The field **biCompression** indicates whether the image is compressed. Member function **readBMP** will only read uncompressed.bmp images.

5.6   *The Color Table*

In section 4.1 we described how personal computers use a color table to expand the range of colors that can be displayed on limited hardware. The bitmap file can optionally contain such a color table. When a color table is present, the pixel values stored in the file are actually indexes into the color table. The color displayed on the screen is whatever RGB color the index mapped to in the color table. As described in Chapter 4, we cannot use such images due to possible color averaging effects from the warp and blend tools developed in Part II. The images processed by ICT will not actually need a color table because either 24-bit color images or 8-bit monochrome images are produced by ICT. The pixels stored in the image files by function **writeBMP** are the actual values that are displayed on the screen. Regardless, we need to be able to read a color table should it exist in the image file. The **readBMP** file ignores any color table it finds because it is assuming the pixels in the file are literal not indexes. Windows bitmap files come in four color variations:

1. Two colors (1 bit per pixel).
2. 16 colors (4 bits per pixel).
3. 256 colors (8 bits per pixel).
4. 16.7 million colors (24 bits per pixel).

In the 2-color, 16-color, and 256-color formats, the color table contains an entry for each possible color. Each color is specified using an RGB triple of the type described in Chapter 4 along with a fourth byte that is not used. The structure that holds one entry in the color table is called an RGBQUAD and is described in windows.h as:

```
typedef struct tagRGBQUAD{
    BYTE RGBBlue;
    BYTE RGBGreen;
    BYTE RGBRed;
    BYTE RGBReserved;
} RGBQUAD;
```

Because the BYTE data type is defined in windows as unsigned char, each data member of an RGBQUAD has 256 possible values. Thus the 24 usable bits in a single RGBQUAD value can represent any possible color in an RGB color space. True color .bmp files do not contain color tables because the pixels themselves are RGB color values.

5.7   *True Colors*

In the case of a 256-color image, each pixel is stored as a single byte. As mentioned earlier, in this case we assume the image pixels are not indexes into a color table but represent actual intensities that are to be displayed on the screen directly.

In the case of a true color image, each pixel is stored as a 3-byte triple. One byte is reserved for each of the red, green, and blue component colors. Now consider all of the first-occurring bytes in each true color pixel in an image. These first-occurring bytes would make up all of the blue pixels of the image. The set of all blue pixels in a true color image are sometimes referred to collectively as the blue color plane, or simply, the blue image; similarly there is a red image and a green image. Thus we see that each true color image is actually stored as a set of three color-separable 8-bit images: one 8-bit red image, one 8-bit green image, and one 8-bit blue image. We make use of this property of true color .bmp images during scene generation, which is described in Chapter 13.

True color .bmp images can very quickly consume significant amounts of disk space. For this reason several compression schemes have been defined for .bmp images. Most of these approaches are based on the assumption that consecutive pixel values in a given image row or column do not change rapidly; in fact, a significant percentage of the time they are the same. There is a family of compression schemes based on this assumption. This type of compression is called *run-length encoding;* several RLE approaches are described in [FOLE90] and [PETZ92].

Padded Pixels

It is important to note here that the physical width of each image record in a .bmp file must be a multiple of 4 bytes. Such a record is called DWORD aligned because all of the bytes in a scan line of the image fit into a round number of DWORDs (a DWORD is defined as unsigned long, which occupies 4 bytes). Presumably, this requirement permits optimal processing in a 32-bit environment. This requirement is placed on true color .bmp images as well as those .bmp formats that use a color table. The consequence of this requirement is that the **memImage** object contains a data member called **paddedWidth**. Data member **paddedWidth** is the smallest multiple of four that is greater than or equal to the width of the image. A related data member, called **pads**, is the actual number of bytes needed to round out the actual width to its actual **paddedWidth**.

Win16 and Win32 Versions of Class memImage

There are two versions of class **memImage**. A 16-bit version of class **memImage** is found in the file memImage.cpp. A 32-bit version is found in file memimg32.cpp. Both versions of this class share the header file memImage.h. Be certain to use the correct version of this class when you are building the ICT application. Two versions of **memImage** are required since the Win16 file access functions **lread** and **lwrite** are not supported in Win32. The 32-bit version of class **memImage** was created by making the function substitutions indicated in Table 5.2:

Here are the listings for the 16-bit version of the **memImage** member functions described in this chapter:

```
memImage::memImage (char *fileName, short imHeight, short
imWidth,
   short imAccessMode, char rw, short colorSpec){
   char msgBuffer[MAXPATH];
   if (colorSpec != ONEBITMONOCHROME && colorSpec != REDCOLOR &&
     colorSpec != GREENCOLOR && colorSpec != BLUECOLOR &&
     colorSpec != RGBCOLOR && colorSpec != EIGHTBITMONOCHROME &&
     colorSpec != 0){
     sprintf(msgBuffer,"memImage: ColorSpec not valid: %d", colorSpec);
     StatusPrint(msgBuffer);
     valid = 0;
```

Table 5.2   Win16 and Corresponding Win32 File Access Functions

Win16 Function	*Win32 Function*
lcreat, lopen	CreateFile
lread	ReadFile
lwrite	WriteFile
llseek	SetFilePointer
lclose	CloseHandle

```
        return;
     }
   if(rw != 'R' && rw != 'r' && rw != 'W' &&rw != 'w'){
      sprintf(msgBuffer,"memImage: rw must be R or W: %c", rw);
      StatusPrint(msgBuffer);
      valid = 0;
      return;
   }
   if(imAccessMode != RANDOM && imAccessMode != SEQUENTIAL){
      sprintf(msgBuffer,"memImage: accessMode must be RANDOM or SEQUENTIAL: %d",
      imAccessMode);
      StatusPrint(msgBuffer);
      valid = 0;
      return;
   }
   if((rw == 'W' || rw == 'w') && (imHeight <= 0 || imWidth <= 0 ||
      colorSpec == 0)){
      sprintf(msgBuffer,
      "memImage: length, width and colorSpec must be > 0 for write access");
      StatusPrint(msgBuffer);
      valid = 0;
      return;
   }
   short myBitsPerPixel, myStatus;
   valid = 1;
   myBitsPerPixel = mapColorSpecToBitsPerPixel(colorSpec);
   // Get a preview of the file if opened for reading so we know which
   // BMP reader is appropriate
int myHeight, myWidth;
if(imHeight == 0 || imWidth == 0 || colorSpec == 0){
   myStatus = readBMPHeader(fileName, &myHeight, &myWidth, &myBitsPerPixel);
   if(myStatus != 0){
      valid = 0;
       sprintf(msgBuffer,
         "memImage: Unable to open BMP header for read access");
      StatusPrint(msgBuffer);
      return;
   }
   imHeight = myHeight;
   imWidth = myWidth;
   if(colorSpec == 0)colorSpec =
      mapBitsPerPixelToColorSpec(myBitsPerPixel);
}
//
// Assign the memImage properties
imageHeight = imHeight;
imageWidth = imWidth;
bitsPerPixel = myBitsPerPixel;
theColorSpec = colorSpec;
accessMode = imAccessMode;
```

```
      if(rw == 'W' || rw == 'w'){
        DWORD numRows = imageHeight;
        if (accessMode == SEQUENTIAL) numRows = 1;
        allocate(numRows,imageWidth);
        if(!isValid()){
          StatusPrint("memImage: Could not allocate memory for write");
        }
      }
      if(accessMode == SEQUENTIAL){
      // Write or Read the BMP header
        if(rw == 'W' || rw == 'w')myStatus = writeBMP(fileName);
        if(rw == 'R' || rw == 'r')
        myStatus = readBMP(fileName, colorSpec);

        if(myStatus != 0) valid = 0; // Indicate the file could not be opened
      }
      if(accessMode == RANDOM){
        if((rw == 'W' || rw == 'w') && colorSpec == RGBCOLOR){
          StatusPrint("memImage: RANDOM 24 bit BMPs not supported for writing");
          valid = 0;
          return;
        }
        if((rw == 'W' || rw == 'w') && colorSpec != RGBCOLOR)
          myStatus = writeBMP(fileName);

        if(rw == 'R' || rw == 'r'){
        int myHeight, myWidth;
        short myBitsPerPixel;
        myStatus = readBMPHeader(fileName, &myHeight, &myWidth, &myBitsPerPixel);
        if(myStatus != 0){
          valid = 0; // Indicate that the file could not be opened
          sprintf(msgBuffer,"memImage: Unable to open BMP header");
          StatusPrint(msgBuffer);
          return;
        }
        readBMP(fileName, theColorSpec);
        if(myStatus != 0) valid = 0; // Indicate the file could not be opened
       }
      }
}

memImage::~memImage (){
  farfree(bytes);
  if(accessMode == SEQUENTIAL && fp > 0) _lclose(fp);
}


memImage::memImage (short height, short width){
// Allocates a memory resident 8-bit image
  valid=0;
```

```
    accessMode = RANDOM;
    imageHeight = height;
    imageWidth = width;
    theColorSpec = EIGHTBITMONOCHROME;
    bitsPerPixel = 8;
    allocate(height, width);
}

memImage::memImage (memImage *m){
    imageHeight = m->imageHeight;
    imageWidth = m->imageWidth;
    bitsPerPixel = m->bitsPerPixel;
    accessMode = m->accessMode;
    theColorSpec = m->theColorSpec;
    if(m->valid==1) allocate(m->imageHeight, m->imageWidth);
}

void memImage::allocate(short height, short width){
    long totalBytes;
    void far *buffer;
    float bytesPerPixel = (float)bitsPerPixel/8.;
    float fWidthInBytes = (float)width * bytesPerPixel;
    //handle the 1bpp case
    short widthInBytes = (short)fWidthInBytes;
    if (fWidthInBytes > (float) widthInBytes) widthInBytes++;
    paddedWidth = (widthInBytes/4)*4;
    if(paddedWidth!=widthInBytes) paddedWidth+=4;
    pads=paddedWidth-widthInBytes;
    totalBytes=(long)paddedWidth*(long)height;

    buffer = farcalloc(totalBytes,sizeof(BYTE));
    if (!buffer){
      valid = 0;     // Not enough memory for image
      return;
    }
    valid=1;
    bytes =(BYTE HUGE *)buffer;
    clear();       // zero the memory area
}

void memImage::clear(){
    int x, y;
    BYTE HUGE *myTemp;
    myTemp = bytes;
    int rows = imageHeight;
    if (accessMode == SEQUENTIAL) rows = 1;
    for (y = 1; y <= rows; y++){
      for (x = 1; x <= paddedWidth; x++){
      *myTemp = 0;
      myTemp++;
```

```
        }
      }
    }
HBITMAP memImage::getBmp(HDC dc){
    HBITMAP hBitmap;
    hBitmap=CreateBitmap(paddedWidth,imageHeight,1,8,bytes);
    return hBitmap;
}


void memImage::display2(HDC dc, short outWidth, short
outHeight){
    HBITMAP hBitmap,holdBitmap;
    HDC newdc;


    Handle hloc;
    PBITMAPINFO pbmi;
    HBITMAP hbm;


    RGBQUAD pal[256];
    hloc = LocalAlloc(LMEM_ZEROINIT | LMEM_MOVEABLE,
        sizeof(BITMAPINFOHEADER) + (sizeof(RGBQUAD) * 256));
    pbmi = (PBITMAPINFO) LocalLock(hloc);
    for(short a=0; a<256; a++){
        pal[a].rgbRed=a;
        pal[a].rgbGreen=a;
        pal[a].rgbBlue=a;
        pal[a].rgbReserved=0;
    }


    pbmi->bmiHeader.biSize = sizeof(BITMAPINFOHEADER);
    pbmi->bmiHeader.biWidth = imageWidth;
    pbmi->bmiHeader.biHeight = imageHeight;
    pbmi->bmiHeader.biPlanes = 1;
    pbmi->bmiHeader.biBitCount = 8;
    pbmi->bmiHeader.biCompression = BI_RGB;


    memcpy(pbmi->bmiColors, pal, sizeof(RGBQUAD) * 256);
    //create a bitmap data structure containing the memimage bits
    hBitmap = CreateDIBitmap(dc, (BITMAPINFOHEADER FAR*) pbmi, CBM_INIT,
        bytes, pbmi, DIB_RGB_COLORS);
    LocalFree(hloc);
    // create a memory DC
    newdc = CreateCompatibleDC(dc);
    // select the bitmap into the memory DC
    holdBitmap =(HBITMAP)SelectObject(newdc,hBitmap);
    // Blt the memimage bits to the desired dc
    int localHeight = imageHeight;
    int localWidth = imageWidth;
```

```
    if (localHeight > outHeight) localHeight = outHeight;
    if (localWidth > outWidth) localWidth = outWidth;
    int yDelta = imageHeight - localHeight;
    int xDelta = imageWidth - localWidth;
    if(yDelta < 0) yDelta = 0;
    if(xDelta < 0) xDelta = 0;

BitBlt(dc,0,0,localWidth,localHeight,newdc,0,yDelta,SRCCOPY);
  SelectObject(newdc,holdBitmap);
  DeleteObject(hBitmap);
  DeleteDC(newdc);
}


short memImage::makeMask(HDC dc, POINT far *thePoints, intnumVertices){
  HBITMAP hBitmap,holdBitmap;
  HDC newdc;
  hBitmap = CreateBitmap((int)imageWidth, (int)imageHeight, (UINT)1, (UINT)1,
    (const void HUGE *)bytes);
  if(hBitmap == 0){
    StatusPrint("CreateMask: Unable to create internal bitmap");
    return 1;
  }


  // create a memory DC
  newdc=CreateCompatibleDC(dc);
  //  Select the bitmap into the memory DC
  holdBitmap=(HBITMAP)SelectObject(newdc,hBitmap);
  // Clear the memory dc by drawing a filled black rectangle
  RECT myRect;
  SetRect(&myRect, 0,0,imageWidth, imageHeight);
  FillRect(newdc,&myRect,
  (HBRUSH)GetStockObject(BLACK_BRUSH));
  // Create the image mask by drawing a filled white polygon
  HPEN hpen = CreatePen(PS_SOLID, 1, 0xFFFFFFFFL);
  SelectObject (newdc, hpen);
  SelectObject (newdc, GetStockObject (WHITE_BRUSH));
  SetPolyFillMode(newdc, WINDING);
  Polygon(newdc, thePoints, numVertices);
  // Display the mask
  BitBlt(dc,0,0,imageWidth,imageHeight,newdc,0,0,SRCCOPY);
  // Copy the completed mask image back to the memImage buffer
  DWORD dwCount = (DWORD)paddedWidth * (DWORD)imageHeight;
  // the bitmap is stored using a width that is a 2-byte multiple
  GetBitmapBits(hBitmap, dwCount, bytes);
  SelectObject(newdc,holdBitmap);
  DeleteObject(hBitmap);
  DeleteDC(newdc);
  return 0;
}
```

```
void memImage::copy(memImage *outImage, short xoffset, short
  yoffset){int x, y;
  for (x = 1; x <= imageWidth; x++){
    for (y = 1; y < imageHeight; y++){
      BYTE thePixel = getMPixel(x, y);
      if(thePixel != 0)
        outImage->setMPixel((long)x + (long)xoffset, (long)y +
          (long)yoffset,
         thePixel);
    }
  }
}


BYTE memImage::getMPixel (long x, long y){
  //input x and y are assumed to be 1 relative
  long addr;
  BYTE HUGE * myTemp = bytes;
  if(accessMode == SEQUENTIAL) y = 1;
  if (y < 1 || y > imageHeight || x < 1 || x > imageWidth) return 0;
  addr = ((y - 1) * (long)paddedWidth) + x - 1;
  myTemp = myTemp + addr;
  return *myTemp;
}


BYTE memImage::getMPixel (long x, long y, char aColor){
//  input x and y are assumed to be 1 relative
//  returns the desired pixel from a color image
  long addr;
  BYTE HUGE *thePixel;
  BYTE HUGE *myTemp = bytes;
  if(accessMode == SEQUENTIAL) y = 1;
  if (y < 1 || y > imageHeight || x < 1 || x > imageWidth) return 0;
  addr = ((y - 1) * (long)paddedWidth) + ((x - 1)*3); // 3 bytes/color
                                                      // pixel
  myTemp = myTemp + addr;
  thePixel = myTemp;
  if(aColor == 'B') return *thePixel;
  if(aColor == 'G') return *(thePixel + 1);
  if(aColor == 'R') return *(thePixel + 2);
  StatusPrint("getMPixel: unknown color value");
  return 0;
}


short memImage::setMPixel (long x, long y, BYTE value){
// input x and y are assumed to be 1 relative
  long addr;
  BYTE HUGE *myTemp = bytes;
  if(accessMode == SEQUENTIAL) y = 1;
```

```
    if (y < 1 || y > imageHeight || x < 1 || x > imageWidth) return (0);
    addr = ((y - 1) * (long)paddedWidth) + x - 1;
    myTemp = myTemp + addr;
    *(myTemp) = value;
    return value;
}


short memImage::getHeight (){
  return (imageHeight);}


short memImage::getWidth (){
  return (imageWidth);}


short memImage::getAccessMode (){
  return (accessMode);}


short memImage::getColorSpec (){
  return (theColorSpec);}


BYTE HUGE * memImage::getBytes (){
  return (bytes);}


short memImage::isValid(){
//  valid = 1 indicates the constructor did not encounter errors.
  if(valid == 0)
    return (0);
  else
    return (1);
}


short memImage::writeBMP(char *fileName){
  char msgText [MAXPATH];
  BITMAPFILEHEADER bf;
  BITMAPINFOHEADER bi;
  RGBQUAD palinfo[256];
  DWORD a;
  valid = 1;

  bi.biSize=(long)sizeof(BITMAPINFOHEADER);
  bi.biWidth=(long)imageWidth;
  bi.biHeight=(long)imageHeight;
  bi.biPlanes=1;
  if (theColorSpec == RGBCOLOR) bi.biBitCount=24;
  else
   if(theColorSpec == ONEBITMONOCHROME) bi.biBitCount=1;
  else
    bi.biBitCount=8;
```

```
bi.biCompression=BI_RGB;
bi.biSizeImage=(long)imageHeight*(long)paddedWidth;
bi.biXPelsPerMeter=1;
bi.biYPelsPerMeter=1;
bi.biClrUsed=256;
bi.biClrImportant=256;

bf.bfType=0x4d42;
bf.bfSize=((long)sizeof(BITMAPFILEHEADER)
  +(long)bi.biSize
  +(long)bi.biSizeImage)/4;
bf.bfReserved1=0;
bf.bfReserved2=0;
bf.bfOffBits=(long)sizeof(BITMAPFILEHEADER)
  +(long)sizeof(BITMAPINFOHEADER)
  +(long)sizeof(RGBQUAD)*256;

for(a=0; a <256; a++){
  palinfo[a].rgbRed=a;
  palinfo[a].rgbGreen=a;
  palinfo[a].rgbBlue=a;
  palinfo[a].rgbReserved=a;
}
fp = _lcreat(fileName,0);
if(fp == NULL) {
  sprintf(msgText, "writeBMP: Couldn't open output image. %s", fileName);
  StatusPrint(msgText);
  valid = 0;
  return 1;
}
_lwrite(fp, &bf, sizeof(BITMAPFILEHEADER));
_lwrite(fp, &bi,sizeof(BITMAPINFOHEADER));
_lwrite(fp, palinfo, sizeof(RGBQUAD) * 256);
size_t numItems = 1;
int myIndex;
BYTE HUGE *theBytes = bytes;
if (accessMode == RANDOM){
  for(myIndex = 1; myIndex <= imageHeight; myIndex++){
    numItems = _lwrite(fp, theBytes, paddedWidth);
    if(numItems == -1) {
     sprintf(msgText,
     "writeBMP: _lwrite error. %s",fileName);
     StatusPrint(msgText);
     _lclose(fp);
     valid = 0;
     return 1;
   }
   theBytes += paddedWidth;
 }
```

```
    }
  if (accessMode == RANDOM) _lclose(fp);
  return 0;
}

short memImage::readBMP(char *fname, short colorSpec){
  BITMAPFILEHEADER bmFH;
  BITMAPINFOHEADER *pbmIH;
  BITMAPINFO *pbmInfo;
  WORD PalSize=256;
  char transfer[3];
  LONG x,y,index,counter,pad24,pad8;
  unsigned long bmWidth, bmHeight, bmImgSize, bmScanWidth, bmScanWidth8;
  char msgText[MAXPATH];
  if ( colorSpec == RGBCOLOR && accessMode == RANDOM) {
    sprintf(msgText, "readBMP: Invalid colorSpec: %d", colorSpec);
    StatusPrint(msgText);
    valid=0;
    return 1;
  }
  valid = 1;
  fp = _lopen(fname, OF_READ);
  if( fp == NULL ) {
    sprintf(msgText, "readBMP: Couldn't open image. %s", fname);
    StatusPrint(msgText);
    valid=0;
    return 2;
  }

  SetCursor( LoadCursor( NULL, IDC_WAIT ) );
  _lread(fp, (LPSTR) &bmFH, sizeof(BITMAPFILEHEADER) );
  if( bmFH.bfType != 0x4D42 ){ // if type isn't "BM" ...
    sprintf(msgText, "readBMP: Not a .BMP image. %s", fname);
    StatusPrint(msgText);
    _lclose(fp);
    valid = 0;
    return 3;
  }

  pbmIH = (BITMAPINFOHEADER *)
    GlobalLock(GlobalAlloc(GMEM_FIXED, sizeof(BITMAPINFOHEADER)));
    _lread(fp, (LPSTR) pbmIH, sizeof(BITMAPINFOHEADER));
    bitsPerPixel = 8;
    if(colorSpec == RGBCOLOR) bitsPerPixel = 24;
    WORD fileBitsPerPixel = (WORD) pbmIH->biBitCount;
    if(fileBitsPerPixel != 1 && fileBitsPerPixel != 8 &&
      fileBitsPerPixel != 24 ){
      sprintf(msgText,
        "readBMP: Pixel size mismatch. Requested: %d file: %d %s",
```

```
      bitsPerPixel, pbmIH->biBitCount, fname);
    StatusPrint(msgText);
    _lclose(fp);
    valid = 0;
    return 4;
}


if( (DWORD) pbmIH->biCompression != BI_RGB ){
    sprintf(msgText,
      "readBMP: Compressed images not supported. %s", fname);
    StatusPrint(msgText);
    _lclose(fp);
    return 5;
}


GlobalUnlock( (HANDLE) pbmIH );
GlobalFree( (HANDLE) pbmIH );


pbmInfo = (BITMAPINFO *)
    GlobalLock(   GlobalAlloc( GHND, PalSize +
      sizeof(BITMAPINFOHEADER) ) );
pbmInfo->bmiHeader = *pbmIH;


bmWidth = (DWORD) pbmInfo->bmiHeader.biWidth;
bmHeight = (DWORD) pbmInfo->bmiHeader.biHeight;
imageHeight = bmHeight;
imageWidth = bmWidth;
bmImgSize = (DWORD) pbmInfo->bmiHeader.biSizeImage;
// must be an even WORD size !!!
bmScanWidth8=((bmWidth*8+31)/32)*4;
bmScanWidth=((bmWidth*24+31)/32)*4;


long widthInBytes = bmWidth * 3;
short remainder = widthInBytes % 4;
pad24 = 0;
if (remainder > 0)pad24 = 4 - remainder;
// we are reading from a 24 bit BMP in order to create an 8-bit BMP
// calculate the number of pads needed for the 8-bit BMP
short remainder8 = bmWidth % 4;
pad8 = 0;
if(remainder8 > 0) pad8 = 4 - remainder8;


bmImgSize= bmScanWidth8*bmHeight;
pbmInfo->bmiHeader.biSizeImage = bmImgSize;


DWORD numRows = bmHeight;
if (accessMode == SEQUENTIAL) numRows = 1;
allocate(numRows, bmWidth);
```

```
      if(valid==0){
        sprintf(msgText, "readBMP: Couldn't allocate memory. %s", fname);
        StatusPrint(msgText);
        _lclose(fp);
        return 6;
    }


    _llseek(fp, bmFH.bfOffBits, 0);
    if (accessMode == RANDOM){
      BYTE HUGE *theBytes = bytes;
      short numItems, myIndex;
      if(bitsPerPixel == fileBitsPerPixel){
      for(myIndex = 1; myIndex <= imageHeight; myIndex++){
        numItems = _lread(fp, theBytes, paddedWidth);
        if(numItems == -1) {
          sprintf(msgText,
          "readBMP: _lread error. %s",fileName);
          StatusPrint(msgText);
          _lclose(fp);
          valid = 0;
          return 1;
        }
        theBytes += paddedWidth;
      }
    }
    else {        // we are reading 8 bpp from a 24-bpp file
      index = 0;
      long rowWidth = widthInBytes + pad24;
      char *transfer = new char[rowWidth + 1];
      for(y = 0; y < bmHeight; y++){
        _lread(fp, transfer, rowWidth);
        for(x = 0; x < bmWidth * 3; x += 3){
          bytes[index] = transfer[x + (4 - colorSpec - 1)];
          index++;
        }
        index += pad8;
      }
      delete transfer;
    }     // end else
  }
  GlobalFree( (HANDLE)GlobalHandle( HIWORD( pbmInfo ) ) );
  if (accessMode == RANDOM) _lclose(fp);
  SetCursor( LoadCursor( NULL, IDC_ARROW ) );
  return 0;
}


short memImage::readNextRow(){
  short myStatus;
  myStatus = _lread(fp, bytes, paddedWidth);
  if (myStatus == 0) return 1;
```

```
    else
    return 0;
}

void memImage::close(){
  _lclose(fp);
  fp = 0;
}

short memImage::writeNextRow(){
  short myStatus;
  myStatus = _lwrite(fp, bytes, paddedWidth);
  if (myStatus == 0) return 1;
  else
  return 0;
}

short readBMPHeader(char *fname, int *height, int *width,
short *bitsPerPixel){
  BITMAPFILEHEADER bmFH;
  BITMAPINFOHEADER *pbmIH;
  BITMAPINFO *pbmInfo;
  WORD PalSize=256;
  HFILE fp;
  unsigned long imageSize;
  char errText[MAXPATH];

  fp = _lopen(fname, OF_READ);
  if( fp == NULL ){
    sprintf(errText, "readBMPHeader: Can't open %s",fname);
    StatusPrint(errText);
    return 1;
  }

  _lread(fp,  (LPSTR) &bmFH, sizeof(BITMAPFILEHEADER));
   if( bmFH.bfType != 0x4D42 ){   // if type isn't "BM" ...
     sprintf(errText, "readBMPHeader: Not a bitmap image: %s",fname);
     StatusPrint(errText);
     _lclose(fp);
     return 2;
   }
   pbmIH = (BITMAPINFOHEADER *)
     GlobalLock(   GlobalAlloc( GMEM_FIXED,sizeof(BITMAPINFOHEADER)));
   _lread(fp, (LPSTR) pbmIH, sizeof(BITMAPINFOHEADER));
   *bitsPerPixel = (WORD) pbmIH->biBitCount;
   if( (DWORD) pbmIH->biCompression != BI_RGB){
     sprintf(errText, "Compressed image. Not accepted: %s",fname);
     StatusPrint(errText);
     _lclose(fp);
```

```
        return 3;
    }
GlobalUnlock( (HANDLE) pbmIH );
GlobalFree( (HANDLE) pbmIH );
pbmInfo = (BITMAPINFO *)
    GlobalLock(   GlobalAlloc( GHND, PalSize +
        sizeof(BITMAPINFOHEADER) ) );
pbmInfo->bmiHeader = *pbmIH;
*width = (DWORD) pbmInfo->bmiHeader.biWidth;
*height = (DWORD) pbmInfo->bmiHeader.biHeight;
imageSize = (DWORD) pbmInfo->bmiHeader.biSizeImage;
GlobalFree((HANDLE)GlobalHandle(HIWORD(pbmInfo)));
_lclose(fp);
return 0;
}
```

Entering the Third Dimension

This chapter describes how graphical objects are represented in a three-dimensional world, how to view the graphical world from different viewpoints, how to move the graphical objects around in this world, and finally how to display these graphical objects on a computer screen. We assume the reader has little or no prior knowledge of the topics discussed here. Those who are familiar with these topics may wish to skip to the next chapter.

From this point forward, we shall use the term *model* to refer to a graphical object in order to avoid potential confusion between graphical objects and C++ objects. In Chapter 2 we said that a visual effect scene consists of a set of models. Here we use a slightly narrower definition of the term. In this chapter only, when we refer to a model, we are referring to the model's coordinates. A model then, can be either the boundary of a digitized photograph (image), or a line drawing without an associated image, that is, a shape-based model. Figure 6.1 shows several examples of models.

6.1   Coordinates

The graphical world we refer to here is really a three-dimensional *coordinate system* like that shown in Figure 6.2a. Specific locations in this coordinate

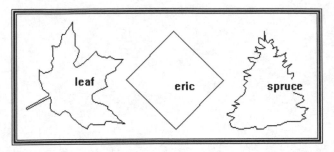

Figure 6.1 Example models.

system are called *points, coordinates,* or *vertices.* As mentioned earlier, a model consists of a set of points. Let's now consider each of these topics in more detail.

Figure 6.2*a* illustrates what is formally called the right-handed Cartesian coordinate system, named after Rene DeCartes who invented it in the early 1600s. You probably remember from high school that the large straight arrows in Figure 6.2*a* represent axes that point in positive directions; these are labeled X, Y, and Z. The point where all three axes intersect is called the *origin.* Throughout this text we refer to the right-handed Cartesian coordinate system as the *world coordinate system.*

Your right hand is a convenient device for remembering the basic properties of the right-handed coordinate system. Figure 6.2*b* shows a person's right hand with the thumb pointed in the positive direction along the X axis. The pointer finger is oriented along the positive Y Axis. The index

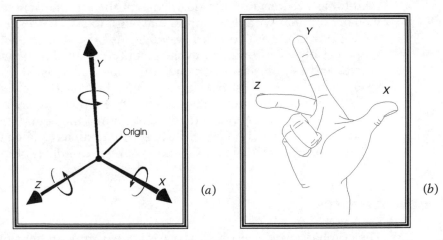

Figure 6.2 The right-handed Cartesian coordinate system.

finger points back toward you, in the positive Z direction. If you now imagine a point in the palm of your right hand as the coordinate system's origin, the lines created by moving from the origin to the end of each finger tip represent the positive direction of motion along each of the three axes, as illustrated in Figure 6.2. Conversely, a motion that begins at a finger tip and moves toward the origin is motion in a negative direction.

A precise location in the world coordinate system is described by specifying a *coordinate*, which consists of a distance from the origin along each of the three axes in the order X, Y, and Z. For example, the location 10 units in the positive X direction, 20 units in the positive *Y* direction, and 30 units in the negative Z direction is written: (10, 20, −30).

Units

The units along each axis can be whatever we wish them to be. The most important point about units is to be consistent when using them. We do not assume specific units in the coordinate system used in ICT. An image is located in the world coordinate system by assuming it occupies one unit per pixel. This means that the spatial resolution of the coordinate system is independent of the spatial resolution at which images are captured.

6.2   *Angles and the Right-Handed Rule*

With your right hand positioned as shown in Figure 6.2*b*, notice that it is possible to rotate an object about each axis. The *right-handed rule* says that positive angles of rotation describe a circular motion in the counterclockwise direction around the axis when viewed from any location on the positive axis, looking toward the origin. Arrows rotating in positive directions about each axis are shown in Figure 6.2*a*. Conversely, a negative angle describes a motion around an axis in the clockwise direction again, assuming the viewer is looking toward the origin from a point on any positive axis.

We shall refer to the three rotation angles as r*x*, r*y*, and r*z*. We are accustomed to using degrees as a unit of measure when describing angles. The graphics transformations described later in this chapter, however, require that angles be specified in *radians*. There is nothing magical about radians, they are just another way of describing an angle. Angles measured in degrees may be converted to radians by remembering that there are pi (3.1415926 . . .) radians for each 180 degrees. The ICT software declares the constant DTR (Degrees-to-Radians) as a conversion factor equal to 3.1415926/180.0. Multiplying an angle specified in degrees by this factor will convert it to an equivalent angle in radians.

6.3 *Basic Coordinate Transformations*

In this section we describe how to move models around in three dimensions. There are three basic ways a model can be moved or changed in a three-dimensional coordinate system: a change in location, called a *translation*; a change in orientation, called a *rotation*; and a change in size, called a *scale* operation. By applying combinations of rotation, scale, and translation operations to a model, we can cause it to move to any location and orientation in the coordinate system.

It's All Relative

Notice that we have been talking about these transformations in a relative sense. For example, if an object is rotated 45 degrees about the X axis, it is rotated from its present location and orientation. In this sense, the transformations we will be dealing with are always applied relative to a model's current position and orientation. We now describe three fundamental graphic transformations.

Translation

The operation of simply moving a model from one three-dimensional location to another is called a translation. In order to move the model, we move all the points in the model. If the point (x, y, z) is a model coordinate prior to the translation, then the translated point (x', y', z') is given by:

$$x' = x + t_x$$
$$y' = y + t_y$$
$$z' = z + t_z$$

where t_x, t_y, and t_z are the amounts to move along the X, Y, and Z axes respectively. Note that translation is relative in the sense that xd indicates an amount to move along the X axis relative to the model's current location. A model's initial location must be known in order to know where the model will end up after a particular transform is applied.

Rotation

A point in the world coordinate system can be rotated about any of the three axes. We will need to keep track of rotation angles for each axis. We use r_x, r_y, and r_z to indicate the rotation angles about the X, Y, and Z axes respectively. We may obtain the rotated point (x', y', z') from an initial point (x, y, z) by rotating about the Z axis by an angle r_z using:

$$x' = x \cos (r_z) - y \sin(r_z)$$
$$y' = y \cos (r_z) + x \sin (r_z)$$
$$z' = z$$

Similarly, rotating about the X axis:

$$x' = x$$
$$y' = y \cos (r_x) - z \sin (r_x)$$
$$z' = y \sin (r_x) + z \cos(r_x)$$

Finally, rotating about the Y axis:

$$x' = z \sin (r_y) + x \cos(r_y)$$
$$y' = y$$
$$z' = z \cos (r_y) - x \sin(r_y)$$

So far we have discussed only rotating points. To rotate a model, we simply rotate all the points in the model. A model's *orientation* refers generally to the values of the model's three rotation angles. A model's *location* is defined here as its average location, or *centroid*. Centroids are described in detail in Chapter 7.

Scaling

The size of a model can be enlarged or reduced using a scaling operation. The amount of scaling to apply to the model is expressed by a number whose range is centered about one. That is, applying a scale factor of one to a point will result in a scaled coordinate (x', y', z'), which is equal to the old coordinate. In other words, no scaling has occurred. A scale factor of 0.5 means that the value along each axis of the new point is half as much as the original point. A scale factor may be applied along each axis. Three scale factors result: s_x, s_y, and s_z. The mathematical expression for the scaled cornerpoint is:

$$x' = xs_x$$
$$y' = ys_y$$
$$z' = zs_z$$

Scaling objects that are not centered about the origin must be handled in a manner similar to the way we described for rotating objects that are not located at the origin. We must first center the model about the origin by applying a translation, apply the scale factor, and then translate the model back to its original location.

Combining Transformations

So far we have described rotating points and models that are centered about the origin. What if the model we want to rotate is not centered at the origin? The answer is that even if the model we wish to rotate is not centered about the origin, we can still apply the equations above if we first move (i.e., translate) the model so that it is centered about the origin, apply the rotation, and then translate the model back to its original location. To do this type of rotation, then, requires two additional translations besides the rotation itself. We will return to this subject later in section 6.8, where we discuss how to combine many transformations together.

6.4   *The Viewer*

Models located in the world coordinate system can be viewed from a known location and orientation collectively called the *viewpoint*. The viewpoint consists of two of the types of transformations we have already described: a translation and a set of three rotation angles. Each of these transformations is relative to the origin. One way to visualize the viewpoint is to imagine the viewer as being translated a certain distance from the origin and then, from that location, viewing the world in the direction indicated by three view angles: v_x, v_y, and v_z.

6.5   *Those Handy Matrices*

It turns out that in order to move the models as we wish, we often need to combine the transformations described above together. A computationally efficient way to do this is to rearrange the transformation equations given previously into a matrix form. Once in matrix form several transformations can be combined by multiplying the appropriate matrices together. This combined or *composite* transformation matrix can then be applied to all of the points in a model.

Conventions

First a few words about matrices. In order to multiply two matrices together we essentially multiply rows of the first matrix with columns of the second matrix. The only requirement for this definition to work in all cases is that the number of rows in the first matrix must be equal to the number of columns in the second matrix. Consider now that a single point (x, y, z) can also be thought of as a matrix with either one row or one column, depending on whether it is written as:

$$[x, y, z] \quad \text{or} \quad \begin{bmatrix} x \\ y \\ z \end{bmatrix}$$

Since the same point can be expressed as a matrix with either a single row or a single column, there are two different ways to multiply a point by a matrix:

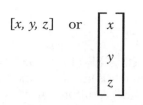

$$[x, y, z] \quad \times \quad \begin{bmatrix} a, b, c \\ d, e, f \\ g, h, i \end{bmatrix} \quad \text{or} \quad \begin{bmatrix} a, d, g \\ b, e, h \\ c, f, i \end{bmatrix} \quad \times \quad \begin{bmatrix} x \\ y \\ z \end{bmatrix}$$

Notice that the rows and columns of the 3 × 3 matrix were exchanged depending on whether the coordinate was written as a row vector in the first equation or as a column vector in the second equation. You can expand the multiplication out to satisfy yourself that the resulting transformed coordinate will have exactly the same value in either of these cases. By the way, when the rows and columns of a matrix are interchanged as they are in the example above, we say the matrix has been *transposed*. The point is that many graphics texts use the first convention; others use the second. If one is not aware of the difference, confusion can result. To be clear, in this book we use the second convention shown above. This form is consistent with that found in [Fole90].

6.6   *Homogeneous Coordinates*

Even though the graphics transformations we have described involve only three dimensions, the transformation matrices we provide in the following sections will have four rows and columns. The fourth row and column accommodate what are called *homogeneous coordinates*. Homogeneous coordinates came about primarily to enable translation, a simple addition, to be expressed as a matrix multiplication. The matter of homogeneous coordinates is elaborated further in texts such as [FOLE90] and [HEAR86]. For our purposes, only one adjustment needs to be made in the way we represent a point in order to use homogeneous coordinates. In addition to X, Y, and Z coordinates, the number one is added to the coordinate notation. For example, the point (10, 20, −30) now becomes (10, 20, −30, 1). Adding the extra one in the fourth position now permits points to be translated with the translation matrix, which will be provided below. In using homogeneous coordinates, we gain a consistent notation for representing and compositing together each of the graphic transformations considered here.

6.7 Introduction to Class tMatrix

Now for some good news. A C++ class library named **tMatrix** (short for transformation matrix) is developed in this section, which encapsulates all of the matrix forms of the graphic transformations discussed in the previous section. In the sections that follow we introduce each of the transformations along with the appropriate **tMatrix** member function that performs the transformation. A **tMatrix** object can be thought of as a set of one or more graphic transformations that can be applied to a model in a scene.

Creating a tMatrix Object

There are two **tMatrix** constructors:

```
tMatrix();
tMatrix(tMatrix *aMatrix);
```

The first constructor simply creates an initialized **tMatrix** object. The second constructor essentially creates a copy of the **tMatrix** object, which is passed in as the only argument.

Now let's look at the **tMatrix** private data members. A **tMatrix** object has a private matrix for each of the basic transformations we have mentioned thus far: **scMat** for scaling operations; **trMat** for translations; and three rotation matrices, **rxMat**, **ryMat**, and **rzMat**. One additional matrix **theMatrix** is used to store what is called the composite transformation. The role this matrix plays will become clear shortly.

The following are the three public member functions that implement the graphic transformations:

```
void scale(float sx, float sy, float sz);
void rotate(float rx, float ry, float rz);
void translate(float tx, float ty, float tz);
```

where s*x*, s*y*, s*z* are the scale factors in the X, Y, and Z directions; r*x*, r*y*, and r*z* are the rotation angles in radians about the X, Y, and Z angles respectively; and t*x*, t*y*, and t*z* are the desired translations in the X, Y, and Z directions.

6.8 Composite Transformations

Once a **tMatrix** object has been created, transformation operations are added to the **tMatrix** object by calling an appropriate member function for each desired transformation. Each time an operation is added to the **tMatrix** object, the matrix corresponding to the operation itself is multiplied with the matrix **theMatrix**. **theMatrix** then contains the composite of all transformations that have been applied. A second way to composite many transformations together is to use the **multiply** member function with two **tMatrix** objects, each containing transformations:

```
void multiply(tMatrix *matrix1, tMatrix *matrix2);
```

Multiplying and Copying Matrices

Two traditional C functions are also bundled with the **tMatrix** class, a matrix multiplication function called **matmult** and a matrix copy function called **matcopy**. These two functions are used by many of the **tMatrix** member functions.

6.9 The Identity Matrix

There is a special matrix, called the *identity,* which is analogous to the number 1 in arithmetic. In the same way that any number multiplied by the number 1 is equal to itself, any matrix multiplied by the identity matrix is also unchanged. Let's consider another use for the identity. In arithmetic, the *inverse* of any number is defined as its reciprocal. For example, the inverse of the number 7 is 1/7. It follows that any number multiplied by its inverse is equal to the number 1. In the case of matrices, any matrix multiplied by its inverse matrix (we discuss the inverse matrix in Chapter 9) will equal the identity matrix. We will make good use of these properties in Chapter 9. Here is a 4 × 4 identity matrix:

$$\begin{bmatrix} 1, & 0, & 0, & 0 \\ 0, & 1, & 0, & 0 \\ 0, & 0, & 1, & 0 \\ 0, & 0, & 0, & 1 \end{bmatrix}$$

The **tMatrix** member function **setIdentity** will initialize matrix **theMatrix** with the identity matrix shown above. Matrix **theMatrix** is also initialized to its identity each time a **tMatrix** object is created.

6.10 Applying a Transformation

The function **transformPoint** applies whatever transformation is contained in the **tMatrix** object's internal matrix (theMatrix) to the point (**xIn**, **yIn**, **xIn**) passed in:

```
void transformPoint(float xIn, float yIn, float zIn,
float *xOut, float *yOut, float * zOut);
```

The transformed point is returned in the coordinate (**xOut**, **yOut**, **zOut**). In order to transform an entire model with this function, this function must be called for each point in the model. Since a model's coordinates are actually stored in a **shape3d** object, we have provided a function that applies a **tMatrix** transformation matrix to a **shape3d** object and we therefore defer this discussion to Chapter 7.

Here is a listing of the **tMatrix** header file tMatrix.h:

```
class tMatrix{
  public:
  void scale(float sx, float sy, float sz);
  void rotate(float rx, float ry, float rz);
  void translate(float tx, float ty, float tz);
  void multiply(tMatrix *matrix1, tMatrix *matrix2);
  void setIdentity();
  void transformPoint(float xIn, float yIn, float zIn, float *xOut, float
    *yOut, float * zOut);
  short invertg();
  void transpose();
  tMatrix();
  tMatrix(tMatrix *aMatrix);
  ~tMatrix();
  void Display(char *);

  protected:
  float theMatrix[4][4]; // Composite transformation matrix
  float rxMat[4][4]; // X rotation matrix
  float ryMat[4][4]; // Y rotation matrix
  float rzMat[4][4]; // Z rotation matrix
  float scMat[4][4]; // Scaling matrix
  float trMat[4][4]; // Translation matrix
};
void matmult(float result[4][4],float mat1[4][4],
  float mat2[4][4]);
void matcopy(float dest[4][4],float source[4][4]);
```

6.11 Graphic Transformations—Matrix Style

Following are the matrix forms of the transformations we discussed in section 6.3. By multiplying these forms out in long hand you will see that these equations are equivalent to the nonmatrix forms discussed in section 6.3. Here are the matrices for the translation, scale, and the three rotation transformations:

Translation Matrix

$$
\begin{bmatrix}
1, & 0, & 0, & t_x \\
0, & 1, & 0, & t_x \\
0, & 0, & 1, & t_x \\
0, & 0, & 0, & 1
\end{bmatrix}
$$

Scale Matrix

$$
\begin{bmatrix}
s_x, & 0, & 0, & 0 \\
0, & s_y, & 0, & 0 \\
0, & 0, & s_z, & 0 \\
0, & 0, & 0, & 1
\end{bmatrix}
$$

X-Axis Rotation Matrix

$$
\begin{bmatrix}
1, & 0, & 0, & 0 \\
0, & \cos(r_z), & -\sin(r_x), & 0 \\
0, & \sin(r_x), & \cos(r_x), & 0 \\
0, & 0, & 0, & 1
\end{bmatrix}
$$

Y-Axis Rotation Matrix

$$
\begin{bmatrix}
\cos(r_y), & 0, & \sin(r_y), & 0 \\
0, & 1, & 0, & 0 \\
-\sin(r_y), & 0, & \cos(r_y), & 0 \\
0, & 0, & 0, & 1
\end{bmatrix}
$$

Z-Axis Rotation Matrix

$$\begin{bmatrix} \cos(r_z), & -\sin(r_z), & 0, & 0 \\ \sin(r_z), & \cos(r_z), & 0, & 0 \\ 0, & 0, & 1, & 0 \\ 0, & 0, & 0, & 1 \end{bmatrix}$$

6.12 Adding a Viewpoint

Now that we have a way to define graphic transformations and apply them to models in the scene, suppose we wish to use these transformations to change the point from which the scene is viewed. Recall from Chapter 3 that the viewpoint can be changed by specifying a translation and rotation in the scene file. The viewer translation and rotation are composited into a **tMatrix** object and then multiplied together with the **tMatrix** object created for each model as the scene is either previewed or rendered. The only difference is that moving the viewpoint has the exact opposite effect of moving a model in the scene. In other words, we simply negate the translation and rotation transformations to produce the desired effect. For example, if the viewer moves to the left, all the models in a scene move to the right in response. The following example code uses **viewMatrix**, a pointer to a **tMatrix** object, to build a viewer transformation matrix:

```
tMatrix *viewMatrix = new tMatrix();  // Create the tMatrix object
float DTR = 3.1415926 / 180.0;
float xRadians = viewRotateX * DTR;
float yRadians = viewRotateY * DTR;
float zRadians = viewRotateZ * DTR;
viewMatrix->rotate(-xRadians, -yRadians, -zRadians);
viewMatrix->translate(-viewTranslateX, -viewTranslateY, -
viewTranslateZ);
```

6.13 Adding True Perspective

All of the graphic transformations described so far operate in a purely three-dimensional space; that is, after a model has been transformed as needed, it remains in the three-dimensional coordinate system. We need now to display the transformed model on a two-dimensional computer screen. The process of creating a two-dimensional view of models located in a three-dimensional coordinate system is called *projection*. Consider the following example: Suppose you are looking out your living room window at the cars passing by on the street. Suppose also that your neighbor across the street is also looking at the same cars passing by through her living room window. You and your neighbor have different views of the same cars since your locations and orientations relative to the cars are different.

Figure 6.3 illustrates the relationship between a single transformed point in the three-dimensional world coordinate system $P(x, y, z)$, the viewpoint C, the view screen, and the projected point, which is located on the view screen $S(x_p, y_p)$. We wish to determine projected points for each model in our scene.

We can obtain an expression for the projected points from Figure 6.3 by remembering a bit of high school geometry and recognizing that the triangles SCZ_1 and PCZ_2 are similar. From geometry we know that the ratios of the same sides of similar triangles are equal. To be more precise:

$$d/(z + d) = x_p/x$$

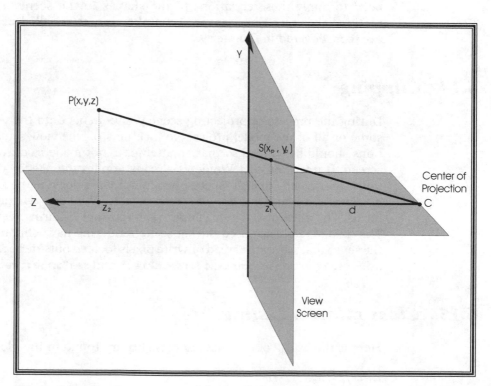

Figure 6.3 The view screen and center of projection.

Solving for x_p we obtain:

$$x_p = x(d/(z + d))$$

Since the same relationship holds for the y coordinate:

$$y_p = y(d/(z + d))$$

One of the areas to be generally concerned about when creating projections is the case where the object to be projected is located on the plane $z = 0$. In this case no projection occurs and care must be taken that the projection equations (which often divide by z) do not result in a divide-by-zero error. To check our equations we inspect the equation for xp in the case of $z = 0$ and obtain:

$$x_p = x(d/(0 + d))$$
$$x_p = x$$

This result is correct and does not result in a divide-by-zero. Now that we have the equations that will place our transformed models on the screen we need to apply these equations to the shapes in the scene. This transformation takes place in a **shape3d** member function called **transformAnd-Project**, covered in Chapter 9.

6.14 Clipping

During the process of projecting scene components onto the view screen, if some or all of the model projects to locations off the view screen these portions should be clipped so that an attempt is not made to draw off the view screen. It turns out that Windows already applies the needed clipping functions. This means that the scene preview software does not need to check for portions of a shape that are off-screen because Windows will do the clipping for us. The other area where clipping is important is during scene rendering. The **memImage** objects used during scene rendering have clipping built in, in the sense that requests to read or write pixels located outside **memImage** boundaries are ignored (see **memImage::setMPixel** and **memImage::getMPixel**).

6.15 Class tMatrix Listing

Here is the listing of the **tMatrix** class library found in the file tMatrix.cpp:

```
tMatrix::tMatrix(){
  setIdentity();
}
```

```
tMatrix::tMatrix(tMatrix *aMatrix){
  matcopy(theMatrix, aMatrix->theMatrix);
}


void tMatrix::multiply(tMatrix *matrix1, tMatrix *matrix2){
  setIdentity();
  matmult(theMatrix, matrix1->theMatrix, matrix2->theMatrix);
}


void tMatrix::setIdentity(){
  theMatrix[0][0]=1; theMatrix[1][0]=0;
  theMatrix[2][0]=0; theMatrix[3][0]=0;
  theMatrix[0][1]=0; theMatrix[1][1]=1;
  theMatrix[2][1]=0; theMatrix[3][1]=0;
  theMatrix[0][2]=0; theMatrix[1][2]=0;
  theMatrix[2][2]=1; theMatrix[3][2]=0;
  theMatrix[0][3]=0; theMatrix[1][3]=0;
  theMatrix[2][3]=0; theMatrix[3][3]=1;
  matcopy(rxMat, theMatrix);
  matcopy(ryMat, theMatrix);
  matcopy(rzMat, theMatrix);
  matcopy(scMat, theMatrix);
  matcopy(trMat, theMatrix);
}


tMatrix::~tMatrix()
{} //no objects were declared with new ==> nothing to free

void tMatrix::scale(float sx, float sy, float sz){
  float mat[4][4];
  scMat[0][0]=sx; scMat[1][0]=0; scMat[2][0]=0; scMat[3][0]=0;
  scMat[0][1]=0; scMat[1][1]=sy; scMat[2][1]=0; scMat[3][1]=0;
  scMat[0][2]=0; scMat[1][2]=0; scMat[2][2]=sz; scMat[3][2]=0;
  scMat[0][3]=0; scMat[1][3]=0; scMat[2][3]=0; scMat[3][3]=1;
  matmult(mat, scMat, theMatrix);
  matcopy(theMatrix,mat);
}


void tMatrix::translate(float tx, float ty, float tz){
  float mat[4][4];
  trMat[0][0]=1; trMat[1][0]=0; trMat[2][0]=0; trMat[3][0]=tx;
  trMat[0][1]=0; trMat[1][1]=1; trMat[2][1]=0; trMat[3][1]=ty;
  trMat[0][2]=0; trMat[1][2]=0; trMat[2][2]=1; trMat[3][2]=tz;
  trMat[0][3]=0; trMat[1][3]=0; trMat[2][3]=0; trMat[3][3]=1;
  matmult(mat, trMat, theMatrix);
  matcopy(theMatrix, mat);
}


void tMatrix::rotate(float rx,float ry,float rz){
  float mat1[4][4];
  float mat2[4][4];
```

```
rxMat[0][0]=1; rxMat[1][0]=0; rxMat[2][0]=0; rxMat[3][0]=0;
rxMat[0][1]=0; rxMat[1][1]=cos(rx);
rxMat[2][1]=-sin(rx);rxMat[3][1]=0;
rxMat[0][2]=0; rxMat[1][2]=sin(rx);
rxMat[2][2]=cos(rx);rxMat[3][2]=0;
rxMat[0][3]=0; rxMat[1][3]=0;
rxMat[2][3]=0; rxMat[3][3]=1;
matmult(mat1, rxMat, theMatrix);

ryMat[0][0]=cos(ry); ryMat[1][0]=0;
ryMat[2][0]=sin(ry); ryMat[3][0]=0;
ryMat[0][1]=0; ryMat[1][1]=1;
ryMat[2][1]=0; ryMat[3][1]=0;
ryMat[0][2]=-sin(ry); ryMat[1][2]=0;
ryMat[2][2]=cos(ry); ryMat[3][2]=0;
ryMat[0][3]=0; ryMat[1][3]=0;
ryMat[2][3]=0; ryMat[3][3]=1;
matmult(mat2, ryMat, mat1);

rzMat[0][0]=cos(rz); rzMat[1][0]=-sin(rz);
rzMat[2][0]=0;rzMat[3][0]=0;
rzMat[0][1]=sin(rz);
rzMat[1][1]=cos(rz);
rzMat[2][1]=0; rzMat[3][1]=0;
rzMat[0][2]=0; rzMat[1][2]=0;
rzMat[2][2]=1; rzMat[3][2]=0;
rzMat[0][3]=0; rzMat[1][3]=0;
rzMat[2][3]=0; rzMat[3][3]=1;
matmult(theMatrix, rzMat, mat2);
}

void matmult(float result[4][4],float mat1[4][4],float
mat2[4][4]){
  for (int i=0; i<4; i++)
    for (int j=0; j<4; j++) {
      result[j][i]=0;
      for (int k=0; k<4; k++)
        result[j][i]+ =mat1[k][i] * mat2[j][k];
    }
}

void matcopy(float dest[4][4],float source[4][4]){
  for (int i=0; i<4; i++)
    for (int j=0; j<4; j++)
      dest[j][i]=source[j][i];
}

void tMatrix::transpose(){
  float mat1[4][4];
  for (int i=0; i<4; i++)
    for (int j=0; j<4; j++)
```

```
        mat1[i][j] = theMatrix[j][i];
   matcopy(theMatrix, mat1);
}


void tMatrix::transformPoint(float xIn, float yIn, float
zIn, float *xOut, float *yOut, float *zOut){
   *xOut = (xIn * theMatrix[0][0]) + (yIn * theMatrix[1][0]) +
      (zIn * theMatrix[2][0]) + theMatrix[3][0];
   *yOut = (xIn * theMatrix[0][1]) + (yIn * theMatrix[1][1]) +
      (zIn * theMatrix[2][1]) + theMatrix[3][1];
   *zOut = (xIn * theMatrix[0][2]) + (yIn * theMatrix[1][2]) +
      (zIn * theMatrix[2][2]) + theMatrix[3][2];
}


void tMatrix::display(char *heading){
   char msgText[80];
   StatusPrint(heading);
   sprintf(msgText,"%6.2f\t%6.2f\t%6.2f\t%6.2f\t",
   theMatrix[0][0],theMatrix[1][0],theMatrix[2][0],theMatrix[3][0];
   StatusPrint(msgText);

   sprintf(msgText,"%6.2f\t%6.2f\t%6.2f\t%6.2f\t",
   theMatrix[0][1],theMatrix[1][1],theMatrix[2][1],theMatrix[3][1]);
   StatusPrint(msgText);

   sprintf(msgText,"%6.2f\t%6.2f\t%6.2f\%6.2f\t",
   theMatrix[0][2],theMatrix[1][2],theMatrix[2][2],theMatrix[3][2]);
   StatusPrint(msgText);

   sprintf(msgText,"%6.2f\t%6.2f\t%6.2f\t%6.2f\t",
   theMatrix[0][3],theMatrix[1][3],theMatrix[2][3],theMatrix[3][3]);
   StatusPrint(msgText);
}


short tMatrix::invertg(){
#define MAXROWS 4
#define MAXCOLS MAXROWS // MAXCOLS defined for readability
//
//   Invert a tMatrix object.
//   Approach:  Augment the forward graphic transformation matrix with four
//   b vectors which collectively make up the 4×4 identity matrix.
//   The augmented b vectors are contained in the tMatrix object bVector.
//   Solve the system using Gaussian elimination and partial pivoting.
//   Back-substitute each of the four processed b vectors to obtain the
//   inverse. Gaussian elimination is described in more detail in:
//
//   Numerical Methods for Scientists and Engineers, J. D. Hoffman,
//   McGraw-Hill, 1992, Section 1.3.
//
   int i, j, k, maxValue;
```

```
float aTemp;
char msgText[80];
tMatrix *bVector = new tMatrix();

for (i = 0; i < MAXROWS; i++){
maxValue = i;
for (j = i + 1; j < MAXROWS; j++)    // Partial pivot (swap rows) if necessary
  if(fabs(theMatrix[i][j]) > fabs(theMatrix[i][maxValue])).maxValue = j;
  if(maxValue != i){
    for (k = i; k < MAXCOLS; k++){
      aTemp = theMatrix[k][i];
      theMatrix[k][i] = theMatrix[k][maxValue];
      theMatrix[k][maxValue] = aTemp;
    }
    for (k = 0; k < MAXCOLS; k++){
      aTemp = bVector->theMatrix[k][i];
      bVector->theMatrix[k][i] = bVector->theMatrix[k][maxValue];
      bVector->theMatrix[k][maxValue] = aTemp;
    }
  }
  for (j = i + 1; j < MAXROWS; j++){
    float aFactor = theMatrix[i][j] / theMatrix[i][i];
      for (k = MAXCOLS - 1; k >= i; k--){
        if(fabs(theMatrix[i][i]) < 1.0E-06){
          sprintf(msgText,
          "invertg: i: %d j: %d k: %d pivot element cannot be zero!",i,j,k);
          StatusPrint(msgText);
          return -1;
        }
        theMatrix[k][j] -= theMatrix[k][i] * aFactor;
      }
      for (k = MAXCOLS - 1; k >= 0; k--)
        bVector->theMatrix[k][j] -= bVector->theMatrix[k][i] * aFactor;
  }
}
//
// Backsubstitute the augmented b vectors to obtain the inverse
  int col, row;
  float aSum;

  for (col = 0; col < MAXCOLS; col++){
    for (j = MAXROWS - 1; j >= 0; j--){
      aSum = 0.0;
      if(j != MAXROWS - 1){
        for (k = j + 1; k < MAXCOLS; k++){
          aSum += (theMatrix[k][j] * bVector->theMatrix[col][k]);
        }
      }
      if(fabs(theMatrix[j][j]) < 1.0E-06){
        StatusPrint("invertg: Zero Diagonal Not Allowed. Exiting");
```

```
        return -1;
      }
    bVector->theMatrix[col][j] =
      (bVector->theMatrix[col][j] - aSum) / theMatrix[j][j];
  }
}
// Copy the inverse into theMatrix
for (col = 0; col < MAXCOLS; col++){
  for(row = 0; row < MAXROWS; row++)
    theMatrix[col][row] = bVector->theMatrix[col][row];
}
delete bVector;
return 0;
}
```

C H A P T E R

7

Handling Shapes

In this chapter we address the need for a set of services that display and process three-dimensional polygons, which we refer to as *shapes*. These shapes are used in many places throughout ICT, including the scene preview tool and the image warping tool, both to be developed in Part II. This set of services has been encapsulated in the **shape3d** class library. More specifically, the **shape3d** class library provides a set of services that store, retrieve, and process two-dimensional and three-dimensional shape information.

A **shape3d** object can be thought of in a more traditional graphics sense as an *n*-sided polygon. A **shape3d** object manages a list of connected three-dimensional vertices. The ICT application uses **shape3d** objects in many areas. For example, during scene preview, models are displayed on the screen by drawing their associated shapes (see Figure 6.1 in Chapter 6). We begin by looking at the **shape3d** header file shape3d.h and describing the **shape3d** class and its data members and functions.

7.1   *A More Precise Definition of Shape*

The **shape3d** header file begins with the definition of two structures. The first structure describes a single three-dimensional coordinate or point (*x*, *y*, *z*). This structure is a basic building block used throughout the ICT:

```
struct point3d{
   float x, y, z;
};
```

By the way, in C++, structures are considered by default to be new data types. This declaration is equivalent to the following structure definition in C:

```
typedef struct {
   float x, y, z;
} point3d;
```

The second structure found in shape3d.h is a bit more unusual. The structure **vertexSet** consists of an integer three-dimensional coordinate, a floating point three-dimensional coordinate, and an integer two-dimensional coordinate:

```
struct vertexSet {
   int x, y, z;
   float tx, ty, tz;
   int sx, sy;
};
```

This structure is named **vertexSet** because it contains a set of three vertices. In fact, each of these three vertices represents the same point at different stages of processing. Imagine for a moment the rectangular shape of the boundary of an image. This shape has four vertices. Let's consider one of these four vertices. The integer three-dimensional coordinate (x, y, z) specifies a location in world coordinates, that is, the absolute location of the point in the right-handed Cartesian coordinate system described in Chapter 6. The floating point coordinate (t_x, t_y, t_z) represents the world coordinate (x, y, z) after it has been moved from its original location to its desired location and orientation by a transformation matrix, also described in Chapter 6. The point (t_x, t_y, t_z) is referred to as the transformed coordinate. Finally, the integer two-dimensional coordinate (s_x, s_y) represents the transformed point after it has been projected to the screen. The point (s_x, s_y) is called a screen coordinate. As we shall see later, keeping these three separate representations of the same point together in a single **shape3d** object has several advantages.

7.2   *The Private and Public Lives of Shapes*

When designing any C++ class we generally want to encapsulate as many of the details as possible while, at the same time, maintaining the highest possible level of computational efficiency. For practical purposes, what this means is that we want to declare as many data members and functions **pri**-

vate or **protected** as appropriate. Exactly what is appropriate is generally determined by how the information is used in the application. For example, because there are many occasions in the ICT application where we need to traverse the vertices of a **shape3d** object in a time-efficient manner, we have decided to expose a pointer to the current vertex. In other words, the variable **currentVertex** is declared a **public** data member. We decide, however, that it is important to protect the address of the first vertex in the allocated block of shape vertices, and so **firstVertex** is declared a **private** data member. The data member **currentVertex** can be initialized to point to **firstVertex** by the public member function **initCurrentVertex**. The following code fragment illustrates how these functions and data members are used together to change a **shape3d** object's location on the screen:

```
void shape3d::translateS(long xOffset, long yOffset){
  initCurrentVertex();
  for (int index = 0; index < getNumVertices(); index++){
    currentVertex->sx += offsetX;
    currentVertex->sy += offsetY;
    currentVertex++;
  }
}
```

The **shape3d** member function **translateS** adds the X and Y offsets to each projected (screen) vertex in the **shape3d** object. The first step in this process is to initialize the member function **currentVertex** using the function **initCurrentVertex**. In each pass of the loop that follows, the X and Y offsets are added to the current vertex and the data member **currentVertex** is incremented. The end result is that the **shape3d** object's vertices have been translated by the amount **xOffset** along the X axis and by **yOffset** along the Y axis.

There is only one other **private shape3d** data member that we have not yet discussed: **numAllocatedVertices**. When a **shape3d** object is created, a block of memory is allocated for the number of vertices needed or anticipated. The number of vertices for which memory has been allocated is saved in a private data member **numAllocatedVertices**. If there is not enough memory for the requested vertices then **numAllocatedVertices** is set to zero by the shape constructor. The **isValid** member function (based on the value of **numAllocatedVertices**) returns TRUE if the **shape3d** object was created successfully, otherwise **isValid** returns FALSE. Here is the complete header file for class **shape3d**:

```
#define MAXVERTICES 128
void StatusPrint(char *);

struct point3d{
  float x, y, z;
};
```

```
struct vertexSet{
  int x,y,z;
  float tx, ty, tz;
  int sx, sy;
};



class shape3d{
private:
  int numVertices;
  int numAllocatedVertices;
  vertexSet *firstVertex; // the base address for the vertices
public:
  vertexSet *currentVertex;
  int color;
  int minX, minY, maxX, maxY;
  float minTX, maxTX, minTY, maxTY, minTZ, maxTZ;
  float originX, originY, originZ;
  shape3d(point3d *UL, point3d *UR, point3d *LR, point3d *LL);
  shape3d (char *fileName, short modelType);
  shape3d(int allocatedVertices = 4);
  shape3d(char *pathName);
  shape3d(shape3d *transformedShape);
  ~shape3d();
  void screenBoundingBox();
  void worldBoundingBox();
  void transformBoundingBox();
  void getTCentroid(float *centroidX, float *centroidY, float *centroidZ);
  void getWCentroid(float *centroidX, float *centroidY, float *centroidZ);
  void translateW(float offsetX, float offsetY, float offsetZ);
  void translateT(float offsetX, float offsetY, float offsetZ);
  void translateS(long offsetX, long offsetY);
  short readShape(char *pathName);
  short readBMPFile(char *fileName);
  short writeShape(char *pathName);
  void printShape(char *);
  void transformAndProject (tMatrix *modelMatrix);
  void initCurrentVertex();
  short addWorldVertex(int x, int y, int z);
  short deleteLastWorldVertex();
  short getLastWorldVertex(int *x, int *y, int *z);
  short getPreviousWorldVertex(int *x, int *y, int *z);
  void invertY(short screenHeight);
  int getNumVertices();
  void setNumVertices(int numVertices);
  short isValid();
  float averageX();
  float averageY();
};
```

7.3   Creating Shapes

There are five constructors for class **shape3d**, which means that a **shape3d** object can be created in five different ways. The following constructor definitions are found in the file shape3d.h:

```
shape3d(point3d *UL, point3d *UR, point3d *LR, point3d *LL);
shape3d(int numVertices = 4);
shape3d(char *pathName);
shape3d(shape3d *transformedShape);
shape3d (short *myStatus, char *fileName, short modelType);
```

Each **shape3d** constructor is now described.
    The constructor:

```
shape3d(point3d *UL, point3d *UR, point3d *LR, point3d *LL);
```

creates and populates a four-vertex **shape3d** object from four three-dimensional points. This constructor can be used, for example, to create a **shape3d** object from the four cornerpoints of an image.
    The constructor:

```
shape3d(int allocatedVertices = 4);
```

creates a **shape3d** object and allocates memory for the number of vertices specified by the argument **allocatedVertices**. If the argument **allocatedVertices** is not supplied by the caller, the syntax of the function prototype indicates that a **shape3d** object will be created that has sufficient memory for four vertices. It is important to note that this constructor does not fill the **shape3d** object with any vertex data. Thus the data member **numAllocatedVertices** indicates how much memory has been allocated in terms of vertices, and the **private** data member **numVertices** indicates how many vertices have actually been inserted into the shape3d object. These two variables are used to manage the **shape3d** vertex memory.
    The constructor:

```
shape3d(char *pathName);
```

creates a **shape3d** object by reading a shape file with the indicated pathname.
    The constructor:

```
shape3d(shape3d *transformedShape);
```

creates a new **shape3d** object from a pointer to the **shape3d** object supplied by the constructor's single argument. This constructor essentially creates a copy of the shape that is passed to it.

The constructor:

```
shape3d (short *myStatus, char *fileName, short modelType);
```

creates a **shape3d** object from a model of either type SHAPE or type IMAGE. This constructor is used during scene preview to populate the scene list with models. The first argument is a return status indicating whether shape creation was successful. The second argument is the name of the file to be opened. The **modelType** argument has one of two possible constant values: SHAPE or IMAGE. If the model is of type SHAPE, the **file-Name** argument is assumed to refer to a shape file.

If the model is of type IMAGE, then the **fileName** argument is assumed to refer to a .bmp format image file and the image file header is read using the member function **readBMPFile**. The size of the image is determined, and a four-vertex **shape3d** object is created from the image's four cornerpoints. The cornerpoint vertices are defined by assuming that the image is positioned in the *X-Y* plane at Z = 0 and that its lower-left corner is located at the origin (0,0,0) of the world coordinate system (discussed in Chapter 6).

7.4   *Getting and Setting Shape Vertices*

This section describes how to determine or set the number of vertices in a **shape3d** object and how to access individual vertices. The following two public **shape3d** member functions enable the number of vertices to be obtained or set respectively:

```
int getNumVertices();
void setNumVertices(int numVertices);
```

As its name implies, the member function **addWorldVertex** adds the indicated world coordinate to the **shape3d** object and increments the private data member **numVertices**. The function **addWorldVertex** returns a status of zero if the vertex is successfully added. Since memory is allocated for a shape ahead of time, no more than **numAllocatedVertices** vertices may be added to a shape. Suppose, for example, that memory for 128 vertices has been allocated, and that 128 vertices have already been added to the **shape3d** object. If function **addWorldVertex** is now called, a message is posted to the process log indicating that no additional vertices may be added, and a value of −1 is returned.

```
short addWorldVertex(int x, int y, int z);
```

Member function **deleteLastWorldVertex** deletes the last vertex and decrements **numVertices**.

```
short deleteLastWorldVertex();
```

Member function **getLastWorldVertex** returns the last world coordinate system vertex in the **shape3d** object. That is, the coordinate pointed to by **currentVertex** is returned.

```
short getLastWorldVertex(int *x, int *y, int *z);
```

Member function **getPreviousWorldVertex** returns the world coordinate system vertex that is one vertex prior to the last vertex.

```
short getPreviousWorldVertex(int *x, int *y, int *z);
```

7.5   *Reading and Writing a Shape File*

The world coordinates of a **shape3d** object can be saved in a text file, called a *shape file,* for later use. The reason the transformed and screen vertices of a **shape3d** object are not also saved in the shape file is that these coordinates can be calculated from the world coordinates and a transformation matrix. Since a form of the transformation matrix is already stored in the scene file for each model, all we need to save in the shape file is the number of vertices and the world vertices themselves. Shape files are saved and retrieved respectively using two public member functions **writeShape** and **readShape**:

```
short writeShape(char *pathName);
short readShape(char *pathName);
```

The function **readShape** reads a shape file and creates a **shape3d** object that contains the world vertices described in the shape file. An example shape file is shown here:

```
// An example shape file with a comment line
12
7,268,0
741,269,0
741,32,0
725,30,0
```

706,34,0

685,40,0

663,37,0

595,43,0

567,33,0

545,27,0

507,28,0

473,27,0

The shape file format is quite simple. The first record contains a single integer that indicates the number of vertices in the shape file. Each record that follows contains one three-dimensional coordinate, expressed in the right-handed Cartesian coordinate system discussed in Chapter 6. Although the example above shows integer coordinates, floating point coordinates could be used as well. Any shape file may be displayed using ICT by placing it in a scene file and using the scene preview menu item (the precise steps are described in Chapter 3). The member function **readShape** expects the total number of records in the shape file to equal the number of vertices indicated in the first record plus one for the first record itself. Records beginning with the characters "//" are treated as comments. The shape file suffix is .shp.

As its name indicates, member function **writeShape** saves a **shape3d** object's world vertices in a shape file.

```
short writeShape(char *pathName);
```

The name of the shape file created by **writeShape** is indicated by the **pathName** argument. The format of the file is the same as described for function **readShape**. Although any valid Windows **pathName** is permitted, the convention used by ICT is the suffix .shp.

The function **printShape** displays the three versions of the shape3d vertices. The contents of a shape3d object are posted to the process log. The single argument contains an explanatory message that is also posted to the process log prior to printing the shape to enhance readability of the log. Function **printShape** is used primarily for debugging purposes.

```
void printShape(char *);
```

7.6 Bounding Boxes and Centroids

A **shape3d** object has two important properties, a centroid, and a bounding box, which are described in this section. The **shape3d** member functions:

```
void worldBoundingBox();
void transformBoundingBox();
void screenBoundingBox();
```

calculate the bounding box of the shape coordinates using either the world, transformed, or screen coordinates respectively. The bounding box used in ICT is defined as the smallest rectangle that encloses the **shape3d** object's screen vertices. The bounding box is obtained by traversing the screen vertices and determining the minimum and maximum *X* and *Y* coordinates. The resulting coordinates are stored in the shape's data members: **minX**, **minY**, **maxX**, and **maxY**. The bounding box is used by the image warp tool described in Chapter 9. Similarly, the data members **minTX**, **maxTX**, **minTY**, **maxTY**, **minTZ**, and **maxTZ** describe what might be called a minimum bounding volume, since the *Z* dimension is included. This bounding volume is the smallest rectangular solid that encloses the transformed **shape3d** object. The bounding volume is used during the process of applying a graphic transformation to a shape object (described in Chapter 12).

The functions **getTCentroid** and **getWCentroid** first calculate the transformed coordinate bounding box or world coordinate bounding box respectively, and then calculate the average value along each axis from the bounding box maximum and bounding box minimum. The resulting average coordinate is located in the exact center of the **shape3d** object. As you may have noticed, this middle coordinate is called a *centroid* (see Figure 7.1). Note that the coordinate (**centroidX**, **centroidY**, **centroidZ**) returned by **getTCentroid** and **getWCentroid** is a floating point even in the case of **getWCentroid**, because an average value has been calculated.

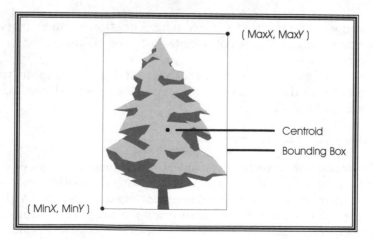

Figure 7.1   A model's centroid and bounding box.

The data members **originX**, **originY**, and **originZ** record the shape's centroid. The centroid is used later during depth sorting to determine the order in which the models in a scene are rendered.

7.7 *Moving Shapes*

The functions described in this section all affect a **shape3d** object in some way by changing at least one of its three sets of vertices.

As their name indicates, the functions **translateW**, **translateT**, and **translateS** translate the world, transformed, or screen vertices respectively of a **shape3d** object by the indicated offsets.

```
void translateW(float offsetX, float offsetY, float offsetZ);
void translateT(float offsetX, float offsetY, float offsetZ);
void translateS(long offsetX, long offsetY);
```

Next we describe the following **shape3d** member functions:

```
void invertY(short screenHeight);
transform3d (tMatrix *modelMatrix);
transformAndProject (tMatrix *modelMatrix, float tx, float ty,
float tz);
```

Member function **invertY** inverts the screen Y coordinates of a **shape3d** object. The Y axis is inverted by subtracting the current y coordinate from the height of the screen:

$$y' = \text{screenHeight} - y$$

where y' is the inverted y coordinate. Function **invertY** is used to convert Windows screen Y axis coordinates into the right-handed Cartesian Y axis coordinates.

Member function **transform3d** applies the graphic transformation contained in the argument matrix **modelMatrix** to all the world vertices in the **shape3d** object:

```
transform3d (tMatrix *modelMatrix);
```

The transformed vertices are saved in the **shape3d** object's vertex memory and correspond one-to-one in position with the world vertices.

Member function **transformAndProject** transforms the points in a shape using the supplied transformation matrix. This means that the transformed and screen versions of the shape coordinates are calculated from the **shape3d** object's set of world coordinates. First, the transformed vertices are calculated by applying the supplied transformation matrix to the **shape3d** object's world coordinates. Second, the transformed points are projected to the screen. The **shape3d** object's centroid is also calculated for later use by the depth-sorting function. Function **transformAndProject** is described in greater detail in Chapter 9.

Here is a listing of the **shape3d** class library:

```
shape3d::shape3d (char *fileName, short modelType){
  char msgText[MAXPATH], shapePath[MAXPATH];
  char *shapeDir;
  short aStatus;
  if (modelType == IMAGE) {
    // First try to open a corresponding shape file. If it doesn't exist,
    // use the image file and set the shape to a rectangle.
    shapeDir = ictPreference->getPath(ShapeFileDirectory);
    getShapePath(fileName, shapeDir, shapePath);

    aStatus = readShape(shapePath);
    if (aStatus != 0) {
      sprintf(msgText,"shape3d. Can't open shape file: %d %s",aStatus,
        shapePath);
      StatusPrint(msgText);
      numAllocatedVertices = 0;
      aStatus = readBMPFile(fileName);
      if (aStatus != 0) {
        sprintf(msgText,"shape3d. ReadBMPFile error: %d %s",aStatus,
          fileName);
        StatusPrint(msgText);
        numAllocatedVertices = 0;
      }
    }
  }
  else { // The model is of type SHAPE
    aStatus = readShape(fileName);
    if (aStatus != 0) {
      sprintf(msgText,"shape3d. ReadShape error: %d %s",aStatus, fileName);
      StatusPrint(msgText);
      numAllocatedVertices = 0;
    }
  }
}


shape3d :: shape3d(char *pathName){
  readShape(pathName);
}


shape3d :: ~shape3d(){
  if(is Valid()) free(firstVertex);
}
```

```
shape3d::shape3d(int numVerts){
  numVertices = 0;
  numAllocatedVertices = numVerts;
  void *nullPointer = calloc(numAllocatedVertices, sizeof(vertexSet));
  if(nullPointer == 0){
    StatusPrint("shape3d: Unable to allocate shape object");
    numAllocatedVertices = 0; // signal an error
    return;
  }
  firstVertex = (vertexSet *) nullPointer;
  currentVertex = firstVertex;
  // zero the shape memory
  for (int index = 0; index < numAllocatedVertices; index++){
    currentVertex->sx = 0;  // screen coordinate
    currentVertex->sy = 0;
    currentVertex->x = 0; // initial coordinate
    currentVertex->y = 0;
    currentVertex->z = 0;
    currentVertex->tx = 0.0;  // transformed coordinate
    currentVertex->ty = 0.0;
    currentVertex->tz = 0.0;
    currentVertex++;
  }
  initCurrentVertex();  //re-initialize the vertex pointer
}


shape3d::shape3d(shape3d *transformedShape){
  numVertices = transformedShape->numVertices;
  numAllocatedVertices = numVertices;
  void *nullPointer = calloc(numVertices, sizeof(vertexSet));
  if(nullPointer == 0) {
    StatusPrint("shape3d: Unable to allocate shape object");
    numAllocatedVertices = 0; //signal an error
    return;
  }
  firstVertex = (vertexSet *) nullPointer;
  currentVertex = firstVertex;
  transformedShape->initCurrentVertex();
  for (int index = 0; index < numVertices; index++){
    currentVertex->sx = transformedShape->currentVertex->sx; // screen coord.
    currentVertex->sy = transformedShape->currentVertex->sy;
    currentVertex->x = transformedShape->currentVertex->tx; // initial coord.
    currentVertex->y = transformedShape->currentVertex->ty;
    currentVertex->z = transformedShape->currentVertex->tz;
    currentVertex->tx = 0.0;   // transformed coord.
    currentVertex->ty = 0.0;
    currentVertex->tz = 0.0;
    currentVertex++;
    transformedShape->currentVertex++;
```

```
      }
  }

  shape3d :: shape3d(point3d *UL, point3d *UR, point3d *LR, point3d *LL){
    numVertices = 4;
    numAllocatedVertices = numVertices;
    void * nullPointer = calloc(numVertices, sizeof(vertexSet));
    if(nullPointer == 0) {
      StatusPrint("shape3d: Unable to allocate shape object");
      numAllocatedVertices = 0; //signal an error
      return;
    }
    firstVertex = (vertexSet *) nullPointer;
    currentVertex = firstVertex;
    currentVertex->sx = 0;currentVertex->sy = 0;
    currentVertex->x = UL->x;   // initial coordinate
    currentVertex->y = UL->y;
    currentVertex->z = UL->z;
    currentVertex->tx = 0.0; // transformed coordinate
    currentVertex->ty = 0.0;currentVertex->tz = 0.0;
    currentVertex++;
    currentVertex->sx = 0;currentVertex->sy = 0;
    currentVertex->x = UR->x;
    currentVertex->y = UR->y;
    currentVertex->z = UR->z;
    currentVertex->tx = 0.0;
    currentVertex->ty = 0.0;currentVertex->tz = 0.0;
    currentVertex++;
    currentVertex->sx = 0;currentVertex->sy = 0;
    currentVertex->x = LR->x;
    currentVertex->y = LR->y;
    currentVertex->z = LR->z;
    currentVertex->tx = 0.0;
    currentVertex->ty = 0.0;currentVertex->tz = 0.0;
    currentVertex++;
    currentVertex->sx = 0;currentVertex->sy = 0;
    currentVertex->x = LL->x;
    currentVertex->y = LL->y;
    currentVertex->z = LL->z;
    currentVertex->tx = 0.0;
    currentVertex->ty = 0.0;currentVertex->tz = 0.0;
  }

  short shape3d :: readShape(char *pathName){
    char msgText[MAXPATH], theText[MAXPATH], *theKeyWord;
    ifstream filein(pathName);
    if (filein.fail()){
      sprintf(msgText,"readShape: Unable to open file: %s",pathName);
      StatusPrint(msgText);
```

```
      return -1;
  }
  filein >> ws;
  int lineCounter = 0;
  int checkCounter = 0;   //make certain numVertices vertices are read in
  int counter = 0;
  numVertices = 0;
  while(strcmpi(theKeyWord=getNextLine((char *)theText, &lineCounter,
    &filein, 0), "EOF") != 0){
  if (counter == 0){
    numVertices = atoi(theKeyWord);
    void * nullPointer = calloc(numVertices, sizeof(vertexSet));
    if (nullPointer == 0){
      sprintf(msgText, "ReadShape: could not allocate shape memory");
      StatusPrint(msgText);
      numAllocatedVertices = 0;
      filein.close();
        return -1;
      }
      numAllocatedVertices = numVertices;
      firstVertex = (vertexSet *) nullPointer;
      currentVertex = firstVertex;
    }
    else { // get a coordinate
      char *xValue = strtok(theKeyWord,",");
      char *yValue = strtok(NULL,",");
      char *zValue = strtok(NULL,",");
      if(xValue != NULL) currentVertex->x = atoi(xValue);
      if(yValue != NULL) currentVertex->y = atoi(yValue);
      if(zValue != NULL) currentVertex->z = atoi(zValue);
      currentVertex++;
      checkCounter++;
    }
    counter++;
  }
  short myStatus = 0;
  if (checkCounter != numVertices) {
  sprintf(msgText,"Vertex miscount in input file: %s", pathName);
  StatusPrint(msgText);
  myStatus= -1;
  }
  filein.close();
  return myStatus;
}

short shape3d :: readBMPFile(char *fileName){
  char msgText[MAXPATH];
  short myStatus, bitsPerPixel;
  int height, width;
```

```
        myStatus = readBMPHeader(fileName, &height, &width, &bitsPerPixel);
        if (myStatus != 0) return(myStatus);
        sprintf(msgText,"%s Height: %d Width: %d Bits/Pixel: %d",
          fileName, height, width, bitsPerPixel);
        StatusPrint(msgText);
        numVertices = 4;
        void *nullPointer = calloc(numVertices, sizeof(vertexSet));
        if(nullPointer == 0) {
          StatusPrint("shape3d::readBMPFile: Unable to allocate shape object");
          numAllocatedVertices = 0; //signal an error
          return -1;
        }
        firstVertex = (vertexSet *) nullPointer;
        currentVertex = firstVertex;
        numAllocatedVertices = numVertices;
        currentVertex->sx = 0;currentVertex->sy = 0;
        currentVertex->x = 0.0;
        currentVertex->y = 0.0;
        currentVertex->z = 0.0;
        currentVertex->tx = 0.0;
        currentVertex->ty = 0.0;currentVertex->tz = 0.0;
        currentVertex++;
        currentVertex->sx = 0;currentVertex->sy = 0;
        currentVertex->x = (float) width;
        currentVertex->y = 0.0;
        currentVertex->z = 0.0;
        currentVertex->tx = 0.0;
        currentVertex->ty = 0.0;currentVertex->tz = 0.0;
        currentVertex++;
        currentVertex->sx = 0;currentVertex->sy = 0;
        currentVertex->x = (float) width;
        currentVertex->y = (float) height;
        currentVertex->z = 0.0;
        currentVertex->tx = 0.0;
        currentVertex->ty = 0.0;currentVertex->tz = 0.0;
        currentVertex++;
        currentVertex->sx = 0;currentVertex->sy = 0;
        currentVertex->x = 0.0;   // initial coordinate
        currentVertex->y = (float) height;
        currentVertex->z = 0.0;
        currentVertex->tx = 0.0; // transformed coordinate
        currentVertex->ty = 0.0;currentVertex->tz = 0.0;
        return 0;
}

short shape3d::writeShape(char *pathName){
  char msgText[MAXPATH];
  int index;
  ofstream fileOut(pathName);
```

```
     if (fileOut.fail()){
       sprintf(msgText,"writeShape: Unable to open file: %s",pathName);
       StatusPrint(msgText);
       return -1;
     }
     fileOut << numVertices << '/n';
     initCurrentVertex();

     for (index = 1; index <= numVertices; index ++){
       fileOut <<    currentVertex->x << ',' << currentVertex->y << ',' <<
       currentVertex->z << '\n';
       currentVertex++;
         }
         fileOut.close();
         return 0;
}

void shape3d::printShape(char *comment){
  char msgText[MAXPATH];
  int index;
  sprintf(msgText,"%s numVertices: %d", comment, numVertices);
  StatusPrint(msgText);
  initCurrentVertex();
  for (index = 1; index <= numVertices; index ++){
    sprintf(msgText,"%d,%d,%d\t%6.2f,%6.2f,%6.2f\t%d,%d",
    currentVertex->x, currentVertex->y, currentVertex->z,
    currentVertex->tx, currentVertex->ty, currentVertex->tz,
    currentVertex->sx, currentVertex->sy);
    StatusPrint(msgText);
    currentVertex++;
  }
  return;
}


void shape3d::screenBoundingBox(){
  initCurrentVertex();
  minX = maxX = currentVertex->sx;
  minY = maxY = currentVertex->sy;
  for (int index = 0; index < numVertices; index++){
    if(currentVertex->sx > maxX) maxX = currentVertex->sx;
    if(currentVertex->sx < minX) minX = currentVertex->sx;
    if(currentVertex->sy > maxY) maxY = currentVertex->sy;
    if(currentVertex->sy < minY) minY = currentVertex->sy;
    currentVertex++;
  }
}


void shape3d::initCurrentVertex(){
  currentVertex = firstVertex;
}
```

```
int shape3d::getNumVertices(){
  return numVertices;
}


void shape3d::setNumVertices(int nv){
  numVertices = nv;
}


void shape3d::worldBoundingBox(){
  initCurrentVertex();
  minX = maxX = currentVertex->x;
  minY = maxY = currentVertex->y;
  for (int index = 0; index < numVertices; index++){
    if(currentVertex->x > maxX) maxX = currentVertex->x;
    if(currentVertex->x < minX) minX = currentVertex->x;
    if(currentVertex->y > maxY) maxY = currentVertex->y;
    if(currentVertex->y < minY) minY = currentVertex->y;
    currentVertex++;
  }
}


void shape3d::transformBoundingBox(){
  initCurrentVertex();
  minTX = maxTX = currentVertex->tx;
  minTY = maxTY = currentVertex->ty;
  minTZ = maxTZ = currentVertex->tz;
  for (int index = 0; index < numVertices; index++){
    if(currentVertex->tx > maxTX) maxTX = currentVertex->tx;
    if(currentVertex->tx < minTX) minTX = currentVertex->tx;
    if(currentVertex->ty > maxTY) maxTY = currentVertex->ty;
    if(currentVertex->ty < minTY) minTY = currentVertex->ty;
    if(currentVertex->tz > maxTZ) maxTZ = currentVertex->tz;
    if(currentVertex->tz < minTZ) minTZ = currentVertex->tz;
    currentVertex++;
  }
}


void shape3d::invertY(short screenHeight){
  initCurrentVertex();
  for (int index = 0; index < numVertices; index++){
    currentVertex->y = screenHeight - currentVertex->y;
    currentVertex++;
  }
}


short shape3d::addWorldVertex(int x, int y, int z){
  if (numVertices == numAllocatedVertices){
    StatusPrint("addWorldVertex: Not enough memory to add vertex");
    return -1;
  }
```

```
  currentVertex->x = x;
  currentVertex->y = y;
  currentVertex->z = z;
  currentVertex++; // advance the vertex pointer
  numVertices++;
  return 0;
}


short shape3d::deleteLastWorldVertex(){
  if(numVertices < 1) return -1;
  currentVertex--;
  numVertices->-;
  return 0;
}


short shape3d::getLastWorldVertex(int *x, int *y, int *z){
  if(numVertices < 1) return -1;
  *x = (currentVertex - 1)->x;
  *y = (currentVertex - 1)->y;
  *z = (currentVertex - 1)->z;
  return 0;
}


short shape3d::getPreviousWorldVertex(int *x, int *y, int *z){
  if(numVertices < 2) return -1;
  *x = (currentVertex - 2)->x;
  *y = (currentVertex - 2)->y;
  *z = (currentVertex - 2)->z;
  return 0;
}


float shape3d::averageX(){
  screenBoundingBox();
  return((maxX - minX)/2.0);
}


float shape3d::averageY(){
  screenBoundingBox();
  return((maxY - minY)/2.0);
}


void shape3d::transformAndProject (tMatrix *modelMatrix){
  float cX, cY, cZ;
  getWCentroid(&cX, &cY, &cZ);  // calculate and save the world coord centroid
  translateW(-cX, -cY, -cZ);  // move world coords to the origin
  initCurrentVertex();
  float maxtX, maxtY, maxtZ, mintX, mintY, mintZ;
  // Transform the shape using the perspective matrix
  for (int index = 0; index < numVertices; index++){
```

```
        modelMatrix->transformPoint(
          (float)currentVertex->x, (float)currentVertex->y,
            (float)currentVertex->z, &currentVertex->tx, &currentVertex->ty,
            &currentVertex->tz);
      if(index == 0){
        maxtX = mintX = currentVertex->tx;
        maxtY = mintY = currentVertex->ty;
        maxtZ = mintZ = currentVertex->tz;
      }
      // Calculate the transformed object centroid for depth sorting later
      if(currentVertex->tx > maxtX) maxtX = currentVertex->tx;
      if(currentVertex->tx < mintX) mintX = currentVertex->tx;
      if(currentVertex->ty > maxtY) maxtY = currentVertex->ty;
      if(currentVertex->ty < mintY) mintY = currentVertex->ty;
      if(currentVertex->tz > maxtZ) maxtZ = currentVertex->tz;
      if(currentVertex->tz < mintZ) mintZ = currentVertex->tz;
      currentVertex++;
    }
    originX = mintX + (maxtX - mintX)/2.0;
    originY = mintY + (maxtY - mintY)/2.0;
    originZ = mintZ + (maxtZ - mintZ)/2.0;
    //
    // Project to the screen
    initCurrentVertex();
    float d = -512.0; // Distance from screen to center of projection:(0,0,-d)
    for (index = 0; index < numVertices; index++){
      float w = (d / (currentVertex->tz + d));
      currentVertex->sx = currentVertex->tx * w;
      currentVertex->sy = currentVertex->ty * w;
      currentVertex++;
    }
    translateW(cX, cY, cZ);  // move world coords back
    translateS(cX, cY);      // move Screen coords back
}


void shape3d::
getWCentroid(float *centroidX, float *centroidY, float *centroidZ){
  if(numAllocatedVertices > 0){
    initCurrentVertex();
  float maxX = currentVertex->x, maxY = currentVertex->y,
    maxZ = currentVertex->z;
  float minX = currentVertex->x, minY = currentVertex->y,
    minZ = currentVertex->z;

  for (short index = 0; index < numVertices; index++){
    if(currentVertex->x > maxX) maxX = currentVertex->x;
    if(currentVertex->x < minX) minX = currentVertex->x;
    if(currentVertex->y > maxY) maxY = currentVertex->y;
    if(currentVertex->y < minY) minY = currentVertex->y;
    if(currentVertex->z > maxZ) maxZ = currentVertex->z;
```

```
      if(currentVertex->z < minZ) minZ = currentVertex->z;
      currentVertex++;
   }
  originX = minX + ((maxX - minX) / 2.0);
  originY = minY + ((maxY - minY) / 2.0);
  originZ = minZ + ((maxZ - minZ) / 2.0);
  *centroidX = originX;
  *centroidY = originY;
  *centroidZ = originZ;
  }
}


void shape3d::translateW(float offsetX, float offsetY, float offsetZ){
  initCurrentVertex();
  for (int index = 0; index < numVertices; index++){
    currentVertex->x += (int)offsetX;
    currentVertex->y += (int)offsetY;
    currentVertex->z += (int)offsetZ;
    currentVertex++;
  }
}


void shape3d::translateT(float offsetX, float offsetY, float offsetZ){
  initCurrentVertex();
  for (int index = 0; index < numVertices; index++){
    currentVertex->tx += offsetX;
    currentVertex->ty += offsetY;
    currentVertex->tz += offsetZ;
    currentVertex++;
  }
}


void shape3d::translateS(long offsetX, long offsetY){
  initCurrentVertex();
  for (int index = 0; index < numVertices; index++){
    currentVertex->sx += (int)offsetX;
    currentVertex->sy += (int)offsetY;
    currentVertex++;
  }
}


char *getNextLine(char *theText, int *lineNumber, ifstream *filein,
  short minLineLength){
  int aComment, theLength = 80;
  char *theKeyWord;
  aComment = TRUE;
  while (aComment){
    filein->getline(theText, theLength);   //ignore comments and empty lines
    if(filein->eof()){
```

```
        strcpy(theText,"EOF ");
        theKeyWord = strtok(theText," ");
        return(theKeyWord);
    }
    (*lineNumber)++;
    //
    // Minimum line length <= 4 to accomodate CR/LFs from scenefile maker
    // utility
    if (strncmp(theText,"//",2) == 0 || strlen(theText) <= minLineLength)
      aComment = TRUE;
    else
      aComment = FALSE;
    }
    theKeyWord = strtok(theText," ");
    return(theKeyWord);
}


void getShapePath(char *modelPath, char *shapeDir, char
*shapePath){
  char drive[MAXDRIVE], dir[MAXDIR], file[MAXFILE], ext[MAXEXT];
  fnsplit(modelPath,drive,dir,file,ext);
  short theLength = strlen(file);
  if(theLength > 0){
    *(file+theLength-1) = '\0';  // shorten the filename
    strcpy(shapePath,shapeDir);
    strcat(shapePath,file);
    strcat(shapePath,".shp");
  }
  else {
    StatusPrint("GetShapePath: Empty fileName");
  }
}


short shape3d::isValid(){
  if(numAllocatedVertices == 0) return FALSE;
  else
  return TRUE;
}
```

Image Compositing Tools

In Part I, we concentrated on building up an infrastructure of class libraries and services upon which the image compositing tools presented in this book are based. Now, in Part II, we develop a set of tools that can be used together to create a variety of visual effects images and sequences.

8

Creating Cutouts

8.1   What Is a Cutout?

One of the capabilities we need in order to create special effects scenes is the basic ability to remove a part of an image that is of interest and save it in a separate image file. We call such images *cutouts* because they have been cut out from another image. In this chapter, we describe a technique for creating cutout images and then show how the cutout tool code is added to the ICT starter application.

8.2   Tracing the Boundary

First let's consider an example of how the cutout tool works. Figure 8.1 shows a closeup shot of a young boy named Eric. We shall subsequently refer to this image as the ICT test image. Suppose we wish to remove Eric from the test image so we can later place him in another visual effect scene. Using the cutout tool, we can simply trace a line around Eric's head using the mouse. Let's try this now. Start the ICT application and select the `File | Open Image...` menu item. Now use the file browser to open the image x:\ict\gallery\ericglas.bmp. The image is displayed on the screen in

Figure 8.1   The ICT test image.

its own MDI child window, as shown in Figure 8.1. This scrollable image window is an instance of the **imageWindow** class supplied as part of the ICT starter application. Next, activate the cutout tool by checking the menu item **Tools|Create Cutout**. This action enables the **imageWindow** object to respond to mouse events (more on this in section 8.3). Now, use the left mouse button to trace around Eric's head. Point the cursor at the first location on the boundary and click the left mouse button. A small white dot appears. Now move the mouse to a second point along the boundary of Eric's head and click the left mouse button again. A white line connects the first and second points you selected. Continue on until the entire boundary is traced. When you have finished, your screen should resemble that shown in Figure 8.2. If, along the way, you wish to undo a point, press the right mouse button once. The undo line is drawn in black. Now you can continue tracing from the previous point. Ideally, the undo line could restore the original image intensities.

Although this interface could be improved upon, it is adequate for our present needs. Once the boundary has been traced completely, double click the left mouse button. This action indicates to ICT that you have finished tracing the boundary. A dialog box now appears as shown in Figure 8.3 ask-

Figure 8.2   A cutout image boundary.

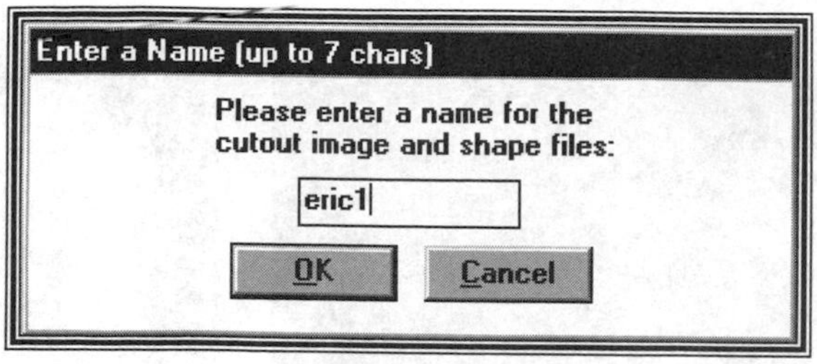

Enter a Name (up to 7 chars)

**Please enter a name for the
cutout image and shape files:**

eric1|

OK   Cancel

Figure 8.3   The cutout image dialog box.

ing for a name. Three files are actually created in this step: the cutout image itself, an alpha image, and a shape file. All of these files will be given a name based on the name you enter here. Each of these files are described in detail in later chapters. After clicking on the OK button, the screen flashes briefly showing, in white, the area inside the boundary you traced. An example is shown in Figure 8.4. Finally, the original image reappears. If all has gone well, the message box at the bottom of the screen displays the message: "Cutout Created Successfully."

At this point, the cutout image has been placed in the x:\ict\cutout directory with the name you supplied along with the letter *c* in the last position and a .bmp suffix. For example, if you had entered the name "Eric1" in the dialog box, the cutout image would have the name Eric1c.bmp. The letter *c* is added by ICT to indicate the image is in color. The alpha image has also been stored in the ICT cutout directory with the name "Eric1a.bmp." The letter *a* is added by ICT to indicate the image is an alpha image. As we shall see later, the operation of the scene generator depends on a small number of file naming conventions such as the ones we have just described. If the images Eric1c.bmp and Eric1a.bmp are displayed, we see what appears in Figure 8.5. Eric, our subject, has been removed from the original image. All pixels outside the boundary we traced now appear to have van-

ericglas.bmp

Figure 8.4   A cutout mask image.

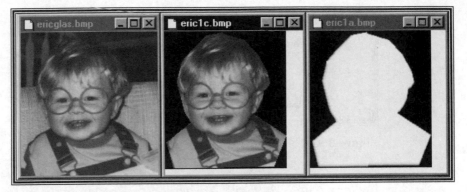

Figure 8.5 A cutout image and its alpha image.

ished. If the pixels in the image file itself were examined, one would observe that the missing pixels have a value of zero. In the chapters that follow we shall see that pixels with zero value are treated in such a way that they appear transparent in the final effect scenes.

Now our attention turns to the unusual-looking image named Eric1a.bmp, shown on the right side of Figure 8.5. This image is called an *alpha image* and it is one of the major subjects of Chapter 10. The alpha image should display all pixels located inside the boundary we traced as being predominantly white in color. Pixels located inside the cutout area and along the boundary have a soft, cottony appearance. The significance of this image is described in Chapter 10.

As we mentioned earlier, a shape file has also been created that contains the vertices of the boundary we traced earlier. In the case of our example, this file has the name Eric1.shp and is stored by default in the ICT shape directory x:\ict\shape. This shape file is used later during scene preview when we wish to manipulate in three dimensions the cutout image we just created. Use of the shape file during scene preview enables us to see the actual boundary of the cutout, instead of the rectangular boundary of the cutout image.

8.3 *Implementation: Trapping Mouse Events*

Now we discuss the software implementation of the cutout tool. The cutout tool just described is implemented by enabling the **imageWindow** object to receive and process Windows mouse click event messages. An **imageWindow** object is a scrollable image window that appears on the screen after an image file has been opened from the **File|Open Image...** menu item. We begin by adding the necessary entries to the response table definition of the

imageWindow class. One entry is made in the response table for each event we wish to intercept:

```
DEFINE_RESPONSE_TABLE1(imageWindow, TWindow)
   ...
   EV_WM_LBUTTONDOWN,
   EV_WM_RBUTTONDOWN,
   EV_WM_LBUTTONUP,
   EV_WM_RBUTTONUP,
   EV_WM_LBUTTONDBLCLK,
   EV_WM_RBUTTONDBLCLK,
END_RESPONSE_TABLE;
```

The ICT starter application created in Chapter 2 can now pass to us messages from Windows indicating whether the left or right mouse button has been pressed. To be more precise, each time a mouse button is clicked inside an **imageWindow** object, that **imageWindow** object receives one of several possible messages indicating whether the left or right mouse button has been clicked and the screen location of the mouse when either the left or right button was clicked. Furthermore, the **imageWindow** object receives messages indicating whether a particular mouse button is in the UP or DOWN state.

The specific entry added earlier to the **imageWindow** response table for the event "Left mouse button down" is EV_WM_LBUTTONDOWN. The constant EV_WM_LBUTTONDOWN is defined by Windows in the file windows.h. Similar messages are defined for "right mouse button down," "left mouse button double click," and so on. There is now an entry for each of these messages in the **imageWindow** response table. Notice that function names do not appear after each of the mouse event messages listed in the **imageWindow** response table. This means that the functions being called in response to incoming Windows messages have standard names. The standard naming convention for response functions is to precede the words following the last underscore in the windows message name by the letters *Ev*. So, in the case of the EV_WM_LBUTTONDOWN message, the standard response function has the name **EvLButtonDown**. We could just as easily have used our own function name and added it after the comma in the appropriate entry in the response table. Moving along, let's now look at the code that responds to a left mouse button click. There are actually two Windows messages of concern here. The first of these is the left button down message:

```
void    imageWindow::EvLButtonDown(UINT, TPoint& point){
  if(theClient->cutoutEnabled){
    if (firstPress == FALSE) {
      firstPress = TRUE;
      aShape = new shape3d(MAXVERTICES);
      StatusPrint("LButtonDown event: Created shape object");
```

```
      }
   }
}
```

The first statement of the **EvLButtonDown** response function ensures that this function does not respond unless the cutout tool has first been activated from the menu:

```
if(theClient->cutoutEnabled){
```

Here, the variable **theClient** points to the ICT MDI client window. The variable **cutoutEnabled**, which is a data member of the client window class, is set to a value of one if the cutout tool has been activated. Next the function determines whether the left mouse button has been pressed since the cutout tool was activated. This condition is indicated by the variable **firstPress**. If the variable **firstPress** is FALSE, the implication is that the user is starting to create a new cutout. In this case, the variable **first-Press** is set to TRUE. A new **shape3d** object is then created with enough storage for MAXVERTICES vertices. Finally, an informative message indicating that a new **shape3d** object has been created is displayed in the status bar located at the bottom-left portion of the screen. This message is also written into the process log. To summarize, the EV_WM_LBUTTONDOWN message is used to create a new **shape3d** object on the first mouse click. New boundary points are actually added to the shape object in response to the EV_WM_LBUTTONUP message, as we see next in the **EvLButtonUp** response function.

The listing for function **EvLButtonUp** appears below. As with the function **EvLButtonDown**, the first statement in function **EvLButtonUp** causes the function to respond only if the **Tools|Create Cutout** menu item has been selected. The next section of code displays a message indicating that a point is being added to the cutout shape object:

```
sprintf(msgText, "Adding point %d: (%d, %d)",
   aShape->getNumVertices(), point.x, point.y);
StatusPrint(msgText);
```

Next, the mouse coordinates at the time the mouse was clicked are supplied to us in the point object, which is an instance of the OWL **TPoint** class. The *x* and *y* screen coordinates are added to the shape object **aShape**. Recall from Chapter 6 that the view screen is located in the world coordinate system on the plane $z = 0$. Therefore we set the Z coordinate to zero in the third argument of **addWorldVertex**.

```
short myStatus;
myStatus = aShape->addWorldVertex(point.x, point.y, 0);
```

8.4   *Drawing Lines*

Now we are ready to draw line segments in the image area contained in the **imageWindow** object. The general approach to drawing these line segments is to first get the **imageWindow** object's device context, then create a Windows pen object to draw with, and then get the previous vertex and draw a line from it to the present vertex. If this is the first vertex in the shape, a single point is drawn. Finally, the device context is released and the pen object deleted.

If you weren't aware of it, most, if not all, Windows graphics operations are accessible via the Windows Graphics Device Interface (GDI). All Windows window objects and their descendants (for example, the imageWindow) have what is called a *device context,* which contains a set of infrastructure items needed to perform graphics operations. More information about the GDI in general can be obtained from sources, such as [PETZ92]. One could think of the **imageWindow** object's device context as the rectangular area on the screen into which the line segments of our cutout boundary will be drawn. We now describe the steps necessary to draw the cutout boundary line segments on the screen.

First we get a handle to the **imageWindow** object's device context using this statement:

```
HDC theDC = GetDC(HWindow);
```

Next we create a Windows **pen** object that is of style PS_SOLID (a solid line), which has a line thickness of one pixel; and the color white, which is specified using an RGB ratio: (255,255,255). The **pen** object is then selected into the device context with the Windows GDI function **SelectObject**:

```
hpen = CreatePen(PS_SOLID, 1, RGB(255, 255, 255));
SelectObject(theDC, hpen);
```

Next we look up the previous world vertex using the **shape3d** member function **getPreviousWorldVertex**. If the status returned is zero, it means that there is no previous vertex, that is, this vertex is the first in the new cutout boundary. If a previous vertex exists, then the function **MoveToEx** is used to position the pen at the location of the previous vertex. The function **LineTo** then draws a line segment (using the selected pen) that originates at the previous vertex and ends at the current vertex. In the case where only one point in the cutout boundary has been defined, the current mouse position is highlighted by drawing a line from it which is one pixel in length. One further note: The function **MoveToEx** is used in place of the older **MoveTo** function because **MoveToEx** is compatible with both Win16 and Win32 environments.

```
myStatus = aShape->getPreviousWorldVertex(&x, &y, &z);
if (myStatus == 0){
  MoveToEx(theDC, x, y, 0L);
  LineTo(theDC, point.x, point.y);
}
else {
  MoveToEx(theDC, point.x, point.y, 0L);      //draw a single point
  LineTo(theDC, point.x+1, point.y+1);
}
```

Now we clean up by releasing the device context and deleting the **pen** object. The order of these two operations is critical. If we do not either select the **pen** out of the device context, or do not release the device context before deleting the **pen** object, then the memory allocated for the pen will not be released properly and a memory leak and/or unpredictable behavior will result:

```
ReleaseDC(HWindow, theDC);
DeleteObject(hpen);
```

Here is a complete listing of function **EvLButtonUp**:

```
void    imageWindow::EvLButtonUp(UINT, TPoint& point){
  if(theClient->cutoutEnabled){
    char msgText[MAXPATH];
    if(firstPress == FALSE) return;
    sprintf(msgText, "Adding point %d: (%d, %d)", aShape->getNumVertices(),
      point.x, point.y);
    StatusPrint(msgText);
    short myStatus;
    myStatus = aShape->addWorldVertex(point.x, point.y, 0); //z = 0
    HPEN hpen;
    HDC theDC = GetDC(HWindow);
    hpen = CreatePen(PS_SOLID, 1, RGB(255, 255, 255));
    SelectObject(theDC, hpen);
    int x, y, z;
    myStatus = aShape->getPreviousWorldVertex(&x, &y, &z);
    if (myStatus == 0){
      MoveToEx(theDC, x, y, 0L);
      LineTo(theDC, point.x, point.y);
    }
    else {
      MoveToEx(theDC, point.x, point.y, 0L);       //draw a single point
      LineTo(theDC, point.x+1, point.y+1);
    }
    DeleteObject(hpen);
    ReleaseDC(HWindow, theDC);
  }
}
```

To summarize the boundary tracing process, each time the mouse is positioned and the left mouse is clicked, a new screen vertex is saved and a line segment is drawn from the previous vertex to the new vertex. To complete the creation of the cutout boundary the left mouse button is double clicked. The **imageWindow** member function that responds to the left mouse double click is **EvLButtonDblClk**. Let's now examine function **EvLButtonDblClk** in more detail.

Intercepting Double-Click Events

Let's start by looking more closely at the double click event. First, an extra step must be taken to enable the **ImageWindow** object to receive double-click event messages. We do this by adding the attribute CS_DBLCLKS to the **ImageWindow** definition as indicated in the following line of code, which is located in the **ImageWindow** constructor:

```
Attr.Style |= WS_VSCROLL | WS_HSCROLL | CS_DBLCLKS;
```

A double-click event is actually two click events that happen in quick succession. If two clicks occur within a certain time interval our application actually receives the following sequence of messages from Windows: WM_LButtonDown, WM_LButtonUp, WM_LButtonDblClk, WM_LButtonUp. The WM_LButtonDblClk message has replaced the second WM_LButtonDown in the message sequence. The main point here is that, by the time the WM_LButtonDblClk message is received, a WM_LButtonUp message from the first click has already been received and processed. Given the way in which we are processing mouse events, it is clear that an extra vertex would have been added to the cutout's shape object as a result of receiving and processing the first WM_LButtonDown message. To compensate, we remove the extra vertex from the shape object:

```
aShape->deleteLastWorldVertex();
```

At this point, a dialog box appears that asks for the name of the new files. The dialog box is an instance of the **nameDialog** class and is shown in Figure 8.3. The **nameDialog** class is defined in the file ctDialog.cpp. The resource ID **IDD_newName** was defined when the dialog box was created in the resource workshop. The name entered by the user is returned in the variable **newName** when the OK button is pressed.

```
if (GetModule()->ExecDialog(
new nameDialog((TWindow *)this, IDD_newName, 0, newName)) == IDOK){
...}
```

Next the **shape3d** object **aShape**, which contains the set of boundary points traced using the mouse, is passed into the function **prepareCutout**, which then, among other tasks, sets to zero all pixels located outside the boundary described by **aShape**.

The argument **HWindow** is a handle to the window in which to draw the polygon (for display purposes only). The argument **imageFileName** is the name of the image from which the cutout is being prepared. The argument **cutoutName** is the name of the cutout image file that will be created. The arguments **PixelWidth** and **PixelHeight** are the width and height of the image from which the cutout is being prepared.

```
prepareCutout(aShape, HWindow, imageFileName, cutoutName,
PixelWidth, PixelHeight);
```

Finally, the shape object is saved to a file and deleted from memory. We defer the discussion of the creation of the alpha image until Chapter 10.

Here is the listing of function **EvLButtonDblClk**:

```
void imageWindow::EvLButtonDblClk(UINT, TPoint& point){
char msgText[MAXPATH], newName[MAXPATH],
cutoutName[MAXPATH];
if(theClient->cutoutEnabled){
  sprintf(msgText, "Save, Exit");
  StatusPrint(msgText);
  aShape->deleteLastWorldVertex();
  if (GetModule()->ExecDialog(
    new nameDialog((TWindow *)this, IDD_newName, 0, newName)) == IDOK){
    char imageFileName[MAXPATH];
    strcpy(imageFileName, theFileName);
    sprintf(msgText, "Creating alpha image");
    StatusPrint(msgText);
    sprintf(cutoutName,"%s",newName);
    StatusPrint(cutoutName);
    short myStatus = prepareCutout(aShape, HWindow, imageFileName,
      cutoutName, PixelWidth, PixelHeight);
    if(myStatus != 0) {
      sprintf(msgText, "Unable to Create Cutout. %d", myStatus);
      StatusPrint(msgText);
      delete aShape;
      theClient->cutoutEnabled = FALSE;
      return;
    }
    delete aShape;
    theClient->cutoutEnabled = FALSE;
    sprintf(msgText, "Cutout Created Successfully");
    StatusPrint(msgText);
    }
```

```
    }
}
```

Here is a listing of the **EvRButtonDown** function, which removes the last point from the cutout boundary and erases the previous line segment in response to a right mouse click:

```
void imageWindow::EvRButtonDown(UINT, TPoint& point){
  if(theClient->cutoutEnabled){
    char msgText[MAXPATH];
    sprintf(msgText, "Deleting: (%d, %d)",point.x, point.y);
    isDirty = TRUE;
    HPEN hpen;
    HDC theDC = GetDC(HWindow);
    hpen = CreatePen(PS_SOLID, 1, RGB(0, 0, 0));   //a black pen
    SelectObject(theDC, hpen);
    short theStatus;
    int x, y, z, px, py, pz;
    aShape->getLastWorldVertex(&x, &y, &z);
    aShape->getPreviousWorldVertex(&px, &py, &pz);
    MoveToEx(theDC, px, py, 0L);
    LineTo(theDC, x, y);
    theStatus = aShape->deleteLastWorldVertex();
    if (theStatus == -1){}
    ReleaseDC(HWindow, theDC);
    DeleteObject(hpen);
  }
}
```

In summary, we have created a basic tool that enables any portion of an image of interest to be removed from its background and saved in a separate image file. This removed portion is called a *cutout image*. The ICT automatically creates an alpha image and a shape file each time a cutout is created. The alpha image is used to smooth the edges of the cutout image when it is blended into an output image. This blending process is described further in Chapter 10. The alpha image is stored along with the cutout image in the x:\ict\cutout directory. We also covered the following topics: handling Windows event messages, trapping mouse events, and drawing line segments using Windows GDI functions.

Image Warping

In chapter eight, we introduced the cutout tool, which provides the ability to remove items of interest from any digitized color image. If we wish to create an effect using existing photos from many different sources, we generally do not have control over the relative scales in which each image was taken. Consequently, we need a means of adjusting the sizes of each image. The warp tool presented here allows control over the scaling of captured images from different sources because we are able to change the size of each image as we desire. The warp tool developed in this chapter is actually capable of doing far more than scaling an image.

9.1 What Is a Warp?

The image warping tool rotates, sizes, and positions either a black-and-white or true color image to any desired three-dimensional location and orientation in the world coordinate system. The scene preview tool (described in Chapter 13 and Appendix B) is used to place one or more cutout images in any desired three-dimensional location and orientation. The warp tool then operates on each photo-based model during the scene-rendering process (described in Chapter 13) to cause each cutout image to appear in the output scene as previewed. Using the warp tool together with the scene preview and rendering tools, we can now consider each digitized image or cutout as a two-dimensional photographic surface that can be placed in a three-dimensional world in any way we desire. This capability resembles that provided by a more traditional polygon-based three-dimensional graphics viewing system, with the exception that each polygon can now be filled with a photographic texture instead of shaded intensities. This difference can lead to dramatic-looking scenes, as we shall see in Chapter 14. Now, let's look at the warp tool itself in more detail.

9.2 *The Warp Tool*

The ICT software contains a demonstration tool that interactively warps a test image. You can get a good idea of what a warp is by experimenting with this tool now. The interactive warp tool is selected from the **Tools|Warp Image . . .** menu item. The dialog box shown in Figure 9.1 appears. Any combination of rotation angles and scale factors can be entered in the text boxes. Rotation angles range from zero to 360. Scale factors range from zero to a small positive number such as five. Be aware that setting both x and y scale factors to zero will cause the warped image to disappear. After entering the desired transformations, press the OK button. The warp tool now applies the rotations and scale factors you entered to a test image supplied with ICT. Figure 9.2 shows the test image as well as an example of the ICT warping tool applied to the image. This example shows a simultaneous rotation through both X, Y, and Z axes. To use the terms introduced in Chapter 6, Figure 9.2 is an example of a composite graphic transformation as applied to an image.

Figure 9.1   The warp parameter dialog box.

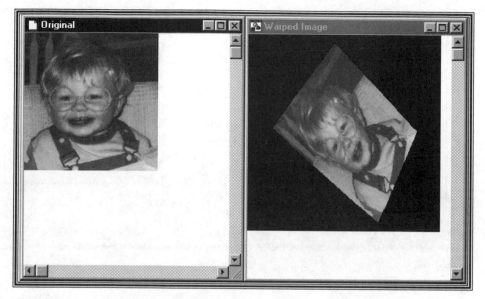

Figure 9.2 A warped image and its original.

Note that opposite sides of the warped image are not parallel to each other. This feature is characteristic of a true perspective warp.

9.3 Forward and Inverse Mappings

There are a great many approaches to warping an image. A good survey of image warping techniques is contained in [WOLB94]. Image warping approaches may be divided into two broad categories: forward mapping and inverse mapping approaches. A *forward mapping* warp applies a graphic transformation to the pixels in the original image shown on the left side of Figure 9.3. Transformed pixels are placed into warped output image shown on the right side of Figure 9.3. Forward mapping approaches are generally implemented by transforming every pixel in the original image. Consequently, a forward mapping warp usually requires the same amount of time to complete, regardless of the transformation factors being applied. In the case where we want to zoom in or magnify an image by applying scale factors greater than one, all of the pixels in the original image must be processed, even though most of the original image pixels may not appear in the output warped image.

An alternate approach is to use what is called an inverse mapping warp. An *inverse mapping* warp works backwards because it begins with

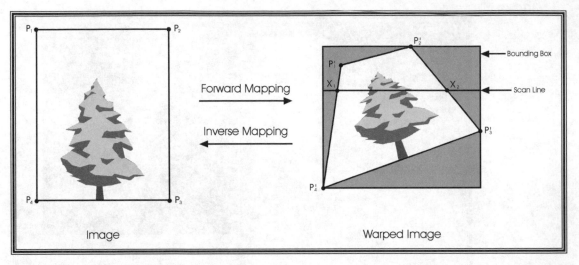

Figure 9.3 Forward and inverse mapping.

the warped image screen coordinates on the right side of Figure 9.3 and applies an inverse graphic transformation to determine which pixels from the original image (on the left side of Figure 9.3) should contribute to each warped image pixel. One advantage of this approach over the forward mapping approach is that every pixel in the original image is not necessarily processed. Only pixels that appear in the output warped image will actually be transformed. This means that the time required to warp an image that is being minimized, for example, will generally be less than the time required to perform a comparable warp using a forward mapping approach. The time required to warp an image using the inverse mapping approach is proportional to the number of pixels that will be visible in the warped image.

9.4 One Pass versus Two

Catmull and Smith [CATM80] introduced the approach of separating a forward mapping warp into two passes. The first pass maps horizontal scan lines from the original image into an intermediate image. The second pass maps vertical lines from the intermediate image into the final warped image. A primary advantage of this approach is that the coordinate mapping equations are designed so that, for example, in the horizontal pass, original image pixels on the ith line are mapped to their respective locations in the ith line of the intermediate image. Similarly, in the vertical pass, pixels on the jth column of the intermediate image are mapped to locations in the jth column of the warped output image. This feature is important from the standpoint of hardware implementation because it simplifies the hardware design.

9.5 *Linear Warp and True Perspective Warp*

If an image located at the origin of our coordinate system is rotated 45 degrees about the Y axis and the viewpoint is located on the positive Z axis, then the left side of the warped image is closer to the viewpoint than the right side of the image. Consequently, the left side of the image will appear longer than the right side of the image, even though both sides of the image are actually the same length. This is an example of the phenomenon of *perspective foreshortening*. Since our eyes present a visual world to us in which the objects in that world are perspective foreshortened, most of us take this phenomenon for granted. The warp algorithm used in ICT uses true perspective because the images it produces exhibit the characteristics we would expect based on our experience in the natural world. A linear warp does not include the effect of perspective foreshortening, that is, it does not use the perspective projection discussed in Chapter 6 to generate the final screen coordinates. Another way of distinguishing these two types of warp is that a true perspective warp is a linear warp that contains the additional step of projecting the transformed coordinates to the screen. In a linear warp, screen coordinates are obtained by simply ignoring the transformed z coordinate. Consequently, opposite sides of a linear warped image are always parallel.

9.6 *Steps in an Inverse Mapping Warp*

The image warp tool presented here can be technically categorized as a single-pass, inverse-mapping, true-perspective warp.

The specific steps we need to take in order to warp an image using the inverse-mapping approach are as follows:

1. Calculate the forward composite transformation matrix from the desired rotation, scale, and translation graphic transformations (including the viewpoint).

2. Calculate the inverse transformation matrix by inverting the forward transformation matrix calculated in step 1.

3. Use the forward transform and the four original image cornerpoints to calculate:

   a. the three-dimensional world coordinates of the warped image cornerpoints, and

   b. the corresponding projected screen cornerpoint coordinates.

These four screen cornerpoints form a two-dimensional quadrangle bounded by the points P1′, P2′, P3′, and P4′ as shown on the right side of Figure 9.3. This quadrangle represents the boundary of the warped image.

4. Create a **shape3d** object from the screen cornerpoints calculated in step 3.

5. Create a **memImage** object to contain the warped image.

6. Pass over the warped image quadrangle using screen coordinates, one horizontal line at a time. For each pixel coordinate in the warped image quadrangle:

   a. Obtain the world coordinate corresponding to current screen coordinate by interpolation of the vertices of the warped image quadrangle determined in the first part of step 3.

   b. Use the world coordinate determined in the previous step and the inverse transformation to obtain the location in the original image of the desired pixel.

   c. Place an anti-aliased estimate of the pixel from the original image location into the warped image at the current screen coordinate.

7. Clean up: Delete the **shape3d** object, save the warped image if necessary, and delete the **memImage** object.

This approach will apply to a **memImage** object, any single or composite graphic transformation that can be constructed using the **tMatrix** class member functions described in Chapter 6. We now describe each of the above steps in detail.

9.7 *Function iWarp*

The software that implements the warp algorithm described here can be found in the file iwarp.cpp, included in the attached diskette. The image warping algorithm is implemented in a function called **iwarp**, which has the following prototype:

```
short iwarp(memImage *inImage, memImage *outImage,
  float rx, float ry, float rz,
  float sx, float sy, float sz,
  float tx, float ty, float tz,
  tMatrix *viewMatrix,
  long *theXOffset, long *theYOffset);
```

Function **iwarp** accepts the image contained in the **memImage** object pointed to by **inImage** and places the warped output in the **memImage** pointed to by **outImage**. The nine desired graphic transformations are included next: rotation angles (in degrees), scale and translation about the X, Y, and Z axes respectively. The viewpoint of the observer is next included in the form of the **tMatrix** object **viewMatrix**. For reasons that will become clear later, the warped image is always centered in the output image supplied. The difference between the warped image's actual offset resulting from the desired graphic transformations and the center of the output image is returned in the last two **iwarp** arguments **xOffset** and **yOffset**. We discuss these last two arguments in greater detail later in this chapter. Function **iwarp** returns a status of zero if the warping operation occurs successfully, otherwise a status of −1 is returned. Recall now that the first step in the warp process is to determine the forward graphic transformation. We do this by creating a **tMatrix** object and composite together the desired graphic transformations:

```
float DTR = 3.1415926 / 180.;
float XRadians = rx * DTR;
float YRadians = ry * DTR;
float ZRadians = rz * DTR;
tMatrix *forwardMatrix = new tMatrix();
forwardMatrix->scale (sx, sy, sz);
forwardMatrix->rotate(XRadians, YRadians, ZRadians);
forwardMatrix->translate(tx, ty, tz);
```

Next, the forward transformation is composited with the viewpoint transformation by multiplying the respective matrices:

```
tMatrix *viewModelMatrix = new tMatrix();
viewModelMatrix->multiply(viewMatrix, forwardMatrix);
```

The **tMatrix** object **viewModelMatrix** now contains the composite forward mapping. This transformation matrix includes the desired location and orientation of the current model as well as the location and orientation of the viewer. The inverse mapping is obtained from the forward mapping by inverting the forward transformation matrix. Since matrix inversion is provided as a member function of the class **tMatrix** we simply create a new **tMatrix** object called **inverseMatrix** using the constructor that takes a **tMatrix** object as its single argument. This constructor copies the contents of the forward matrix into the new matrix object **inverseMatrix**. The new matrix is then inverted by calling the **tMatrix** member function **invertg**:

```
tMatrix *inverseMatrix = new tMatrix(viewModelMatrix);
inverseMatrix->invertg();
```

Matrix inversion is a process that is described in many linear algebra textbooks. The matrix inversion approach used in the **tMatrix** member function **invertg** is based on a process called *Gaussian elimination*, described in [HOFF92], [SEDG84] and in many other texts. Another discussion and implementation of matrix inversion that is based on an approach called LU decomposition can be found in [PRESS92]. We do not describe matrix inversion here because it is well-documented in the literature.

By the way, there is a test that can be easily applied to determine whether an inverse matrix has been correctly calculated. From our discussion of the identity matrix in Chapter 6, we know that any matrix multiplied by its inverse is equal to the identity matrix. Thus we know that the inverse mapping has been correctly determined if the matrix resulting from multiplication of the inverse transformation matrix by the forward transformation matrix is equal (or very nearly equal) to the identity matrix.

We move on now to step 3 in the warp process and determine the four cornerpoints of the warped image. First, the sizes of the input and output image are determined by calling member functions of the **memImage** class **getWidth** and **getHeight**:

```
int inHeight = inImage->getHeight();
int inWidth = inImage->getWidth();
int outHeight = outImage->getHeight();
int outWidth = outImage->getWidth();
int halfHeight = inHeight/2;
int halfWidth = inWidth/2;
```

Next, a **shape3d** object is created with sufficient memory for four sets of vertices. The **shape3d** object **aShape** is then filled with the world coordinates of the original image boundary cornerpoints. Note in the code fragment that follows that the image is placed in the *X-Y* plane of the world coordinate system. In order to view this image as it would normally appear on the screen, the viewpoint would need to be located on the positive Z axis, looking toward the origin.

```
shape3d *aShape = new shape3d(4);
aShape->addWorldVertex(0, 0, 0);
aShape->addWorldVertex(inWidth, 0, 0);
aShape->addWorldVertex(inWidth, inHeight, 0);
aShape->addWorldVertex(0, inHeight, 0);
```

Next, the forward transformation matrix is applied to the shape object and then the transformed coordinates are projected to the screen. Since this operation is common to both the scene preview and scene render functions (discussed in Chapter 13), these operations have been encapsulated as a member function (**transformAndProject**) of a class that is common to both scene render and scene preview functions, namely the **shape3D** class:

```
aShape->transformAndProject(viewModelMatrix);
```

The following section describes function **transformAndProject** in detail.

9.8 *Function transformAndProject*

The function **transformAndProject** applies a graphic transformation to a set of three-dimensional vertices (stored in a **shape3d** object) followed by a projection to the screen. The function has a single argument, which is a **tMatrix** object that contains the graphic transformation to be applied. The function's prototype is shown here:

```
void shape3d::transformAndProject (tMatrix *modelMatrix, short outHeight,
   short outWidth);
```

The first step is to find the associated shape object's centroid and translate the shape object's vertices to the origin of the world coordinate system:

```
getWCentroid(&cX, &cY, &cZ);
translateW(-cX, -cY, -cZ);
```

Both functions **getWCentroid** and **translateW** are **shape3d** member functions. After these two statements have been executed, the shape object vertices have been moved so that the shape object's new centroid is located at the origin: (0,0,0). Now each vertex in the shape object is visited and transformed by multiplying with the transformation matrix. The multiplication is accomplished by the **tMatrix** member function **transformPoint**:

```
initCurrentVertex();
for (index = 0; index < numVertices; index++){
  modelMatrix->transformPoint(
    (float)currentVertex->x, (float)currentVertex->y, (float)currentVertex->z,
      &currentVertex->tx, &currentVertex->ty, &currentVertex->tz);
}
```

One additional calculation is carried out here: The three-dimensional centroid of the transformed shape object is now calculated so it can be used later during depth sorting (discussed in Chapter 11). The following statements initialize the variables **mintX**, **maxtX**, **mintY**, **maxtY**, **mintZ**, **maxtZ**, which represent the bounding box of the transformed shape:

```
if(index == 0){
  maxtX = mintX = currentVertex->tx;
  maxtY = mintY = currentVertex->ty;
  maxtZ = mintZ = currentVertex->tz;
}
```

The bounding box of the transformed shape object is updated as the loop passes over each vertex in the shape:

```
if(currentVertex->tx > maxtX) maxtX = currentVertex->tx;
if(currentVertex->tx < mintX) mintX = currentVertex->tx;
if(currentVertex->ty > maxtY) maxtY = currentVertex->ty;
if(currentVertex->ty < mintY) mintY = currentVertex->ty;
if(currentVertex->tz > maxtZ) maxtZ = currentVertex->tz;
if(currentVertex->tz < mintZ) mintZ = currentVertex->tz;
currentVertex++;
```

After all the vertices have been transformed, the bounding box is known and the centroid of the transformed shape (**originX**, **originY**, **originZ**) can be calculated. The variables **originX**, **originY**, and **originZ** are **shape3d** data members:

```
originX = mintX + (maxtX − mintX)/2.0;
originY = mintY + (maxtY − mintY)/2.0;
originZ = mintZ + (maxtZ − mintZ)/2.0;
```

One task now remains: to add the true perspective effect. This is accomplished by projecting the transformed world coordinates to the screen. Figure 6.3 illustrates the geometry used to carry out the projection. The projection equations are also discussed in section 6.13. Recall from section 6.13 that the projection equations produce perspective effects in the output image consistent with a center of projection located at the point (0,0,-d). We actually would prefer the center of projection to be located in the center of the output effect image. A convenient method of adjusting the location of the center of projection is to subtract half the output image's width ($w/2$) from the world x coordinate and half the output image's height ($h/2$) from the world y coordinate before applying the projection equation. Immediately after applying the projection, we add back half the image x and y dimensions, thus returning the image to its original location. This adjustment effectively moves the image temporarily so that the center of projection appears to be located at the center of the output image. Since we arbitrarily set the value of d to -512, the effective center of projection is located at the world coordinate ($w/2$, $h/2$, 512).

```
float d = −512.0;
halfOutHeight = outWidth/2;
halfOutWidth = outWidth/2;
for (index = 0; index < numVertices; index++){
  float w = (d / (currentVertex->tz + d));
  currentVertex->sx = (currentVertex->tx − halfOutWidth) * w;
  currentVertex->sy = (currentVertex->ty − halfOutHeight) * w;
  currentVertex->sx += halfOutWidth;
  currentVertex->sy += halfOutHeight;
  currentVertex++;
}
```

Now a cleanup step must be performed. We need to reverse the original translation of the shape object to the origin. The world and screen vertices are returned to their original locations:

```
translateW(cX, cY, cZ);
translateS(cX, cY);
```

The transformed shape object coordinates remain centered about the origin for use in a later step in the warp process. Following is the complete listing for the **transformAndProject** function:

```
void shape3d::transformAndProject (tMatrix *modelMatrix,
short outHeight, short outWidth)){
  float cX, cY, cZ;
  getWCentroid(&cX, &cY, &cZ);  // calculate and save the world coord
    centroid translateW(-cX, -cY, -cZ);  // move world coords to the origin
  initCurrentVertex();
  float maxtX, maxtY, maxtZ, mintX, mintY, mintZ;
  // Transform the shape using the perspective matrix
  for (int index = 0; index < numVertices; index++){
    modelMatrix->transformPoint(
      (float)currentVertex->x, (float)currentVertex->y, (float)currentVer-
        tex->z, &currentVertex->tx, &currentVertex->ty, &currentVertex->tz);
      if(index == 0){
      maxtX = mintX = currentVertex->tx;
      maxtY = mintY = currentVertex->ty;
      maxtZ = mintZ = currentVertex->tz;
    }
    // Calculate the transformed object centroid for depth sorting later
    if(currentVertex->tx > maxtX) maxtX = currentVertex->tx;
    if(currentVertex->tx < mintX) mintX = currentVertex->tx;
    if(currentVertex->ty > maxtY) maxtY = currentVertex->ty;
    if(currentVertex->ty < mintY) mintY = currentVertex->ty;
    if(currentVertex->tz > maxtZ) maxtZ = currentVertex->tz;
    if(currentVertex->tz < mintZ) mintZ = currentVertex->tz;
    currentVertex++;
  }
  originX = mintX + (maxtX - mintX)/2.0;
  originY = mintY + (maxtY - mintY)/2.0;
  originZ = mintZ + (maxtZ - mintZ)/2.0;
  //
  // Project to the screen
  initCurrentVertex();
  float d = -512.0;
halfOutHeight = outWidth/2;
halfOutWidth = outWidth/2;
for (index = 0; index < numVertices; index++){
  float w = (d / (currentVertex->tz + d));
  currentVertex->sx = (currentVertex->tx - halfOutWidth) * w;
```

```
    currentVertex->sy = (currentVertex->ty - halfOutHeight) * w;
    currentVertex->sx += halfOutWidth;
    currentVertex->sy += halfOutHeight;
    currentVertex++;
}
```

9.9 *Applying the Inverse Mapping*

At this point we have performed the preparatory tasks needed to apply the inverse mapping warp to the original image. We have calculated the screen coordinates of the boundary of the warped image indicated by the quadrangle P1′P2′P3′P4′ in Figure 9.3. We have also calculated the corresponding three-dimensional world coordinates for each of the screen cornerpoints. We now implement step 6 of our plan as described in section 9.2. A pass is made over the bounding box of the projected image one scan line at a time. The right side of Figure 9.3 shows one such scan line and its relation to the bounding box and the projected quadrangle P1′P2′P3′P4′. For each scan line in the bounding box, the interval X1,X2 must be calculated. For all pixels inside the interval X1,X2, we map pixels from the original image to the warped image using the inverted graphic transformation matrix. Pixels outside the interval X1,X2 are ignored. The code fragment that follows shows the outer loop, which ranges from **minY** to **maxY** of the bounding box. The function **get-Intervals** accepts as input the shape object **aShape**, which contains the screen quadrangle and its world coordinate counterpart and the current scan line *y*. Function **getIntervals** returns the number of *x* coordinates found in the input shape object that intersect the scan line *y*. Since the projected shape will always be four sided and convex, **numXCoordsFound** should always be equal to two. The *x* coordinates defining the interval X1,X2 are returned in the array **screenXCoords**. Function **getIntervals** also returns the corresponding three-dimensional world coordinate for each screen *x* coordinate found. These world coordinates are found in the arrays **tXCoords**, **tYcoords**, and **tZCoords**. Thus the world coordinate corresponding to the screen *x* coordinate found in **screenXCoords[0]** is found in the array elements: **tXCoords[0]**, **tYCoords[0]**, **tZCoords[0]**. The constant MAXVERTICES is passed into function **getIntervals** to indicate the length of the arrays being passed. If more than MAXVERTICES vertices are detected by function **get-Intervals**, the arrays supplied will not be overrun. The inner workings of the function **getIntervals** are described in section 9.11.

```
for (y = minY; y <= maxY; y++){
  myStatus = getIntervals (aShape, y, &numXCoordsFound, MAXVERTICES,
  screenXCoords, tXCoords, tYCoords, tZCoords);
```

```
    if(myStatus != 0){
      sprintf(msgText,"iwarp: getInterval error: %d",myStatus);
      StatusPrint(msgText);
      return 2;
}
```

Before describing the inner loop we need to recall that the inverse-mapping approach applies the inverse transform to a three-dimensional world coordinate. The inverse transform maps the world coordinate to a location in the original image. The function **getIntervals** supplies the world coordinates of each endpoint of the interval X1,X2 located on the current scan line. We interpolate the three-dimensional world coordinates of each pixel within the interval X1,X2 from the known world coordinates at the interval endpoints. The following code fragment sets up the interpolation constants. Since the image surface being warped is planar, changes in x, y, and z on a per-pixel basis are linear. Because this is true, we need only calculate the interpolation constants once per scan line. The change along the y axis in the world coordinate system per pixel is stored in the variable **yIncrement**. The variable **yIncrement** is equal to the change in y over the entire interval **dy** divided by the length of the interval on the current scan line **dsx**.

```
if (numXCoordsFound == 2){
  float dx = tXCoords[1] - tXCoords[0];
  float dy = tYCoords[1] - tYCoords[0];
  float dz = tZCoords[1] - tZCoords[0];
  float dsx = screenXCoords[1] - screenXCoords[0];

  if(dsx > 0.0){
  xIncrement = dx/dsx;
  yIncrement = dy/dsx;
  zIncrement = dz/dsx;
}
else{
  xIncrement = 0.0;
  yIncrement = 0.0;
  zIncrement = 0.0;
}


xIn = tXCoords[0];
yIn = tYCoords[0];
zIn = tZCoords[0];
```

Having calculated the world x, y, and z interpolation increments, we now begin the inner loop that visits each pixel in the interval X1,X2.

```
for(x = screenXCoords[0];x <= screenXCoords[1]; x++){
```

The actual mapping step is carried out using function **transformPoint**:

```
inverseMatrix->transformPoint
(xIn, yIn, zIn, &xOut, &yOut, &zOut);
```

Here the interpolated world coordinate (**xIn**, **yIn**, **zIn**) is mapped, using the inverse transformation matrix, to a coordinate in the original image (**xOut**, **yOut**, **zOut**).

We know that the image either is being reduced or is being viewed actual size if the *x, y,* or *z* axis scale factors are less than or equal to one. In this case we simply retrieve the pixel located at the point (**xOut**, **yOut**, **zOut**) using the function **getMPixel**. We need to add half the image's width and height back to the new coordinates in order to map the transformed coordinates back to the original image coordinate system.

```
if (sx <= 1.0 && sy <= 1.0 && sz <= 1.0)
   intensity = inImage->
     getMPixel((long)(xOut + halfWidth + 0.5),
     (long)(yOut + halfHeight + 0.5));
```

Similarly, we know that a magnification or zoom-in is being accomplished if any scale factor is greater than one. In the case of an image magnification, if pixels are simply transferred from the original image to the warped image, the resulting warped image will have a blocky appearance. This condition is called *aliasing*. A technique exists called *adaptive super-sampling,* which overcomes this aliasing effect. We describe aliasing and adaptive super-sampling in detail in section 9.10.

Once we have obtained the pixel or super-sampled pixel from the input image we copy it to the output image with a call to **setMPixel**, specifying the warped image coordinate. Note that both the *x* and *y* coordinates are loop indexes. The last step then increments the interpolated world coordinates:

```
    else{
    // super-sample....
    }
    outImage->
      setMPixel((long)x + xOffset, (long)y + yOffset, intensity);
    xIn += xIncrement;
    yIn += yIncrement;
    zIn += zIncrement;
  }
```

Here is a listing of function **iwarp**:

```
short iwarp(memImage *inImage, memImage *outImage,
  float rx, float ry, float rz, float sx, float sy, float sz,
```

```
     float tx, float ty, float tz, tMatrix *viewMatrix,
   long *theXOffset, long *theYOffset){
   short x, y;
   char msgText[132];
   short myStatus, numXCoordsFound;
   long screenXCoords[MAXWVERTICES];
   float tZCoords[MAXWVERTICES], tXCoords[MAXWVERTICES],
     tYCoords[MAXWVERTICES];
   //
   // The shape object contains the projected 4 sided polygon and a z
   // coordinate at each of the projected vertices.
   //
   //
   // Build the forward and inverse transformation matrices
   float inverse[4][4];
   tMatrix *forwardMatrix = new tMatrix();
   float DTR = 3.1415926 / 180.;
   float XRadians = rx * DTR;
   float YRadians = ry * DTR;
   float ZRadians = rz * DTR;
   forwardMatrix->scale(sx, sy, sz);
   forwardMatrix->rotate(XRadians, YRadians, ZRadians);
   forwardMatrix->translate(tx, ty, tz);
   tMatrix *viewModelMatrix = new tMatrix();
   viewModelMatrix->multiply(viewMatrix, forwardMatrix);

   tMatrix *inverseMatrix = new tMatrix(viewModelMatrix);
   // copy the original and invert it
   inverseMatrix->invert(inverse);

#ifdef ICTDEBUG
   forwardMatrix->Display("Forward Matrix:");
   inverseMatrix->Display("Inverse Matrix:");
#endif

   int inHeight = inImage->getHeight();
   int inWidth = inImage->getWidth();
   int outHeight = outImage->getHeight();
   int outWidth = outImage->getWidth();
   int halfHeight = inHeight / 2;
   int halfWidth = inWidth / 2;
   //
   // Load a shape object with the original image boundary coordinates
   shape3d *aShape = new shape3d(4);
   aShape->addWorldVertex(0, 0, 0);
   aShape->addWorldVertex(inWidth, 0, 0);
   aShape->addWorldVertex(inWidth, inHeight, 0);
   aShape->addWorldVertex(0, inHeight, 0);
   //
```

```
      // Transform and project the image coords
      aShape->transformAndProject(viewModelMatrix);

#ifdef ICTDEBUG
      aShape->printShape("Transformed Image Boundaries:");
#endif
      aShape->screenBoundingBox();
      short minY = aShape->minY;
      short maxY = aShape->maxY;
      short minX = aShape->minX;
      short maxX = aShape->maxX;
      short transformedXMiddle = minX + ((maxX - minX) / 2);
      short transformedYMiddle = minY + ((maxY - minY) / 2);
      //
      // calculate offsets that will center the warped image in the output image
      float dx = (outWidth / 2.0) - transformedXMiddle;
      float dy = (outHeight/ 2.0) - transformedYMiddle;
      long xOffset = dx + 0.5;
      long yOffset = dy + 0.5;
      aShape->transformBoundingBox();

#ifdef ICTDEBUG
      aShape->printShape("iwarp: input shape");
      //
      // Inverse check.  Map transformed shape cornerpoints into original image
      aShape->initCurrentVertex();
      float xo, yo, zo;
      for (int index = 1; index <= aShape->getNumVertices(); index++){
         float anX = aShape->currentVertex->tx;
         float anY = aShape->currentVertex->ty;
         float anZ = aShape->currentVertex->tz;
         inverseMatrix->transformPoint (anX, anY, anZ, &xo, &yo, &zo);
         aShape->currentVertex++;
         sprintf(msgText, "in: %6.2f %6.2f %6.2f out: %6.2f %6.2f %6.2f",
         anX, anY, anZ, xo + halfWidth, yo + halfHeight, zo);
         StatusPrint(msgText);
      }
#endif
      //
      // Loop through the screen coordinates, filling in with inverse mapped pixels
      for (y = minY; y <= maxY; y++){
      myStatus = getIntervals (aShape, y, &numXCoordsFound, MAXWVERTICES,
         screenXCoords, tXCoords, tYCoords, tZCoords);
         if(myStatus != 0){
            sprintf(msgText,"iwarp: getInterval error: %d",myStatus);
            StatusPrint(msgText);
            return 2;
         }
#ifdef ICTDEBUG
      StatusPrint("y:\tsx  \ttx  \tty  \ttz");
```

```
    for(int i = 0; i < numXCoordsFound; i++){
      sprintf(msgText,"%d\t%ld\t%6.2f\t%6.2f\t%6.2f" , y, screenXCoords[i],
      tXCoords[i], tYCoords[i], tZCoords[i]);
      StatusPrint(msgText);
    }
    if (numXCoordsFound != 2){
      sprintf(msgText,"iWarp: numCoords <> 2. y: %d numCoords %d",
        y, numXCoordsFound);
      StatusPrint(msgText);
    }
#endif
    float xIn, yIn, zIn, xOut, yOut, zOut;
    float xOut1, yOut1, zOut1, xOut2, yOut2, zOut2;
    float xOut3, yOut3, zOut3, xOut4, yOut4, zOut4;
    float fIntensity;
    BYTE intensity;
    float xIncrement, yIncrement, zIncrement;

    if (numXCoordsFound == 2){
      float dx = tXCoords[1] - tXCoords[0];
      float dy = tYCoords[1] - tYCoords[0];
      float dz = tZCoords[1] - tZCoords[0];
      float dsx = screenXCoords[1] - screenXCoords[0];

      if(dsx > 0.0){
        xIncrement = dx/dsx;
        yIncrement = dy/dsx;
        zIncrement = dz/dsx;
      }
      else{
        xIncrement = 0.0;
        yIncrement = 0.0;
        zIncrement = 0.0;
      }
      xIn = tXCoords[0];
      yIn = tYCoords[0];
      zIn = tZCoords[0];

      float dpx, dpy;
      dpx = 1.0 / sx;
      dpy = 1.0 / sy;
      if(dpx > 0.5) dpx = 0.5;
      if(dpy > 0.5) dpy = 0.5;

      for(x = screenXCoords[0];x <= screenXCoords[1]; x++){
        inverseMatrix->transformPoint
          (xIn, yIn, zIn, &xOut, &yOut, &zOut);
          // if (TRUE) // no super-sampling if uncommented
          if (sx <= 1.0 && sy <= 1.0 && sz <= 1.0)  // super-sampling if
                                                    // uncommented
```

```
                intensity = inImage->getMPixel((long) (xOut+ halfWidth + 0.5),
                  (long) (yOut + halfHeight + 0.5));
          else{        // super sample
            fIntensity = 0;
            inverseMatrix->transformPoint
                (xIn – dpx, yIn – dpy, zIn, &xOut1, &yOut1, &zOut1);
            fIntensity = fIntensity + inImage->
            getMPixel((long)(xOut1 + halfWidth + 0.5),
                (long)(yOut1) + halfHeight + 0.5));
            inverseMatrix->transformPoint
                (xIn – dpx, yIn + dpy, zIn, &xOut2, &yOut2, &zOut2);
            fIntensity = fIntensity + inImage->
                getMPixel((long)(xOut2 + halfWidth + 0.5),
                (long)(yOut2 + halfHeight + 0.5));
            inverseMatrix->transformPoint
                (xIn + dpx, yIn – dpy, zIn, &xOut3, &yOut3, &zOut3);
            fIntensity = fIntensity + inImage->
                getMPixel((long)(xOut3 + halfWidth + 0.5),
                (long)(yOut3 + halfHeight + 0.5));
            inverseMatrix->transformPoint
                (xIn + dpx, yIn + dpy, zIn, &xOut4, &yOut4, &zOut4);
            fIntensity = fIntensity + inImage->
                getMPixel((long)(xOut4 + halfWidth + 0.5),
                (long)(yOut4 + halfHeight + 0.5));
            intensity = (BYTE)((fIntensity * 0.250) + 0.5);
          }
          outImage->setMPixel((long)x + xOffset, (long)y + yOffset, inten-
            sity);
          xIn += xIncrement;
          yIn += yIncrement;
          zIn += zIncrement;
        }
      }
    }
    *theXOffset = xOffset;
    *theYOffset = yOffset;
    delete forwardMatrix;
    delete viewModelMatrix;
    delete inverseMatrix;
    delete aShape;
    return 0;
}
```

9.10 *Adaptive Super-Sampling and Anti-Aliasing*

Figure 9.4 diagrams the effect of an image warp that applies a simultane-
ous rotation and magnification. We cause a magnification by using scale
factors greater than one. The diagram on the left side of Figure 9.4 shows

the set of pixels that will be selected by the inverse mapping function as denoted by the rotated rectangle. A rotation is added to this example to underscore the point that we need to rely on the inverse-mapping function to supply the correct neighboring pixel locations. The set of original image pixels selected by the inverse-mapping function during a warp is collectively called the *footprint* of the warped image. The footprint shows the set of pixels in the original image that contribute to the warped output image. The larger the scale factor, the smaller the footprint becomes, indicating that fewer pixels from the original image contribute to the warped image as the level of magnification increases. As mentioned earlier, if pixels selected by the inverse mapping function are simply transferred from the original image to the warped image, the magnified image will take on a blocky appearance. This phenomenon is called *aliasing,* and is also referred to as "the jaggies" or "stairstepping." Figure 9.5 shows an example of aliasing. The warp parameters are rz = 45 degrees and sx = sy = 2.0. One solution to the aliasing problem is to oversample the original image, estimating an intensity from the intensities located at oversampled coordinates. This estimate is then transferred to the warped image. Our method of estimation is to use an arithmetic average. Super-sampling thus uses the inverse-mapping function to obtain neighboring pixel values in the original image. The size of the neighborhood can be made inversely proportional to the scale factor in each dimension. This change in position is calculated in variables **dpx** and **dpy** as shown in the code fragment that follows. Four new neighboring locations in the input image are obtained by calling the **transformPoint** function, passing nearest neighboring locations in the output image. The resulting four pixel values are then averaged and placed into the warped output image.

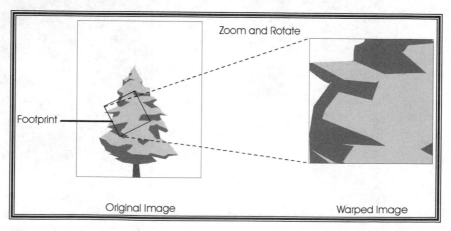

Figure 9.4 A warped image footprint.

```
dpx = 1.0 / sx;
dpy = 1.0 / sy;
if(dpx > 0.5) dpx = 0.5;
if(dpy > 0.5) dpy = 0.5;
```

The super-sampling code is located in the listing at the end of section 9.9. This technique is adaptive because the area in the original image over which the super-sampling occurs can change depending on the scale factors used, and because the super-sampling method is invoked only when scale factors greater than one are used. Figure 9.6 shows an example of adaptive super-sampling. The warp ($rz = 45$, $sx = sy = 2.0$) applied in Figure 9.5 is applied again, with super-sampling added. The blockiness has disappeared and the warped image is said to be *anti-aliased*. Adaptive super-sampling is applied by default in function **iWarp**.

9.11 Getting Screen Intervals (a.k.a. Scan Conversion)

In this section, the function **getIntervals** is described. Function **getIntervals** determines the starting and ending screen x coordinates for each horizontal line of the projected image bounding box. The interval within the two x coordinates is the area on the screen for the given scan line to which the warp algorithm needs to be applied. Function **getIntervals** also calculates the world coordinates for each detected screen x coordinate. The

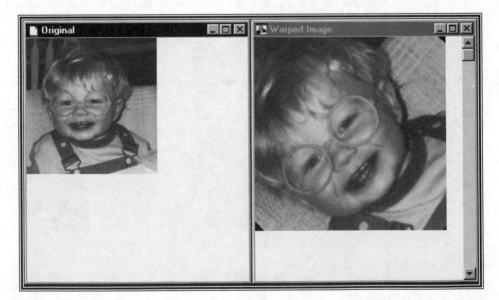

Figure 9.5 A warped image without adaptive super-sampling.

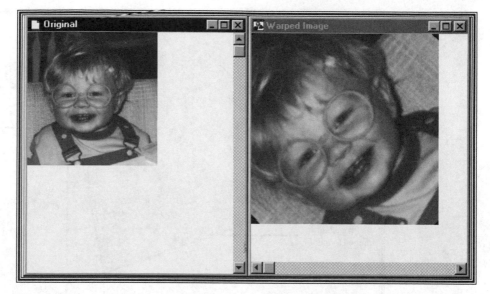

Figure 9.6   A warped image with adaptive super-sampling.

approach used in this function effectively translates from a graphical representation of the warped image boundary (a set of line segments) into an image-processing representation of the warped image (rows of pixels). This type of translation is called *scan conversion* [FOLE90].

Figure 9.7 summarizes the situation we are given. A shape object contains four vertices that represent the boundary of the projected image on the screen. We are given a scan line y and asked to determine at which x coordinates the shape object intersects the line y. Let's begin by considering the shape object as a set of line segments. We know the coordinates of the endpoints of each line segment. We also know the three-dimensional world coordinates at each line segment endpoint. Our approach is to determine the slope and intercept of each line segment, then use this line equation to determine the x coordinate of the location where the line segment intersects the scan line y. If the x coordinate falls within the x interval of the line segment itself, it qualifies as a valid intersection. We then store the located x coordinate and interpolate the three-dimensional world location of the intersection point from the known world locations of the appropriate line segment endpoints. Finally, we must handle the special cases when the projected line segments are either horizontal or vertical.

The next step is to sort the located x coordinates and their world locations in ascending order. Now notice that each vertex is actually part of two different line segments. When applying the algorithm described above to the scan line whose y coordinate is equal to the y coordinate of the vertex

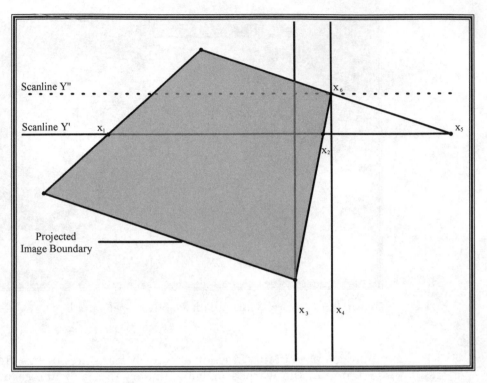

Figure 9.7 Scan conversion geometry.

(denoted by the dotted line in Figure 9.7) the x intercept will be detected twice, once for each line segment to which the vertex belongs. Because of this situation, we need to test for and remove potential duplicate x intercepts. Below is a listing of function **getIntervals**:

```
short getIntervals (shape3d *theShape, short y, short *numCoords,
  short numAllocatedXCoords, long *screenXCoords,
  float *tXCoords, float *tYCoords, float *tZCoords){
  short numShapeVertices = theShape->getNumVertices();
  float m, b;
  BOOL horzFlag, vertFlag;
  long *currentScreenX;
  float *currenttX, *currenttY, *currenttZ;
  currentScreenX = screenXCoords;
  currenttX = tXCoords;
  currenttY = tYCoords;
  currenttZ = tZCoords;
  *numCoords = 0;
  long sx1, sy1, sx2, sy2, minx, maxx, miny, maxy;
  float tx1, tz1, tx2, tz2;
```

```
//
// Calculate how much the transformed shape changed
theShape->transformBoundingBox();
float transformYRange = fabs(theShape->maxTY - theShape->minTY);
int maxTy = theShape->maxTY;
theShape->initCurrentVertex();
theShape->screenBoundingBox();
float screenYRange = abs(theShape->maxY - theShape->minY);
int maxSy = theShape->maxY;
theShape->initCurrentVertex();
float yRatio;

if(screenYRange > 0.0)
  yRatio = transformYRange/screenYRange;
else
  yRatio = 1.0;

float theY = maxTy - (yRatio * (maxSy - (float)y));

for (short index = 1; index <= numShapeVertices; index++){
  sx1 = theShape->currentVertex->sx;
  sy1 = theShape->currentVertex->sy;
  tx1 = theShape->currentVertex->tx;
  tz1 = theShape->currentVertex->tz;
  theShape->currentVertex++;
  // if this is the last line segment, circle around to the beginning
  if(index == numShapeVertices)theShape->initCurrentVertex();
  sx2 = theShape->currentVertex->sx;  //Can't use (currentVertex+1)->x
  sy2 = theShape->currentVertex->sy;
  tx2 = theShape->currentVertex->tx;
  tz2 = theShape->currentVertex->tz;
  theShape->currentVertex--;
  minx = min(sx1, sx2);
  maxx = max(sx1, sx2);
  miny = min(sy1, sy2);
  maxy = max(sy1, sy2);
  getLineEquation(sx1, sy1, sx2, sy2, &m, &b, &horzFlag, &vertFlag);
  if (!(horzFlag || vertFlag)){
    float theX = ((float)y - b) / m;
    long newX = (long) (theX + 0.5);
    if ((newX >= minx && newX <= maxx) && (y >= miny && y <= maxy)){
      if(*numCoords == numAllocatedXCoords){
        StatusPrint("getIntervals: #coordinates > length of array");
        return -1;
      }
      *currentScreenX = newX;
      // determine z by interpolating between line segment endpoints
    float totalDistance = sqrt(((sx2 - sx1) * (sx2 - sx1)) +
      ((sy2 - sy1) * (sy2 - sy1)));
    float partialDistance = sqrt(((newX - sx1) * (newX - sx1)) +
```

```
            ((y - sy1) * (y - sy1)));
        float ratio = partialDistance/totalDistance; // 0 <= ratio <= 1
        if(totalDistance > 0.0){
          *currenttX = tx1 + (ratio * (tx2 - tx1));
          *currenttY = theY;
          *currenttZ = tz1 + (ratio * (tz2 - tz1));
        }
        else {
          *currenttX = 0.0;
          *currenttY = 0.0;
          *currenttZ = 0.0;
          StatusPrint("getIntervals: totalDistance = 0.0. Didn't interpolate");
        }
        currenttX++;
        currenttY++;
        currenttZ++;
        currentScreenX++;
        (*numCoords)++;
      } // end if between sx1 and sx2
  } //end if not horizontal or vertical
  else {
    // handle horizontal and vertical lines
    if (vertFlag && !horzFlag){
      if (y >= miny && y <= maxy){
        *currentScreenX = sx1;
        *currenttX = tx1;
        *currenttY = theY;
        *currenttZ = tz1;
        currentScreenX++;
        currenttX++;
        currenttY++;
        currenttZ++;
        (*numCoords)++;
      }
    }
    if (horzFlag && !vertFlag){
      if(y == sy1) {
        *currentScreenX = sx1;
        *currenttX = tx1;
        *currenttY = theY;
        *currenttZ = tz1;
        currentScreenX++;
        currenttX++;
        currenttY++;
        currenttZ++;
        (*numCoords)++;
        *currentScreenX = sx2;
        *currenttX = tx2;
        *currenttY = theY;
        *currenttZ = tz2;
```

```
              currentScreenX++;
              currenttX++;
              currenttY++;
              currenttZ++;
              (*numCoords)++;
          }
        }
    // if horzFlag and vertFlag are true, its a duplicate point. Ignore it.
    }
    theShape->currentVertex++;
  }
  //
  //   Sort the found x coordinates in ascending order
  insertionSort (screenXCoords, tXCoords, tYCoords, tZCoords, *numCoords);
  removeDuplicates (screenXCoords, tXCoords, tYCoords, tZCoords, numCoords);
  return 0;
}
```

Alpha-Blending

This chapter describes a powerful and effective addition to our toolkit known as *alpha-blending*. The alpha-blending function described here is synonymous with the term *image compositing*. The blending function is quite different in nature from the warping tool described in the last chapter in the sense that the warping algorithm is closely related to three-dimensional graphics. In contrast, the blending function is more closely related to image processing since we operate directly on the pixels of the respective images.

The concept of "blending" two images together using a third image or channel was described by Porter and Duff in 1984 [PORT84]. Careful application of this algorithm permits two or more images to be composited together seamlessly (that is, so that the effects of aliasing are reduced to the point that the eye does not notice). The alpha-blending algorithm also provides the ability to vary the opaqueness of models in a scene, such as shadows or smoke.

10.1   What Is Alpha-Blending?

Let's consider the following example. Suppose you wish to create a picture of your best friend in front of the Eiffel Tower (let's call this image the background image) and all you have is a picture of your best friend and a picture of the Eiffel tower. Using ICT we would create a cutout image of your best friend and then blend or composite the cutout image of your friend into the background image of the Eiffel tower.

The fundamental idea behind blending is that a third channel or image can be used to drive a blending process that combines the cutout and background images together. Figure 10.1 shows this concept in diagram form. The blending tool combines the cutout and background images together using the following equation:

$$B_{ij} = C_{ij}A_{ij} + (1 - A_{ij})B_{ij}$$

where i and j are image column and row indexes and A_{ij} is a factor (called alpha) that has a value between zero and one inclusive. B_{ij} is a pixel in the output image and C_{ij} is a pixel in the cutout image. These quantities are also shown in Figure 10.1. We implement blending by applying the blending equation above to three image objects: A cutout image, a corresponding alpha image, and an output image. Each pixel (i,j) of the cutout image is assumed to be "lined up" or co-located with pixel (i,j) in the cutout's alpha image. The spatial correspondence between these two images and the output image is determined by the transformed and projected model coordinates. Each pixel in the alpha image contains a number that can be interpreted as an alpha factor. The alpha factor can be thought of as a translucency indicator in which a value of zero implies transparency and a value of one implies complete opaqueness. We expand this definition of the alpha factor later in this chapter.

Taking another perspective, the blending equation replaces each background image pixel with a weighted sum of itself and the corresponding cutout image pixel. The weights are provided by alpha image pixel values. It

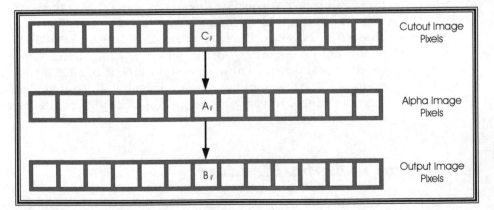

Figure 10.1   Images used during alpha-blending.

follows, then, that if each alpha factor in the alpha image is set to one, the cutout image will replace the background pixel over which it is superimposed. If the alphas are all zero, then blending the cutout image into the background image will have no effect since each pixel in the cutout image will have effectively been made transparent. More interesting things start happening when we use alphas between zero and one.

10.2   Why Is Alpha-Blending Important?

The first application of alpha-blending we describe is that of smoothing the edges of a cutout image being composited so that the effects of aliasing are reduced dramatically. Next a modification of the blending equation is introduced that permits dynamic scaling of the alpha factors in an existing alpha image. We then apply this concept to show how to create a shadow from an existing cutout image. Now let's consider the first alpha-blending application.

10.3   Making an Alpha Image from a Cutout

In Chapter 8 we mentioned that an alpha image is generated automatically by the ICT during the process of making a cutout image. We deferred explaining the purpose of this image until now. The overall process of creating an alpha image is illustrated in Figure 10.2. Let's look at an example. The bottom portion of Figure 10.3 shows a mask image generated from an example tree cutout image. Given our discussion about blending in the previous section, the appearance of this image should now begin to make sense. Each pixel in the alpha image that corresponds to a pixel inside the cutout area (namely inside the tree area) has been set to the value 255 (white). Conversely, all pixels in the alpha image that are outside the cutout area are assigned the value zero (black). This image is a predecessor of the alpha image and it is often called a *mask*. The mask image could be called a *binary image* because it only has two values: 0 and 255.

To convert the mask image into an alpha-image, the edges of the white area in the mask image are smoothed. By smoothing the mask image, alpha factors will be calculated in pixels along the edges of the tree that are greater than zero and less than one. When this mask image is used to blend the cutout and background images together, an effect will be produced where the outermost edges of the tree are made translucent. The end result is that the normal effects of aliasing are reduced because pixels along the edges of the cutout tree image (where one form of aliasing occurs) are being combined with the background.

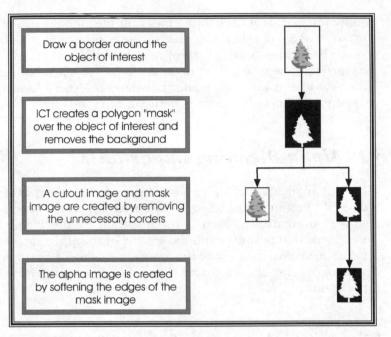

Figure 10.2 Steps to create an alpha image.

10.4 Edge Smoothing

Now let's take a closer look at the edge-smoothing process itself. In order to get the proper effect, we need to be very particular about how edge smoothing in an alpha image is performed. The top part of Figure 10.3 shows three side-view plots of the intensities in one horizontal line of the mask image shown in the bottom half of Figure 10.3. The lower intensity plot is labeled "Unsmoothed." This plot shows the edge profile of the mask image. If we choose to smooth the edges of the mask image by applying a sliding window average filter (also called a block filter), a situation results that is diagrammed in the middle-intensity plot located in the upper part of Figure 10.3. This plot is labeled "Conventional Block Filter." In this case the block filter will "smear" the mask image into areas for which there are no corresponding cutout image pixels. The parts of the image affected are indicated by the small white triangular areas that lie outside the vertical lines denoting the edges of the cutout image. Nonzero alphas in these triangular regions will cause zero-valued pixels from the cutout image to be mixed into the background image and the end result will be that the blended image will exhibit a dark halo. What we want instead is to smooth the mask image in such a way that the alpha factors corresponding to zero pixels in the cutout image remain zero. In other words, we only want to calculate alpha factors where the mask image pixels are greater

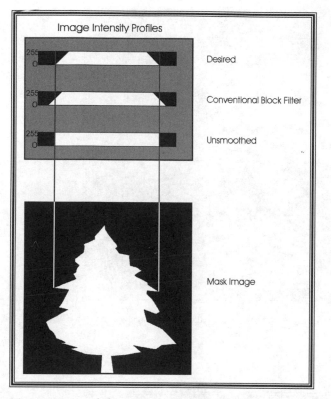

Figure 10.3 Alpha image edge smoothing.

than zero. This approach will produce the result labeled "Desired" in the uppermost portion of Figure 10.3, where the alpha factors along the edges of the tree are less than the maximum and all alphas outside the edges of the tree are zero. Alphas that lie in the interior of the cutout remain their original value denoting full opaqueness: 255.

To show the effect of blending, Figure 10.4 is a visual effect scene created by compositing two maple leaf models based on the same image. The model appearing in the upper-right portion of Figure 10.4 is blended, while the model appearing in the lower-left portion of the figure is not. We will inspect this image closely in order to observe the effect of blending. Figure 10.5 shows the area of each model that is examined in more detail in Figures 10.6 and 10.7. Figure 10.6 shows a closeup of the unblended leaf border. Figure 10.7 shows a closeup of the same portion of the leaf border, which was composited using alpha-blending. The image in Figure 10.7 exhibits less contrast than its nonblended counterpart shown in Figure 10.6. This lack of contrast will cause the model's edges to remain unnoticed by your eye. This is a case where it's what you *don't* see that makes the difference.

Figure 10.4   An example of alpha-blending.

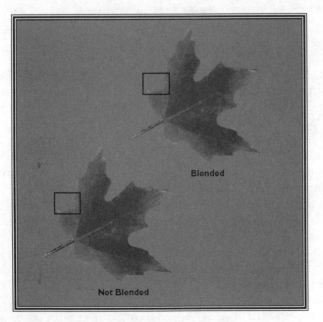

Figure 10.5   Magnification detail.

Figure 10.6 Magnification of compositing example without blending.

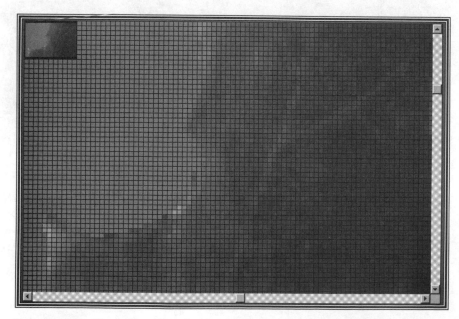

Figure 10.7 Magnification of compositing example with blending.

A cutout image and its corresponding alpha-image can be used during scene generation, as shown in Figure 10.8, to composite the tree into the final scene. By blending the cutout into the final scene, the effects of aliasing are minimized.

The edge-smoothing algorithm described at a high level in the preceding section is implemented as a two-pass process that is found in the functions: **smoothX3NN** and **smoothYNN**. Function **smoothX3NN** is applied to the horizontal lines in the image (which are oriented along the *x* axis of the world coordinate system). Similarly, function **smoothY3NN** is applied to the vertical columns in the image. In order to smooth the mask image in both the *X* and *Y* directions, a call must be made to each of the smoothing functions. The order in which the calls are made will not appreciably change the outcome.

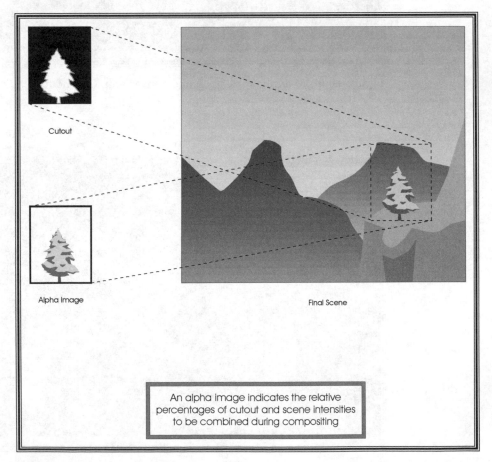

Cutout

Alpha Image

Final Scene

An alpha image indicates the relative percentages of cutout and scene intensities to be combined during compositing

Figure 10.8 The role of the alpha image.

The function **smoothX3NN** makes a pass over the image line by line. As the function traverses the pixels in each line, it calculates the average of the current pixel and one pixel on either side of it. These three pixels make up what is called in image processing an averaging window. Function **smoothX3NN** writes an output pixel into the output alpha image (in the location corresponding to the center of the averaging window) only if the pixel in the center of the averaging window has a corresponding cutout image pixel which is nonzero. Greater smoothing effects can be achieved by using larger averaging windows. For example, a **smoothX4NN** and **smoothY4NN** could easily be constructed and applied to mask images. Here is a listing of the edge smoothing functions that convert a mask image into an alpha-image:

```
void memImage::smoothX3NN(){
  int x, y;
  BYTE HUGE *myTemp = bytes;
  for (y = 1; y <= imageHeight; y++){
    for (x = 1; x < imageWidth; x++){
      if(x == 1 && *myTemp > 0){
        *myTemp = (*(myTemp)+ *(myTemp+1))*0.5;
      }
      else
      if(x == imageWidth && *myTemp > 0){
        *myTemp = (*(myTemp-1) + *(myTemp))*0.5;
      }
      else
      if(x > 1 && x < imageWidth && *myTemp > 0){
        *myTemp = (*(myTemp-1) + *(myTemp)+ *(myTemp+1))*0.33333;
      }
      myTemp++;
    }
    myTemp+=pads;
  }
}


void memImage::smoothY3NN(){
  int x, y, y1, y2, y3, result;
  for (x = 1; x <= imageWidth; x++){
    for (y = 1; y <= imageHeight; y++){
      if(y > 1) y1 = getMPixel(x, y - 1);
      y2 = getMPixel (x, y);
      if(y < imageHeight) y3 = getMPixel (x, y + 1);
      result = 0;
      if(y == 1 && y2 > 0)
        result = (y2 + y3) * 0.5;
      if(y > 1 && y < imageHeight && y2 > 0)
        result = (y1 + y2 + y3) * 0.33333;
      if(y == imageHeight && y2 > 0)
        result = (y1 + y2) * 0.5;
```

```
        setMPixel (x, y, (BYTE)result);
    }
  }
}
```

10.5 *The prepareCutout Function*

Now we describe the ICT functions that create the mask image and smooth it to produce the alpha image used in blending. We pick up where we left off in Chapter 8 at the point where a boundary has been traced around the desired portion of the image and the left mouse button was double clicked. At this point the mask image is first created by drawing a filled polygon from the traced boundary and saving it as the mask image. Next the smoothing functions described in the previous section are applied and the corresponding alpha image is created and saved in the x:\ict\cutout directory. The function that creates the cutout and its alpha image is called **prepareCutout** and is found in the file render.cpp on the accompanying diskette. The major steps taken by **prepareCutout** are:

1. Create a filled polygon from the cutout boundary by calling the Windows API function **Polygon**.
2. Save the resulting filled polygon image as a 1-bit Windows bitmap object.
3. Create an 8-bit/pixel **memImage** object by unpacking the bitmap created in step 2.
4. Smooth the edges of the mask image created in step 3.
5. Remove the excess zero border pixels and save the alpha image created in step 4.

The reason we chose to use the windows **Polygon** function to create the mask itself is that it handles all possible cases with ease. The only drawback in using the function **Polygon** is that it creates a 1-bit binary image that needs to be unpacked into an 8-bit per pixel image. Function **Polygon** draws a polygon in which the pixels inside the mask area have a value of one and all other pixels in the image are zero. The mask itself is created with the **memImage** member function **drawMask**. The resulting 1-bit image is unpacked into an 8-bit mask image by **memImage** member function **unPack**. Function **unPack** also maps the pixels that had a value of one in the 1-bit image to pixels having a value of 255 in the 8-bit image. This step makes maximum use of the allowable dynamic range in the unpacked 8-bit mask image. Here is a complete listing of the function **prepareCutout**:

```
short prepareCutout(shape3d *aShape, HWND HWindow, char
*imageFileName,
```

```
              char *cutoutName, short imageWidth, short imageHeight){
              char msgText[MAXPATH];
              int numVertices = aShape->getNumVertices();
              void *nullPointer;
              nullPointer = calloc (numVertices, sizeof(POINT));
              POINT far *thePoints = (POINT far *)nullPointer;
              aShape->initCurrentVertex();
              for(int myIndex = 0; myIndex < numVertices; myIndex++){
                thePoints->x = aShape->currentVertex->x;
                thePoints->y = aShape->currentVertex->y;
                aShape->currentVertex++;
                thePoints++;
              }
              thePoints =(POINT far *) nullPointer;
              memImage *maskImage = new memImage("OneBit.bmp",imageHeight, imageWidth,
                RANDOM, 'W', ONEBITMONOCHROME); //Memory, write, 1 bit
              if(!maskImage->isValid()){
                sprintf(msgText, "makeMask: Couldn't create 1 bit mask image");
                StatusPrint(msgText);
                return 1;
              }
              HDC hdc = GetDC(HWindow);
              short myStatus = maskImage->drawMask(hdc, thePoints, numVertices);
              ReleaseDC(HWindow, hdc);
              free(nullPointer);

              if (myStatus!= 0){
                sprintf(msgText, "MakeMask: Couldn't create 1 bit mask %d", myStatus);
                StatusPrint(msgText);
                maskImage->close();
                delete maskImage;
                return 2;
              }
              //
              // Create an unpacked (8 bit) mask image
              //
              StatusPrint("Unpacking MaskImage...");
              memImage *unpackedMaskImage = new memImage(imageHeight,imageWidth);
              if(!unpackedMaskImage->isValid()){
              sprintf(msgText,"makeMask: Not Enough memory to create unpacked mask
                image");
              StatusPrint(msgText);
              return 1;
            }
            maskImage->unPack(unpackedMaskImage);
            if(!unpackedMaskImage->isValid()){
              sprintf(msgText,"makeMask: unpack image operation was aborted");
              StatusPrint(msgText);
              return 1;
            }
            maskImage->close();
```

```
delete maskImage;
//  Perform a mask copy on the image, removing extra 0 Borders.
StatusPrint("Removing borders from mask image...");
memImage *originalImage = new memImage(imageFileName,0,0,
  SEQUENTIAL, 'R', 0);
if(!originalImage->isValid()){
  sprintf(msgText,"makeMask: Unable to open original image");
  StatusPrint(msgText);
  return 1;
}


myStatus = createCutout(originalImage, unpackedMaskImage,
  cutoutName, aShape);
if(myStatus){
  sprintf(msgText,"makeMask: Unable to prepare mask and image cutouts");
  StatusPrint(msgText);
  return 1;
}
  delete unpackedMaskImage;
  delete originalImage;
  return 0;
}
```

Drawing the Mask

Function **drawMask** is a **memImage** member function because it actually draws the cutout mask into a Windows device context and then transfers the resulting rectangular area of 1-bit pixels to itself, a **memImage** object. The technique used to create the mask is to first create a memory device context. Then draw the polygon that represents the mask itself into the memory device context. The arguments of function **drawMask** are: **dc**, the screen device context; **thePoints**, a pointer to a Windows POINT structure that contains the screen vertices from which the polygon will be drawn; and **numVertices**, the number of two-dimensional points in the POINT structure. The 1-bit mask image is assigned to this **memImage** object in the line that occurs near the end of the function:

```
GetBitmapBits(hBitmap, dwCount, bytes);
```

The Windows function **GetBitmapBits** copies **dwCount** 1-bit pixels from the windows bitmap object (pointed to by **hBitmap**) to the **memImage** bytes pointer, which is the pointer to the pixels in a **memImage**. Each image row of 1-bit pixels created in the **memImage** object by Windows function **GetBitmap-Bits** is the smallest multiple of two which contains the required number of pixels in a row. This small fact must be accounted for in the **unPack** function described in the next section.

Here is a listing of the **drawMask** function that draws the mask from the shape traced out using the mouse:

```
short memImage::drawMask(HDC dc, POINT far *thePoints,
int numVertices){
  HBITMAP hBitmap,holdBitmap;
  HDC newdc;
  hBitmap = CreateBitmap((int)imageWidth, (int)imageHeight, (UINT)1,
    (UINT)1, (const void HUGE *)bytes);
  if(hBitmap == 0){
    StatusPrint("CreateMask: Unable to create internal bitmap");
    return 1;
  }

  // create a memory DC
  newdc=CreateCompatibleDC(dc);
  // Select the bitmap into the memory DC
  holdBitmap=(HBITMAP)SelectObject(newdc,hBitmap);
  // Clear the memory dc by drawing a filled black rectangle
  RECT myRect;
  SetRect(&myRect, 0,0,imageWidth, imageHeight);
  FillRect(newdc,&myRect, (HBRUSH)GetStockObject(BLACK_BRUSH));
  // Create the image mask by drawing a filled white polygon
  HPEN hpen = CreatePen(PS_SOLID, 1, 0xFFFFFFFFL);
  SelectObject (newdc, hpen);
  SelectObject (newdc, GetStockObject (WHITE_BRUSH));
  SetPolyFillMode(newdc, WINDING);
  Polygon(newdc, thePoints, numVertices);
  // Display the mask on the screen
  BitBlt(dc, 0, 0, imageWidth, imageHeight, newdc, 0, 0, SRCCOPY);
  // Copy the completed mask image back to the memImage buffer
  DWORD dwCount = (DWORD)paddedWidth * (DWORD)imageHeight;
  // The mask is stored in the memImage using a width that is a 2 byte
  // multiple
  GetBitmapBits(hBitmap, dwCount, bytes);
  SelectObject(newdc,holdBitmap);
  DeleteObject(hBitmap);
  DeleteDC(newdc);
  return 0;
}
```

Unpacking the Mask

As its name implies, Class **memImage** member function **unPack** unpacks the 1-bit mask image created by function **drawMask** and creates a corresponding

8-bit **memImage** object that is pointed to by its single argument **outputImage**. The member function **unPack** passes over the input image and, for each bit found in the input image, it creates a corresponding 8-bit pixel in the output **memImage** object that has a value of either zero or 255. Several calculations must be made to determine the proper line width to use since the input **memImage** has an actual width equal to the smallest multiple of two that completely contains the required number of 1-bit pixels in an image line (see previous section). Here is a listing of the function **unPack**:

```
short memImage::unPack(memImage *outputImage){
  if (theColorSpec != ONEBITMONOCHROME){
  StatusPrint("unPack: input image colorSpec must be ONEBITMONOCHROME");
  return 1;
}


if(outputImage->accessMode != RANDOM){
  StatusPrint("unPack: output image access mode must be RANDOM");
  return 2;
}
if (outputImage->theColorSpec == RGBCOLOR ||
  outputImage->theColorSpec == ONEBITMONOCHROME){
StatusPrint(
  "unPack: output image colorSpec must be REDCOLOR, GREENCOLOR,
    or BLUECOLOR");
  return 3;
}
int x, y;
BYTE packedByte;
BYTE HUGE *packedBytes = bytes;
short myWidth = imageWidth / 8;
short remainder = imageWidth % 8;
if (remainder > 0) myWidth++;
if((myWidth/2*2) != myWidth) myWidth++;
for (y = 1; y <= imageHeight; y++){
  short xCounter = 0;
  for (x = 1; x <= myWidth; x++){
    packedByte = *packedBytes;
    for(short bitCounter = 0; bitCounter < 8; bitCounter++){
      xCounter++;
      if(xCounter <=imageWidth){
        if((packedByte >> (7-bitCounter)) & 0x1)
          outputImage->setMPixel(xCounter, imageHeight- (y-1), 255);
        else
          outputImage->setMPixel(xCounter, imageHeight- (y-1), 0);
      }
    }   // end for bitCounter
    packedBytes++;
```

```
      }     // end for x
    }       // end for y
  return 0;
}
```

10.6 Combining Warp and Blend Operations

When a model is both warped and blended, the model's alpha image must be warped using the same graphic transformations used to warp the model image itself. In this way, the alpha image pixels remain in one-to-one correspondence with the pixels in the warped image. The blend operation then occurs between the warped model image, the warped alpha image, and the output image. This process is illustrated in Figure 10.9. The combined warp and blend operations are implemented in the function **iRender**, which is described further in Chapter 13.

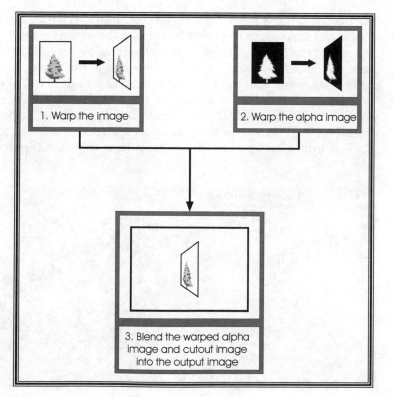

Figure 10.9   Blending a warped image.

10.7 Ghosts and Goblins: Opaqueness and the Alpha Scale Factor

Suppose we wish to uniformly vary the opaqueness of all the alpha scale factors in an alpha image. Instead of creating a new alpha image that contains the scaled alpha factors, it is quite convenient to incorporate a scale factor into the blending equation as follows. First let f equal the new alpha factor that incorporates the alpha scale factor s:

$$f = (A_{ij}/m)s$$

where m is the maximum 8-bit pixel value: 255. Since A_{ij} ranges from zero to 255, the alpha scale factor A_{ij}/m ranges from zero to one. The blending equation may now be rewritten:

$$B_{ij} = fC_{ij} + (1 - f)B_{ij}$$

The new equation simply enables the contribution of the alpha image to the final blended result to be scaled by varying the alpha factor. The alpha scale factor is set to a value of one in the scene file by default. Setting the alpha scale factor to 0.5 would cause a cutout image pixel with a corresponding alpha image pixel value of 255 (the maximum possible) to be combined with the output image pixel in a ratio of 1:1. In other words, the output pixel would be a 50% mixture of both cutout image pixel and background image pixel. Figure 10.10 shows a visual effect scene in which the same model is blended into a background image with four different alpha scale factors.

Figure 10.10 Effects caused by varying the alpha scale factor.

From left to right, the alpha scale factors are: 0.8, 0.6, 0.4 and 0.2. The alpha scale factor can be used in conjunction with sequences to produce morphing effects (see Chapter 14).

Figure 10.11 shows two additional effects created by varying the alpha scale factor. If an alpha scale factor of exactly zero is used, the effect is to erase the model from the background image. The result of this operation is often called a *holdout matt*. This feature is quite useful if, for example, a model image contains a surface such as a window through which we desire the background to be visible. The procedure for making a matt is to create a cutout of the window area and then use the scene preview tool to align the cutout over the window to be erased. By assigning an alpha scale factor of zero to the window cutout model, the window area in the model will be assigned a value of zero. When the model is subsequently blended into a background image, the appropriate portion of the background image will appear in the window area of the model.

The other effect illustrated in Figure 10.11 is that produced by using an alpha scale factor greater than one. The color noise effect is produced when the product of the alpha scale factor, the alpha image pixel intensity, output image pixel intensity, and the model image pixel intensity is greater than 255. Since each pixel is declared in the software as an **unsigned char**, the implementation of the blending equation produces an arithmetic wraparound effect. Since the amount of wraparound varies with each combination of the aforementioned intensities, each blended pixel can produce a different result, giving the increased effect of noise as the magnitude of the alpha scale factor is increased. The alpha scale factors used to produce Figure 10.11 are from left to right: 0, 3, 100, and 100. The effect produced with

Figure 10.11 Additional effects caused by varying the alpha scale factor.

the model on the far right of Figure 10.11 was created using an alpha image consisting of a checkerboard in which the dark squares have intensities of zero and the light squares have intensities of 255.

10.8 *Making Shadows*

Let's consider another use of the alpha scale factor. Suppose we wish to add a shadow to a model. Using a variation of the alpha scale factor idea, we can now simply add another model to the scene file that uses the same image file as the original model. Figure 10.12 shows three models blended into the background without shadows. To add shadows, we first include another copy of each model in the scene file, renaming the model to indicate that it is a shadow. Now we interactively rotate and position each shadow model using the scene preview tool until they appear in the desired perspective.

We could use a more scientific approach to placing the shadows, such as incorporating an illumination source representing the sun for example whose three dimensional position is calculated as a function of the time of year and time of day. From the sun's calculated position, the current viewpoint location and orientation, and the orientation of the surface or surfaces upon which the shadow is cast, we could calculate the correct angles with which to cast a shadow based on the sun's calculated position. Since here we have no need to create such a sophisticated mechanism for generating shadow angles, we elect to simply use the scene preview tool to estimate these angles, given the models that are supplied and the effect we wish to create.

Now that the shadow models have been suitably positioned, how do we make the shadows dark? The answer is that we actually want to subtract

Figure 10.12 Three models without shadows.

an amount from the area of the background image upon which the shadow is cast. The amount to be subtracted can be determined from the alpha values and the alpha scale factor itself. We can cause such a subtraction to occur by making the alpha scale negative. In the case of a negative alpha scale factor s, the blending equation is altered to the following form:

$$B_{ij} = B_{ij} + fC_{ij}$$

Since f will be negative if s is negative, a subtraction is performed as desired. Obviously, the darker the desired shadow, the more negative should be the alpha scale factor. A good starting point is to make alpha scale -0.2, which will subtract 20% of the alpha image value from the background pixels. A lower bound is placed on fC_{ij} so that it cannot have a calculated value less than B_{ij} one. Figure 10.13 shows the same visual effect produced in Figure 10.12, except that shadows have been added.

The two leftmost shadows shown in Figure 10.13 were created by blending the alpha image itself into the background. The shadow of the spruce tree on the right side of Figure 10.13 was created by using the spruce tree image itself as a source of values to subtract from the background image. The result is a more complex and interesting looking shadow. The scene file used to create Figure 10.13 is provided below. Since the shadow of an object can be occluded by the model from which it is derived, the shadow model is always rendered first. Thus each shadow model is positioned before the model from which it is derived in the scene file. The depth-sorting option is disabled when the effect scene is created so that the models will be rendered in the order in which they occur in the scene file. Here is the scene file used to create Figure 10.13:

Figure 10.13 Three models with shadows.

```
scene shadows Still 512,512 Monochrome
Rotation 0,0,0
Translation 0,0,0
MotionPath None


Model bgnd NoBlend NoWarp AlphaScale 1 Image
FileName D:\ICT\GALLERY\g150.BMP
MotionPath None
AlphaImagePath default
Rotation 0,0,0
Scale 1,1,1
Translation 0,0,0


Model lf_shad Blend Warp AlphaScale -0.2 Image
FileName D:\ICT\cutout\mpleafa.BMP
MotionPath None
AlphaImagePath default
Rotation 100,25,0
Scale 0.5,0.5,1
Translation 125,185,0
Model leaf1 Blend Warp AlphaScale 1 Image
FileName D:\ICT\cutout\mpleafc.BMP
MotionPath None
AlphaImagePath default
Rotation 100,25,0
Scale 0.5,0.5,1
Translation 125,195,0


Model sp_shad Blend Warp AlphaScale -0.4 Image
FileName D:\ICT\cutout\sprucec.BMP
MotionPath None
AlphaImagePath default
Rotation 270,0,0
Scale 0.75,0.75,1
Translation 267,171,0


Model spruce Blend Warp AlphaScale 1 Image
FileName D:\ICT\cutout\sprucec.BMP
MotionPath None
AlphaImagePath default
Rotation 0,0,0
Scale 0.75,0.75,1
Translation 310,260,0


Model cs_shad Blend Warp AlphaScale -0.2 Image
FileName D:\ICT\cutout\castle1a.BMP
MotionPath None
AlphaImagePath default
Rotation 235,0,0
```

```
Scale 0.48,0.6,1
Translation -18,69.6,0

Model castle Blend Warp AlphaScale 1 Image
FileName D:\ICT\cutout\castle1c.BMP
MotionPath None
AlphaImagePath default
Rotation 20,0,358
Scale 0.6,0.6,1
Translation -20,230,0
```

10.9   The AlphaImagePath Scene File Option

Each model included in a scene file may optionally specify a specific alpha image pathname. The **alphaImagePath** option in the scene file simply enables any image to be used as an alpha-image. The rectangular area of the alpha image need not be the same size as the model image. In the event that the images are different sizes, the blending function is performed on the smallest common area between the two images. Example 2 in Appendix B shows an example of the test model named "Jenna" blended with an alpha image derived from an image of a checkerboard. The **AlphaImagePath** option makes it possible to experiment with alpha images that you create using, for example, commercially available drawing and image editing tools.

10.10   The Blend Function

We have been describing the blend equation and its variations during the entire course of this chapter. The following listing implements the blending equation and incorporates the modifications for positive and negative alpha scale factors. The only additional comment to be made is that the **blend** function accommodates the possibility that the blended output pixels may be offset by an amount specified in the function's arguments: **xOffset**, and **yOffset**. Here is a listing of function **blend**:

```
short blend(memImage *inImage, memImage *alphaImage,
memImage *outImage,
  float alphaScale, short xOffset, short yOffset){
  //
  //  Blend over the common area in input and mask images
  //
  short inputRows = inImage->getHeight();
  short inputCols = inImage->getWidth();
```

```
short maskRows = maskImage->getHeight();
short maskCols = maskImage->getWidth();

short commonRows = min(inputRows, maskRows);
short commonCols = min(inputCols, maskCols);
//
// each memImage is assumed to be opened for random access
short x, y;
BYTE maskPixel, inPixel, outPixel, addedPixel;
float inWeight, outWeight;
for(y = 1; y <= commonRows; y++){
  for(x = 1; x <= commonCols; x++){
    maskPixel = maskImage->getMPixel(x, y);
    if(maskPixel > 0){
      inPixel = inImage->getMPixel(x, y);
      outPixel = outImage->getMPixel(x + xOffset, y + yOffset);
      inWeight = (float)maskPixel / 255.0 * alphaScale;
      outWeight = 1.0 - inWeight;
      if(alphaScale > 0.0)
        addedPixel = (inWeight * (float)inPixel) + (outWeight
          *(float)outPixel) + 0.5;
      else{
        addedPixel = (float)outPixel + (inWeight *(float)inPixel) + 0.5;
        // make certain shadows won't produce negative values
        if (addedPixel > outPixel) addedPixel = outPixel;
      }
      if (addedPixel < 1) addedPixel = 1;
      if (alphaScale == 0.0) addedPixel = 0;
      outImage->setMPixel(x + xOffset, y + yOffset, addedPixel);
    }
  }
}
return 0;
}
```

10.11 *A Thousand Possibilities*

In this chapter we have seen how the blend tool can be used to smooth edges of cutout images, add shadows to existing models, and alter the opaqueness of any model. Countless additional effects are possible with this technique and we have attempted to provide total flexibility in terms of enabling any image to be used as an alpha image.

11

Hidden Surface Removal

So far we have developed the tools for creating visual effect scenes by arbitrarily placing any number of photographic models in a three-dimensional world. The ICT software provides a graphical viewing system in which these models can be warped and blended so as to appear naturally from any defined observer point of view. There is one important part of this system, however, which we have not yet addressed. Because we can change the point of view from which a particular scene is viewed, we can create many views of the same set of models.

Perhaps we can get an idea of the situation we are addressing by looking at a simple diagram. Figure 11.1 shows a scene that consists of three models, each represented by a sphere, cone, and cube. Two viewpoints are shown; the first is labeled A and the other is labeled B. Now, suppose that we wish to create two scenes: The first scene, called scene A, uses viewpoint A, while the second scene, called scene B, uses viewpoint B. In order to render scene A properly, the model represented by the cube should be in front while the model represented by the sphere is farthest away and is probably partially hidden from the observer by either or both the cone and the cube. In order to render scene B, we wish to see quite a different result. In scene B the model represented by the sphere should appear in front while the cube is farthest away, and may be hidden by either the cone or the sphere.

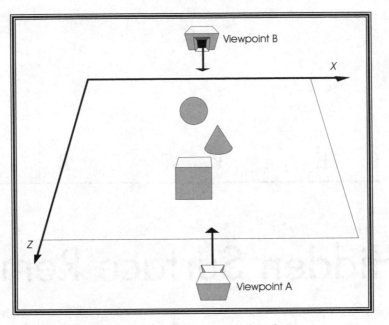

Figure 11.1 Depth sorting from two points of view.

11.1 *The Painter's Algorithm*

If we could predict which parts of the scene were not visible from a given viewpoint, perhaps time could be saved by not rendering those parts of the scene. Unfortunately, it would probably take just as much processing time, if not more, to figure out which parts of the scene are not visible than it would simply to render the entire scene. What we need is a simple way to render the scene so that the models are always rendered in the correct order. Let's take a step back for a moment and think about how we view the objects around us. We observe that the objects that are partially hidden from our sight are usually being blocked by other objects that are closer to us. For example, if we are standing at a point between viewpoint A and the cube shown in Figure 11.1, then the sphere is hidden by the cube because the cube is closer to us than the sphere. If we now move to viewpoint B and turn so that we are again facing the models in Figure 11.1, we notice that the cube is now farthest away and that our view of it can be blocked by either the cone or the sphere because they are now closer to us than the cube.

The general pattern that emerges is that models that are farther away from the observer can be blocked from view by any model that is closer to the observer. It would follow, then, that if we always draw the models that are farther away before those that are closer, we would probably be on the right track. In fact, we have just reasoned our way into describing what is called the *painter's algorithm*, called that, presumably, because painters begin a painting by drawing the background first and gradually work toward the foreground in which objects in the scene are closer to the viewpoint and therefore more detailed.

So, how can we implement this idea? We could just sort the models based on their z coordinates. This idea is attractive since it does not require a great deal of computation; however, this approach could give incorrect results in a great many situations including the case diagrammed in Figure 11.2. Viewpoint C and the models shown in Figure 11.2 all have approximately the same values of z. Consequently, ordering the models by z coordinate will give unpredictable results in such cases. What about using the three-dimensional distance between the viewer and each model? The distance is more costly than a simple z coordinate sort to calculate; however, the distance approach will provide a correct result regardless of the orientation of the models in the scene with respect to the viewpoint. It turns out that this approach will provide us quite acceptable results. The equation for the distance d between two three-dimensional points (x_1, y_1, z_1) and (x_2, y_2, z_2) is:

$$d = sqrt(dx^2 + dy^2 + dz^2)$$

where $dx = x_2 - x_1$ and $dy = y_2 - y_1$ and $dz = z_2 - z_1$. Since the distance equation requires two points, the only question now remaining is which point within a model should be used for the distance calculation. The most convenient choice is to use our handy middle point, or centroid, which we defined in Chapter 9.

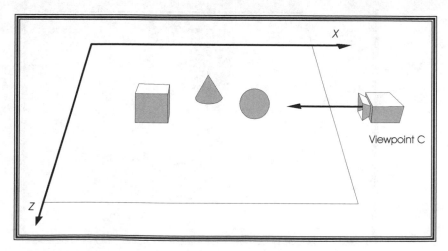

Figure 11.2 A case where depth sorting is needed.

11.2   *Depth Sorting*

To recap: Prior to rendering a scene we will first calculate the three-dimensional distance between the centroid of each model and the viewpoint. We then sort the distances in descending order (largest distance appears first in the sorted list, smallest distance appears last), and finally, render the models in the order in which they occur in the sorted list.

11.3   *Caveats*

This approach will work handily for any case where the models do not actually touch or intersect each other in the world coordinate system. Figure 11.3 shows an example where the models actually cross each other. In such cases, the distance-sorting approach described here will not work. In cases such as the one shown in Figure 11.3, a more detailed approach could be taken that operates at a finer level of granularity, say by depth sorting the individual vertical lines in each model's image. Approaches such as this are significantly more processor intensive and are not of interest to us at this point. Another case where sorting by centroid may not always yield a correct result is the case where there are a large number of models located in close proximity with each other, oriented at relatively random angles to each other. It is pos-

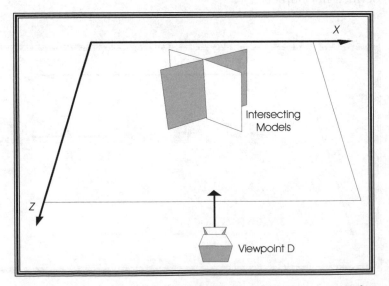

Figure 11.3   A case where simple depth sorting does not work.

sible in such a case that the ordering of centroids with respect to the viewpoint would cause some surfaces to be improperly occluded. In such a case, the render order of models can be determined by considering more than one point. For example, several of the outermost points on a model's surface(s) could be used to estimate the location and orientation of the model as a whole. As you can see, there are many variations of the depth-sorting idea. For our purposes, the centroid-based distance sort will be sufficient.

11.4   The Depth-Sorting Tool

Now we describe the depth-sorting software used in the ICT. Depth sorting is an option that can be toggled from the **Render** menu. The depth-sorting function listed below is used in the scene render process described in Chapter 13. Note that function **depthSort** is a member function of **sceneList**. Here is the **depthSort** function prototype:

```
short sceneList::depthSort(sceneElement *models[], float distances[],
   short *numModels, short depthSortingEnabled);
```

The first argument is an array of pointers to scene models. The second argument is an array of distances from each model to the scene's viewpoint. The third argument **numModels** is returned by **depthSort**. The fourth argument is the flag **depthSortingEnabled**, which is set to TRUE if the models are to be sorted. If **depthSortingEnabled** is FALSE, the **models** array is filled but not sorted.

Function **depthSort** begins by retrieving the viewpoint from the scene list by calling **getViewPoint**:

```
getViewPoint(&viewX, &viewY, &viewZ, &rotateX, &rotateY, &rotateZ);
```

Next, the scene list is traversed and the distance between each model and the viewpoint is calculated. Note that the centroid of each model is assumed to have been previously computed since it is retrieved from the scene list as the point (**originx**, **originy**, **originz**). Each model centroid was calculated during the scene preview step in the function **transformAnd-Project**.

Looking further down in the **depthSort** listing, you will notice the following statements:

```
if(modelCounter == 0 && theModel->warpIndicator == 0 &&
   theModel->blendIndicator == 0) {
     distances[modelCounter] = 2E31;
     models[modelCounter] = theModel;
```

The ICT includes the idea of a backdrop image, which was mentioned in section 2.4. A backdrop image is defined to exist if the first model in the scene file does not include either a warp or blend operation. Such an image is always copied into the output image as the first step in scene rendering. In this case, we assign the backdrop image an arbitrarily large distance so that it can emerge from the depth-sorting algorithm as the first model to be rendered. As the scene list is being traversed during scene penetration, distances are stored in the **distances** array. Pointers to each model are also being stored in the corresponding **models** array. If depth sorting has been selected from the menu item (depth sorting is activated by default), then the list is sorted in descending order by the function **insertionSort2**:

```
if(depthSortingEnabled)
  insertionSort2(distances, (DWORD *)models, *numModels);
```

Note that if depth sorting has not been activated, the models in the scene will be rendered in the order in which they appear in the scene file. For simpler scenes in which the three-dimensional viewpoint-to-model distance is not a desirable way in which to order the rendering of models in a scene, using the model order in the scene file is a convenient way to achieve a desired result. Finally, the function **getDistance** is listed below directly after the listing of function **depthSort**. As its name implies, **getDistance** calculates the three-dimensional distance between two points.

```
short sceneList::depthSort(sceneElement *models[], float distances[],
  short *numModels, short depthSortingEnabled){
  float viewX, viewY, viewZ, rotateX, rotateY, rotateZ;
  float centroidX, centroidY, centroidZ;
  float modelDistance;
  getViewPoint(&viewX, &viewY, &viewZ, &rotateX, &rotateY, &rotateZ);
  // Preview the Scene Models
  scene *theScene = sceneListHead;
  theScene = theScene->nextEntry;  // Skip over the list header
  if(theScene == 0) return -1;
  sceneElement *theModel = theScene->head;
  short modelCounter = 0;

  while (theModel != 0){
    if(modelCounter == 0 && theModel->warpIndicator == 0 &&
    theModel->blendIndicator == 0) {
      distances[modelCounter] = 999999999.9;  // set the distance of the
      models[modelCounter] = theModel;  // backdrop image
    }
    else {
      centroidX = theModel->screenObject->currentShape->originX;
      centroidY = theModel->screenObject->currentShape->originY;
```

```
        centroidZ = theModel->screenObject->currentShape->originZ;
        modelDistance = getDistance(viewX, viewY, viewZ, centroidX,
          centroidY, centroidZ);
        distances[modelCounter] = modelDistance;
        models[modelCounter] = theModel;
      }
    modelCounter++;
    theModel = theModel->nextentry;
  }
  *numModels = modelCounter;
  if(depthSortingEnabled)
  insertionSort2(distances, (DWORD *)models, *numModels);
  return 0;
}


float getDistance(float x1, float y1, float z1, float x2,
float y2, float z2){
  return sqrt(((x1 - x2) * (x1 - x2)) + ((y1 - y2) * (y1 - y2)) +
    ((z1 - z2) * (z1 - z2)));
}
```

12

Creating Photo-Based Animation

In this chapter we add the ingredients necessary to produce photo-based animation. We introduce the concept of a motion path and show how this capability is integrated into ICT. We discuss a sample sequence and show how the scene file and associated motion path files are related. We use the sequence preview tool to view the sequence and show how to produce the images in the sequence. Finally, we discuss the limitations of using photographs in sequences.

With the additions discussed in this chapter we will be able to create sequences of images in which:

- The viewpoint moves.
- Models can move in the scene.
- Both the viewpoint and models can move.
- Models can gradually fade in or fade out of the scene.
- Models can immediately appear or disappear from the scene.

Before we begin our discussion, it is helpful to know that each image in a sequence is called a *frame*.

12.1 Adding Motion

Adding an animation capability to the ICT is really not overly complicated given the infrastructure we have built up so far. We have already created a system whereby an image can be produced from a set of instructions that give the location and orientation of the viewpoint as well as of each model in the scene. What if we could now introduce a shorthand way of providing this location and orientation information for a sequence of images? In order to do this we introduce the concept of a *motion path*. A motion path is shown in Figure 12.1. Suppose one of the models in an effect we wish to create is an image of an airplane. We wish to show the airplane moving along a certain three-dimensional path and we wish this total motion to occur over a sequence of 60 frames. If we could specify the desired location and orientation of the plane at certain key points along its path, then interpolation can be used to fill in the location and orientation information for the frames in between each key point. Each of the dots in Figure 12.1 represents such key points in a motion path; these are called *nodes*. At each node we can specify the frame number, the nine graphic transformations described in Chapter 6 (rotation, scale, and translation), and the alpha scale factor. That's eleven values that need to be supplied at each node. The motion path is actually a list of location, orientation, and translucency information at known points along an intended path of motion.

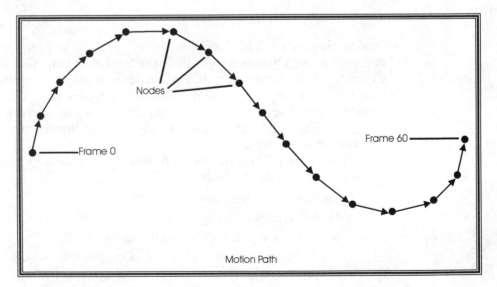

Figure 12.1 A motion path and its nodes.

12.2 *Interpolation*

Interpolation as used here takes advantage of spatial proportions that exist in the known graphic transformations at each node in the motion path and the known number of frames between each node in the motion path. Suppose we want to determine the Y axis translation for each frame in a sequence. The *Y* translation at the first frame in the sequence is known as is the *Y* translation at the end of the sequence. It is also known that the sequence is to last ten frames. The amount the *Y* translation changes from frame to frame, *dy*, is assumed to be linear and can therefore be calculated as:

$$dy = (y_2 - y_1)/(f_2 - f_1)$$

If *f* is a frame counter whose value ranges from f_1 to f_2, then the interpolated *Y* translation *y* is:

$$y = y_1 + (f - f_1)dy$$

Each of the nine graphic transformations (three rotation angles, scale factors, and translations) and the alpha scale factor can be interpolated in this way at each frame in the sequence from their known values at each node along the path of motion.

In ICT, motion path files can be associated with the scene's viewpoint as well as with any model existing in the scene file. These combined capabilities allow sequences to be produced featuring any combination of moving/nonmoving viewpoint and moving/nonmoving models.

12.3 *Getting a Sense of Timing*

If you are new to the subject of animation, one of the key objectives in the production of animation is getting the sequence to flow smoothly. The animation designer needs to have a sense for causing the right amount of motion to occur in the proper number of frames. The human eye is often the best judge of the basic correctness of the general flow of motion in a sequence. Our eyes are very sensitive to "herky-jerky" or erratic motion. The prime reason for the ICT sequence preview function described later is to preview the motion in a sequence so they can be refined to perfection.

To begin getting a handle on this subject, it is helpful to know a few basic facts. For example, a motion picture projector presents 24 frames to your eye each second. A television monitor presents just under 30 frames each second to your eye. We say that television has a *frame rate* of 30 frames per second. So, for example, if you wanted to create a 30-second video clip you would have to produce 30 frames per second times 30 seconds, which equals 900 images! That's quite a lot of work for our humble PC to handle.

12.4 Controlling the Rate of Motion

We can control the rate of movement of either the viewpoint or a particular model by specifying the number of frames over which a given motion is to take place. Let's return to our airplane example. Suppose we wish to move the plane 100 units in the positive X axis direction. Table 12.1 shows a two-node motion path in which the plane is located at the origin in frame zero. The second node in the motion path indicates that the plane has traveled 100 units in the positive *X* direction by frame number 30. If the resulting 30 images could be played back on a television monitor, the elapsed time on the screen for this motion would be one second. If we wished the plane to move twice as fast, we could simply change the frame number in the second node to half its present value: 15. The plane would then move the same number of units along the positive X axis in one half-second.

12.5 Motion File Format

The format of the motion file is quite simple. The motion path file is a text file that contains one line per motion path node. Each node record consists of a set of eleven numbers, as indicated in Table 12.1. The first number is the frame number and it must be an integer; all the remaining numbers are floating points. The delimiter between numbers in a line must be a space. Continuation lines are not supported. Comment lines beginning with the characters "//" are supported. The alpha scale factor ranges from 0 to 1 for most applications.

Table 12.1 A Sample Two-Node Motion Path

Frame Number	Rx	Ry	Rz	Sx	Sy	Sz	Tx	Ty	Tz	Alpha Scale
0	0	0	0	1	1	1	0	0	0	1
30	0	0	0	1	1	1	100	0	0	1

12.6   Sequence Preview

If we want to produce a sequence of any length, we want to be absolutely certain the result will end up as we expect, or else we will need to start over; a very time-consuming prospect. Fortunately, we have the ability to preview the sequence before we render it. Sequence preview can also be used to adjust and fine tune the motion parameters so we can achieve the exact results we desire. The sequence preview uses a different rendering technique from that used in scene preview. We describe both of these animation techniques in detail in the next chapter.

12.7   Using Motion Files

To create a sequence, we use the keyword SEQUENCE in the first line of the scene file, as described in Chapter 3. The scene portion of the scene file must include a line in which the first word is the keyword MOTIONPATH followed by a pathname to the motion file. The scene motion path file is used to determine how many frames of imagery are to be produced. The scene motion path file must be provided for every sequence even if the viewpoint does not move. Each model that is to move must also include an associated MOTIONPATH line with a motion file pathname in its description. The range of frame numbers specified in a model motion file should ideally fall within the range of frame numbers specified in the scene's motion file. If a model's range of frame numbers fall outside the range of frames specified by the scene motion file, the extra frames are ignored. In other words, it's a good idea to make the range of frames specified by the scene motion file greater than or equal to the range of frames specified by any model in the scene file. Let's now consider Figure 12.2, which diagrams a 100-frame sequence in which two models; labeled model1 and model2, are either moving or changing translucency. Various points in the sequence are labeled alphabetically on the right side of the diagram.

When a motion path has been associated with a model in a sequence, all of the model's location and orientation information is taken from the motion path file. To be more specific, from Figure 12.2 we see that model1 does not begin moving until point B has been reached at frame 30 in the sequence. How is the location and orientation of this model specified in each of the first 29 frames in the sequence? The answer is that the first node point of the motion path file is used to supply this information for each of the first 29 frames. Similarly, when point D is reached at frame 60, the model has completed its transformation. For frames 61 to 100, the last node in the motion path file is used to determine the model's location, orientation

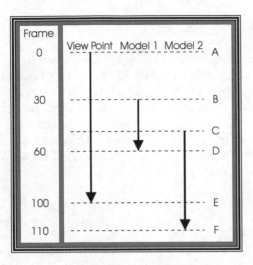

Figure 12.2 A sequence diagram.

and translucency. From Figure 12.2 we see that model2 has specified a motion path that extends to point F at frame 110. As we mentioned before, the scene node's motion file determines the length of the sequence produced. Consequently in our example, the frames 101 through 110 specified in the model2 motion file are ignored.

12.8 *How to Make a Sudden Disappearance*

Now let's consider a case where we wish a model to disappear in the middle of a sequence. Suppose at point D in our sample sequence we wish model1 to simply vanish. We actually have two choices, depending on the warp and blend options selected for the model. The first choice assumes the object is being warped. If the model is being warped, the *x* and *y* scale factors may both be set to zero at frame number 60. These settings will effectively shrink the model into invisibility. We discuss further the exact technique for doing this in the next section. The other possibility for making a model disappear assumes the model is being only blended. In this case, the alpha scale factor can be set to 0.01 at the sixtieth frame. The alpha-blending function will then cause the model to disappear because we have effectively caused it to become transparent. If the model is undergoing both a warp and a blend transformation, the preferred choice is to set the scale factors to zero, since neither the warp function nor blend function will be performed.

If the model is neither blended nor warped, it cannot be removed from a sequence. In this case, the simplest course of action is to specify a null warp transformation ($rx = ry = rz = 0$, $tx = ty = tz = 0$, $sx = sy = sz = 1$) for the model and then set its *x* and *y* scale factors to zero at the desired frame number.

12.9 *Sudden Disappearances: More Details*

Now let's discuss exactly how to set the motion path file parameters to effect an immediate disappearing (or appearing) act. Recall that the location, orientation, and translucency attributes of a model are interpolated for each frame located between the frame numbers that correspond to motion path nodes. Going back to our example in Figure 12.2, if we want model1 to disappear suddenly at frame 60 we could prepare a motion file like that shown in Table 12.2. Note that the scale factor is set to one at frame 30 and zero at frame 60. What will happen here is that the model will gradually shrink from its original size in frame 30 down to nothing in frame 60. This transition will take over 30 frames to accomplish.

If we prepare a path file such as that shown in Table 12.3, the desired result occurs. The third node in the motion path is shown in the fourth row of the table. The last node shows a transition that is to occur between frames 59 and 60. The only difference between the two nodes is that the scale factors have changed from one in frame 59 to zero in frame 60. This change will occur over a single frame and the model will disappear immediately as the frames in the sequence are produced.

12.10 *Sequence File Naming Conventions*

When a sequence is generated by the scene render function the output image file names are generated automatically. The first four characters are taken from the name given to the scene in the scene file. Three characters are reserved for the frame counter and the last character is reserved for the color indicator. The frame counter has a range of 000 to 999. Due to this naming convention, the limit on a sequence's length is 999 frames. This limitation can be easily overcome if necessary by changing the file naming convention. If the sequence is being generated in monochrome, the letter *g* will be used to signify that the green color channel was used (we assume all input images are 24-bit true color .bmp files). If the sequence is generated in color, the letter *c* will appear in the file name's eighth character position.

Table 12.2 First Attempt at a Sudden Disappearance

Frame Number	Rx	Ry	Rz	Sx	Sy	Sz	Tx	Ty	Tz	Alpha Scale
30	0	0	0	1	1	1	45	0	0	1
60	0	70	0	0	0	0	100	0	0	1

Table 12.3 Second Attempt at a Sudden Disappearance

Frame Number	Rx	Ry	Rz	Sx	Sy	Sz	Tx	Ty	Tz	Alpha Scale
30	0	0	0	1	1	1	45	0	0	1
59	0	70	0	1	1	1	100	0	0	1
60	0	0	0	0	0	0	100	0	0	1

12.11 A Sample Sequence

The following scene file, named motion1.scn on the accompanying diskette, defines a sequence that contains three models, each of which have associated motion path files:

```
scene sequence1 Sequence 400,400 Color
Rotation 0,0,0
Translation 0,0,0
MotionPath d:\ict\scene\seq60.pth

Model leaf NoBlend Warp AlphaScale 1 Image
FileName D:\ict\cutout\mpleafc.BMP
MotionPath d:\ict\scene\leaf.pth
AlphaImagePath NONE
Rotation 0,0,0
Scale 1,1,1
Translation 0,0,-500

Model jenna Blend Warp AlphaScale 1 Image
FileName D:\ict\cutout\jenna3c.BMP
MotionPath d:\ict\scene\jenna.pth
AlphaImagePath NONE
Rotation 0,0,0
Scale 1,1,1
Translation 220,0,-500

Model berry Blend Warp AlphaScale 1 Image
FileName D:\ict\cutout\strbrryc.BMP
MotionPath d:\ict\scene\berry.pth
AlphaImagePath NONE
Rotation 0,0,0
Scale 1,1,1
Translation 150,250,-500
```

Here are the three associated motion files. The first path file seq60.pth is associated with the scene description and describes the motion of the viewpoint in the sequence. As you will observe, the two nodes in this motion path are identical to each other with the exception of the frame number. The sequence has a 60-frame duration.

```
// seq60.pth - a viewpoint
// frame rx ry rz sx sy sz tx ty tz alpha
1 0 0 0 1 1 1 0 0 0 1
60 0 0 0 1 1 1 0 0 0 1    //the viewpoint does not change
```

The motion path for the model named **leaf** shows two transformations. The first is a rotation around the *x* axis by 180 degrees, the second is a translation from −500 to zero units. This model is also scaled in both *x* and *y* dimensions throughout the entire sequence.

```
// leaf.pth
// frame rx ry rz sx sy sz tx ty tz alpha
1 0 0 0 0.5 0.5 1 0 0 −500 1
60 180 0 0 0.5 0.5 1 0 0 0 1
```

The motion path for the model named **jenna** also shows two transformations. The first is a rotation around the *y* axis by 360 degrees, the second is a translation from −500 to zero units. This model is also scaled in both *x* and *y* dimensions throughout the entire sequence.

```
// jenna.pth
// frame rx ry rz sx sy sz tx ty tz alpha
1 0 0 0 0.5 0.5 1 0 0 −500 1
60 0 360 0 0.5 0.5 1 0 0 0 1
```

The motion path for the model named **berry** shows two transformations. The first is a rotation around the *z* axis by 180 degrees, the second is a translation from −500 to zero units. This model is also scaled in both *x* and *y* dimensions throughout the entire sequence. This model does not have an associated shape file by design and therefore will appear as a rectangle during the sequence preview.

```
// berry.pth
// frame rx ry rz sx sy sz tx ty tz alpha
1 0 0 0 0.5 0.5 1 150 250 −500 1
60 0 0 180 0.5 0.5 1 150 250 0 1
```

12.12 *Previewing and Rendering a Sequence*

Let's try running our sample sequence. Start up ICT and select the **Tools|Read Scene File...** option. Use the file browser to select the scene file seq1.scn from the x:\ict\scene directory. After clicking the OK button, the status bar should read "Scene File Read Successfully." Now Select the **Preview|Sequence** menu item. The three model shapes should move along their paths in a smoothly animated sequence. The model names are displayed in black instead of red, as they would be in the preview of a single image effect. In order to play the sequence again, click on the button marked with a plus sign, or move the preview dialog box to a different location on the screen (this action causes a Windows Paint message to be generated). Clicking on the OK button will return to the client window. In order to create the actual sequence images, we can now select the **Render|Sequence** menu item. The images will be rendered individually until the entire sequence has been created. Both the sequence preview and sequence rendering processes are described in detail in the following chapter.

12.13 *Limitations of Photo-Based Animation*

There are limitations to using photographs in sequences. The main limitation is the most obvious. Digitized photos are not true three-dimensional objects. We have treated our photo-based models like two-dimensional surfaces that can be manipulated using three-dimensional graphics technology. Combining this idea with the alpha-blending techniques we have discussed makes it possible to create very interesting effects. The tradeoff has always been aligned along the issues of using photos and textures to gain a high degree realism at the expense of a true three-dimensional model versus building true three-dimensional graphics models and giving up a certain element of realism. As the cost of computer processing power continues to decrease, it will become increasingly practical to build three-dimensional graphic models that exhibit truly photographic levels of realism. In these conditions, the emphasis shifts from the process of creating the actual effect imagery toward manageable techniques for collecting or generating the massive quantities of location and texture information needed to support high-resolution three-dimensional graphics models.

12.14 *Play it Again Sam*

Currently, ICT creates a sequence by simply generating a series of images. In order to play the images back in the form of a video, we need to convert the images into a video file format, such as Apple's Quicktime or Microsoft Video for Windows. Since this step involves the purchase of a commercial product, it is considered outside the scope of this book.

12.15 The MotionPath Class

Now let's look at the C++ source code that has encapsulated the capabilities described in Section 12.1 in a class named **motionPath**. The following source code can be found in the files motion.h and motion.cpp on the accompanying diskette. As indicated in the **motionPath** class definition header file motion.h, a **motionPath** object consists of a list of **motionNode** structures and an integer containing the number of nodes in the motion path. As the name implies, a **motionNode** structure represents a single node in a motion path. After a **motionPath** object has been created with the class constructor, the nodes are read from a text file using the member function **readMotion**. In order to determine the amount of memory required for the **motionPath** object, a first pass is made over the motion file. The nodes in the file are counted and this node count is used to allocate memory. The motion file is then repositioned to the beginning and the nodes are read into memory. The **motionNode** member function **read** parses an individual line of text from the motion file and assigns parsed values to the **motionNode** data members. The **motionPath** member function **getNextMotionLine** reads the individual lines in a motion path file and is responsible for screening out comment lines (those beginning with the characters "//").

The **motionPath** member function **getFirstLastFrame** returns the first and last frame numbers identified in the motion file. Finally, the **motionPath** member function **getNode** will return an interpolated motion node given any frame number that lies between the first and last frame numbers. If a frame number less than the first frame is supplied, then the first motion node is returned. If a frame number greater than the last frame is supplied, then the last motion node is returned. Here is a listing of the **motionPath** header file and member functions:

```
class motionPath {
private:
  int allocated;
  void allocate(int);
public:
  int numnodes;
  motionNode *nodes;
  int read(char *);
  int readMotion(char *);
  int getNode(int, motionNode *);
  motionPath(void);
  ~motionPath(void);
  void getFirstLastFrame(int *firstFrame, int *lastFrame);
};
```

```
struct motionNode {
  int nodenum;
  float tx,ty,tz;
  float rx,ry,rz;
  float sx,sy,sz;
  float alpha;
  int read(char *);
  void copy(motionNode);
  void clear(void);
};


void motionPath::allocate(int num){
  if(allocated){
    delete nodes;
    numnodes=0;
    allocated=0;
  }
  if(num>0){
    nodes=new motionNode[num];
    if(nodes!=NULL){
      numnodes=num;
      allocated=1;
    }
  }
}


void motionPath::getFirstLastFrame(int *firstFrame, int *lastFrame){
  *firstFrame = nodes[0].nodenum;
  *lastFrame = nodes[numnodes-1].nodenum;
}


void motionNode::copy(motionNode mn){
  nodenum  n.nodenum;
  tx=mn.tx;
  ty=mn.ty;
  tz=mn.tz;
  rx=mn.rx;
  ry=mn.ry;
  rz=mn.rz;
  sx=mn.sx;
  sy=mn.sy;
  sz=mn.sz;
  alpha=mn.alpha;
}


void motionNode::clear(void){
  nodenum=0;
  tx=0; ty=0; tz=0;
```

Plate 1 A fade-away effect created by progressively reducing a model's opaqueness.

Plate 2 A matt is created (left) by setting the alpha scale factor to zero. Alpha scale factors greater than 1 produce a variety of color noise effects (right).

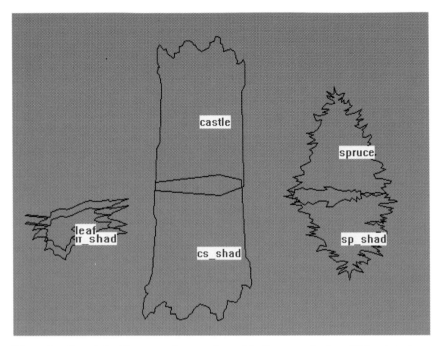

Plate 3 Special effects can be previewed before rendering. This plate is a preview of color Plate 4.

Plate 4 Shadows are created by using a negative alpha scale factor. Details on this technique are found in Chapter 10.

Plate 5 UFOs at Sunset. An example of a multilayer
image compositing technique described in Chapter 14.

Plate 6 An example of the combined use of the Warp and Blend tools
described in Chapters 9 and 10.

Plate 7 Model images used in the cross-dissolve morph sequence shown in plates 8 through 11. Details are described in Chapter 14.

Plate 8 Frame 1 extracted from a cross-dissolve morph sequence.

Plate 9 Frame 2 extracted from a cross-dissolve morph sequence.

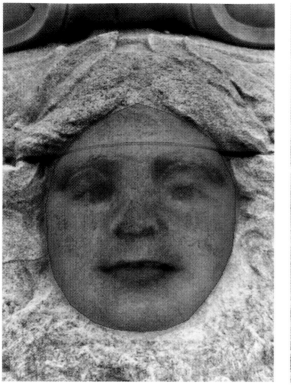
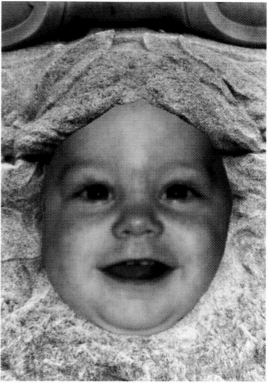

Plate 10 Frame 3 extracted from a cross-dissolve morph sequence.

Plate 11 Frame 4 extracted from a cross-dissolve morph sequence.

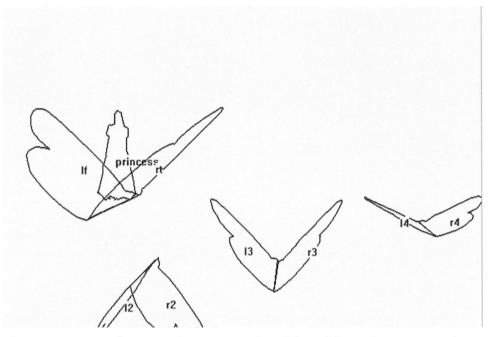

Plate 12 Preview of Plate 13 showing named models and their relative sizes and orientations.

Plate 13 A princess and her consort of butterflies visit a European city.

Plate 14 Disappearing Act. This sequence demonstrates the use of holdout matts (described in Chapter 14) and the ability to vary model opaqueness during generation of a sequence. Frame 1 of the sequence is located in the upper left corner. Frame 2 is located below Frame 1.

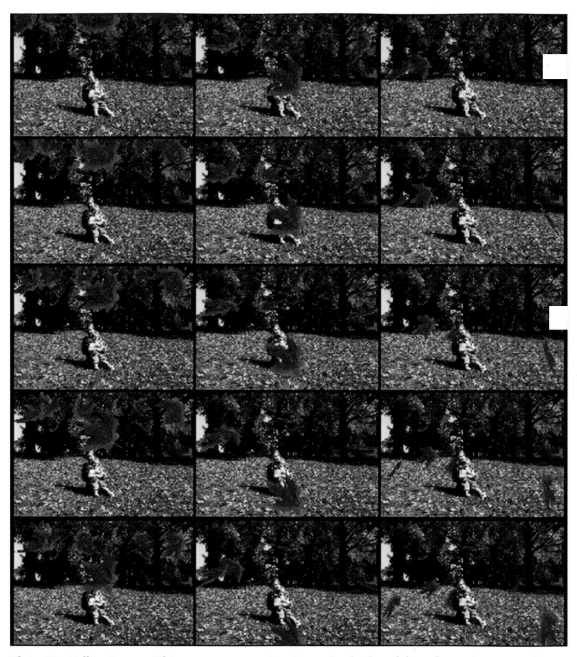

Plate 15 Falling Leaves. This sequence contains six moving leaf models and a stationary mother-and-child model. This effect demonstrates the depth sorting tool described in Chapter 11. Notice the first leaf model which passes over the mother-and-child occludes them, however a second leaf model which passes over the mother-and-child is occluded by them.

```
      rx=0; ry=0; rz=0;
      sx=0; sy=0; sz=0;
      alpha=0;
}

int motionPath::getNode(int frameNumber, motionNode *mn){
   int pn, nn, a;
   float dist, mult, diff;
   //
   // Filter the frameNumber
   int firstFrame, lastFrame;
   getFirstLastFrame(&firstFrame, &lastFrame);
   if(frameNumber < firstFrame) frameNumber = firstFrame;
   if(frameNumber > lastFrame) frameNumber = lastFrame;

   for(a = 0; a < numnodes; a++){
     if(nodes[a].nodenum == frameNumber){
       mn->copy(nodes[a]);
       return 0;
     }
   }
   a = 0;
   while(a < (numnodes - 1)){
     pn = nodes[a].nodenum;
     nn = nodes[a + 1].nodenum;
     if(pn < frameNumber && nn > frameNumber) break;
     a++;
   }
   if(a == (numnodes-1)){
   mn->clear();
   return -1;
   }
   diff = nn - pn;
   mult = (float)(frameNumber - pn) / diff;

   dist = nodes[a + 1].sx - nodes[a].sx;
   mn->sx = nodes[a].sx + dist * mult;

   dist = nodes[a + 1].sy - nodes[a].sy;
   mn->sy = nodes[a].sy + dist * mult;

   dist = nodes[a + 1].sz - nodes[a].sz;
   mn->sz = nodes[a].sz + dist * mult;

   dist = nodes[a + 1].rx - nodes[a].rx;
   mn->rx = nodes[a].rx + dist * mult;

   dist = nodes[a + 1].ry - nodes[a].ry;
   mn->ry = nodes[a].ry + dist * mult;
```

```
       dist = nodes[a + 1].rz - nodes[a].rz;
       mn->rz = nodes[a].rz + dist * mult;

       dist = nodes[a + 1].tx - nodes[a].tx;
       mn->tx = nodes[a].tx + dist * mult;

       dist = nodes[a + 1].ty - nodes[a].ty;
       mn->ty = nodes[a].ty + dist * mult;

       dist = nodes[a + 1].tz - nodes[a].tz;
       mn->tz = nodes[a].tz + dist * mult;
       dist = nodes[a + 1].alpha - nodes[a].alpha;
       mn->alpha = nodes[a].alpha + dist * mult;
       mn->nodenum = frameNumber;
       return 0;
   }

motionPath::motionPath(void){
   allocated = 0;
   nodes = NULL;
   numnodes = 0;
}

motionPath::~motionPath(void){
   if(allocated) delete nodes;
}

int motionPath :: readMotion(char *pathName){
   char msgText[MAXPATH], theText[MAXPATH];
   char *theKeyWord;
   motionNode tempMotionNode;
   ifstream filein(pathName, ios::in|ios::nocreate);
   if (filein.fail()){
     sprintf(msgText,"readMotion: Unable to open file: %s", pathName);
     StatusPrint(msgText) ;
     return -1;
   }
   filein >> ws;
   int lineCounter = 0;
   int nodeCounter = 0;
   short myStatus = 0;

   while(strcmpi(theKeyWord=getNextMotionLine((char *)theText, &lineCounter,
     &filein), "EOF") != 0){
     myStatus = tempMotionNode.read(theKeyWord);
     if(myStatus != 0){
       sprintf(msgText, "Cannot Read: %s Line: %d", pathName, lineCounter);
       StatusPrint(msgText);
       return myStatus;
```

```
      }
      nodeCounter++;
    }
    allocate(nodeCounter);
    if(!allocated){
      dprintf((motion.read: Error in memory allocation\n"));
      return -1;
    }

    // filein.seekg(0L, ios::beg); // Reposition to beginning of file
    filein.close();
    ifstream filein2(pathName);
    nodeCounter = 0;
    while(strcmpi(theKeyWord=getNextMotionLine((char*)theText, &lineCounter,
      &filein2), "EOF") != 0){
      myStatus = nodes[nodeCounter].read(theKeyWord);
      nodeCounter++;
    }
    filein2.close();
    return myStatus;
}

int motionNode::read(char *buffer){
  char *aNodeNum, *anrx, *anry, *anrz, *ansx;
  char *ansy, *ansz, *antx, *anty, *antz;
  char *anAlpha;

  aNodeNum = strtok(buffer," ");
  if(strlen(aNodeNum) > 0)
    nodenum = atoi(aNodeNum);
  else
    return 1;

  anrx = strtok(NULL," ");
  if(strlen(anrx) > 0)
    rx = atoi(anrx);
  else
    return 2;
  anry = strtok(NULL," ");
  if(strlen(anry) > 0)
    ry = atoi(anry);
  else
    return 3;

  anrz = strtok(NULL," ");
  if(strlen(anrz) > 0)
    rz = atoi(anrz);
  else
    return 4;
```

```
      ansx = strtok(NULL," ");
      if(strlen(ansx) > 0)
        sx = atoi(ansx);
      else
        return 5;

      ansy = strtok(NULL," ");
      if(strlen(ansy) > 0)
        sy = atoi(ansy);
      else
        return 6;

      ansz = strtok(NULL," ");
      if(strlen(ansz) > 0)
        sz = atoi(ansz);
      else
        return 7;

      antx = strtok(NULL," ");
      if(strlen(antx) > 0)
        tx = atoi(antx);
      else
        return 8;

      anty = strtok(NULL," ");
      if(strlen(anty) > 0)
        ty = atoi(anty);
      else
        return 9;

      antz = strtok(NULL," ");
      if(strlen(antz) > 0)
        tz = atoi(antz);
      else
        return 10;

      anAlpha = strtok(NULL," ");
      if(strlen(anAlpha) > 0)
        alpha = atoi(anAlpha);
      else
        return 11;
      return 0;
}

char *getNextMotionLine(char *theText, int *lineNumber,
    ifstream *filein){
    int aComment;
    int theLength = 80;
    char *theKeyWord;
    aComment = TRUE;
```

```
    while (aComment){
      filein->getline(theText, theLength); // ignore comments and empty lines
      if(filein->eof()){
        strcpy(theText,"EOF");
        theKeyWord = theText;
        return(theKeyWord);
      }
      (*lineNumber)++;
      if (strncmp(theText,"//",2) == 0 || strlen(theText) == 0)
        aComment = TRUE;
      else
        aComment = FALSE;
    }
    theKeyWord = theText;
    return(theKeyWord);
}
```

13

Putting it All Together: Scene Generation

13.1   *The Scene Generator*

All of the topics we have discussed thus far come together in this chapter. In order to create a visual effects scene, we first preview the scene to place one or more models in desired locations and orientations. This action involves deciding what combinations of graphic transforms we wish to apply to each model. The scene preview tool makes this possible by providing an interactive environment for moving the models around on the screen. This tool enables us to preview the effect of applying combinations of transforms to each model. When all is ready, the scene or sequence render tool is used to create the final output image (or images if the desired effect is a sequence). Each output scene is finally rendered by warping and/or blending each image-based model in the scene according to the instructions we have provided in the scene file.

Two separate processes are used to preview the effect depending on whether we wish to create a single image or a sequence of images. The reason for having separate scene and sequence preview procedures is that the sequence preview procedure uses a technique that produces smooth, flicker-free animation. The scene preview procedure uses a more direct approach of producing a line-drawing on the screen that is less complex; however, it is not suitable for previewing animation because it produces flicker. These two approaches to scene preview will be discussed later in this chapter.

In contrast, only one process is used to render either a still image or a sequence effect. We address the scene preview, sequence preview, and scene/sequence rendering processes later in this chapter. Each of these tools are implemented as member functions of the **sceneList** class, since the preview and render functions depend heavily on the information located in ICT's **sceneList** object.

13.2 *Previewing a Scene*

The first type of preview mode is that of previewing a single image (also called a *still image*). Once the locations and orientations of the models in the scene have been established using the scene preview dialog box, the **sceneList::previewStill** function is called. Since it is possible to move the scene preview dialog box around on the screen during preview, we want to associate the preview functions with the Windows Paint message WM_PAINT. As the following code fragment indicates, both scene and sequence preview functions are included as part of the ICT MDI Client window's **paint** function. By placing the scene and sequence preview messages in the **paint** function, the scene will be redrawn each time the scene preview window is moved around on the screen. The MDI client window's **paint** function is found in the file clientWn.cpp:

```
void ictMDIClient::Paint(TDC& dc, BOOL, TRect&){
  short status;
  if(previewingScene){
    status = mySceneList->previewStill(HWindow, modelMatrix, viewMatrix);
    if(status != 0) exit;
  }
  if(previewingSequence){
    status = mySceneList->previewSequence(HWindow, modelMatrix, viewMatrix);
    if(status != 0) exit;
  }
}
```

The **previewingSequence** and **previewingScene** control variables are set appropriately depending on whether the **Scene|Preview** or **Sequence|Preview** menu items were selected, and the appropriate preview function is called. As mentioned earlier, the ICT MDI client window's **paint** function is invoked in response to the Windows WM_PAINT message. We can explicitly invoke the **previewStill** function by calling the OWL **Invalidate** function. This is true because function **Invalidate** triggers the **paint** function. The **paint** function's single argument is set to TRUE if the window is to be cleared before redrawing the scene. The following example of the use of the **Invalidate** function is taken from the scene preview dialog box member function **increment**. The member function **increment** is called in response to clicking the scene preview button labeled with the plus (+) sign:

```
theClient->Invalidate(TRUE);
```

Let's now examine in more detail what happens when the **Preview|Scene** menu item is selected and the **previewStill** function is invoked. Let's first look at the ICT client response function that is called in response to the **Preview|Scene** menu item selection. From the entry found in the ICT client window response (found in clientWn.cpp) table we see that the function **evPreviewScene** is called in response to the user's selection of the **Preview|Scene** menu item (the details of this mechanism are described in Chapter 2):

```
EV_COMMAND(CM_PREVIEWSCENE, evPreviewScene),
```

The **evPreviewScene** function opens the scene preview modal dialog box, and sets the previewingScene flag to TRUE while the dialog box is opened. This will cause the **paint** function described earlier to redraw the scene being previewed in response to any WM_PAINT messages issued by Windows. The **renderSceneEnabled** variable is set to one after the scene has been previewed. The **renderSceneEnabled** control variable activates the **Render|Scene** menu item. The control variable **isDirty** is used to indicate that the client window has been drawn on and should be erased when any menu item is subsequently selected. Here is a listing of the function **evPreviewScene**:

```
void ictMDIClient::evPreviewScene (){
  previewingScene = TRUE;
  // Execute a modal dialog
  if (GetModule()->ExecDialog(
    new scenePreviewDialog(this,"IDD_ScenePreview", 0, this)) == IDOK){
    renderSceneEnabled = 1;
  }
  previewingScene = FALSE;
  isDirty = 1;
}
```

To recap, what we have seen is that the **previewStill** function is called indirectly through the ICT MDI client window's **Paint** function when the

Preview|Scene menu item is selected. By arranging the function calls in this way, we gain an advantage in that we can cause the scene preview drawing actions to occur not only when we explicitly want them to, but also when the windows operating system detects that part of the scene being previewed needs to be redrawn as a result of actions beyond our direct control, such as the user's moving the scene preview dialog box. This mechanism is also used in response to **Preview|Sequence**, **Render|Scene**, and **Render|Sequence** menu item selections. Now that we understand this interaction between Windows messages and the ICT application, let's take a closer look at the **previewStill** function, which actually performs the drawing operations necessary to preview a single scene. Here is the **previewStill** function prototype:

```
short sceneList::previewStill(HWND theWindow, tMatrix *modelMatrix, tMatrix
   *viewMatrix);
```

The arguments of sceneList member function **previewStill** are as follows:

theWindow: A handle to the window in which to draw the scene being previewed.

modelMatrix: A **tMatrix** object containing the model's graphic transformations. This **tMatrix** object is passed in from the calling function and is used by **previewStill**. It does not contain any specific model transformations.

viewMatrix: A **tMatrix** object containing the location and orientation of the viewer.

The first step in previewing a scene is to create several new objects:

```
motionNode *aMotion = new motionNode;
bundle *xfrm = new bundle();
tMatrix *viewModelMatrix = new tMatrix();
```

And now, here's a bonus! The two **sceneList** member functions that implement the scene preview and sequence preview capability are both actually written to handle sequences as well. It is possible to experiment on your own with these two alternate animation techniques.

The **motionNode** object contains the model's graphic transformations for the frame if the visual effect is a sequence.

The **bundle** object is used to store all the transformations in one structure. It is used only for organizational purposes, as we shall see later.

Finally, a **tMatrix** object is created to contain the composite viewpoint and model transformation that will be applied to each model in the scene. We need to create this composite transformation matrix once for each model in the scene since each model has its own location and orientation. Next, function **getSceneInfo** is called to determine whether the effect is a scene or a sequence. The **sceneList** pointer is advanced to point to the scene object itself. If the effect is a sequence, the first and last frame numbers of the sequence are retrieved from the **motionPath** object associated with the scene list's scene node:

```
getSceneInfo(sceneName, &effectType, &colorMode,
&outputRows, &outputColumns);
//
//  Preview the scene Models
  theScene = sceneListHead;
  theScene = theScene->nextEntry;  //Skip over the list header
  if(theScene == 0) return 0;
  firstFrame = lastFrame = 0;
  if(effectType == SEQUENCE)
    theScene->sensorMotion->getFirstLastFrame (&firstFrame, &lastFrame);
```

Now we enter the sequence loop. Remember that we are using this code to implement scene preview. In the case of rendering a single image, we actually create a sequence of one image. In this case, the variables **firstFrame** and **LastFrame** will be equal and the loop will execute once, producing just one preview image. If the effect type is a sequence, the loop executes once for each frame in the sequence and the view matrix is also constructed once for each frame in the sequence using the information located in the motion path object of the scene node of the scene list.

```
for(frameCounter = firstFrame; frameCounter <= lastFrame;
frameCounter++){
  theModel = theScene->head;  //point to the first model
  if(effectType == SEQUENCE)getViewMatrix(viewMatrix, frameCounter,
    theScene);
  modelCounter = 0;
```

Now we begin to loop through all the models contained in the scene list object. Each model in the scene list object has an associated screen object (called **theModel->screenObject** in the code fragment that follows), which is an instance of a class named **renderObject**. **RenderObject** objects encapsulate all the details of drawing a scene list model onto a particular display device. The function that actually draws lines onto the display device is a member function of class **renderObject**. In this way, the class library supplied on the accompanying diskette can be adapted for use on other display systems by simply adding new member functions to class **renderObject**.

We cover the details of creating and using **renderObject**s later in this chapter.

```
while (theModel != 0){
  if(theModel->screenObject == 0){
```

If the model's screen object pointer is equal to zero, it is assumed that this is the first time a request has been made to preview the scene. In this case, an instance of class **renderObject** is created for each model before it is drawn on the screen. If the **renderObject** named **screenObject** was created successfully, then the **isValid** function returns a value of TRUE. If the **renderObject** could not be created, the model's **statusIndicator** data member is set to one, indicating an error.

```
theModel->statusIndicator = 0;
theModel->screenObject = new renderObject (theModel->fileName,
  theModel->modelType);
  if (!theModel->screenObject->isValid()) {
    theModel->statusIndicator = 1;
    sprintf(msgText, "Preview: Could not create renderObject: %s\0",
      theModel->modelName);
    StatusPrint(msgText);
    delete aMotion;
    delete xfrm;
    delete viewModelMatrix;
    return -1;
  }
}
```

13.3   Backdrop Images

Next we describe the implementation of one of the ideas mentioned in the design discussion in Chapter 2. If the first model in the scene list is neither warped nor blended, a backdrop image is defined to exist and the image is simply copied into the output image as the first step of scene preview. By displaying the backdrop image during scene preview, the other models in the scene can be placed in their desired locations and orientations without guesswork. In the code fragment that follows, the backdrop image object is created only if the first model in the scene list is neither warped nor blended. The first argument in the call to the **memImage** constructor is the name of the .bmp image file to open. The second and third arguments are the image height and image width. These two arguments are both set to zero, indicating to the constructor that the size of the **memImage** object to be created is to be set equal to the size of the image found in the .bmp image file.

```
if(modelCounter == 1 && theModel->warpIndicator == 0 &&
   theModel->blendIndicator == 0) {
     if(backdropImage == 0)
       backdropImage = new memImage(
         theModel->fileName,0,0,RANDOM,'R',GREENCOLOR);
   }
```

13.4 *Previewing a Single Model*

The remaining section of the preview loop is enclosed in an **if** statement. Assuming that the model's **renderObject** has been created successfully, the process of drawing the model now begins. The first step is to create the necessary composite transformation matrix from the set of graphic transformations specified in the model data members. The statement in the code fragment that follows, **modelMatrix->setIdentity()**, initializes the model's transformation matrix. The variables **xOffset** and **yOffset** are used to optionally shift the result of model drawing operations in both the *x* and *y* directions. We will examine the use of these variables later in the chapter; for now, these offsets are initialized to zero. The next step is to retrieve the model transforms from the proper source. If the effect is a sequence and this model is moving (that is, its **motionPath** object pointer is greater than zero), then we retrieve the transforms from the motion path object by calling the function **getNode**. If the effect is a single image, we retrieve the set of nine graphic transforms from the current model's node in the scene list. These values were first defined when the scene list was initially created and possibly underwent further modifications during scene preview. The function **copyTransforms** copies the transforms from the correct source and stores them in a **bundle** object named: **xfrm**. This step is taken to simplify the code statements that follow, which can now assume the correct transforms are located in the **bundle** object, regardless of the type of effect being previewed. Now the model's composite transformation matrix is created from the rotation, scale, and translation factors:

```
if(theModel->statusIndicator == 0){
  modelMatrix->setIdentity();
  long xOffset = 0;
  long yOffset = 0;

  if(effectType == SEQUENCE && theModel->modelMotion > NULL)
    theModel->modelMotion->getNode(frameCounter, aMotion);
```

```
copyTransforms(effectType, theModel, aMotion, xfrm);
modelMatrix->scale(xfrm->sx, xfrm->sy, xfrm->sz);
float xRadians = xfrm->rx * DTR;
float yRadians = xfrm->ry * DTR;
float zRadians = xfrm->rz * DTR;
modelMatrix->rotate(xRadians, yRadians, zRadians);
modelMatrix->translate(xfrm->tx, xfrm->ty, xfrm->tz);
```

Now we are ready to add the viewpoint transformation. We fill the **tMatrix** object **viewModelMatrix** with the matrix product of the **viewMatrix** object that was passed into function **previewStill** and the model's composite transformation matrix, **modelMatrix**, which was created in the previous step. This new matrix contains all the transformations we wish to apply to the current model's **shape3d** object. The function **transformAndProject** applies the composite transformation matrix to the current model's **render-Object**. This **renderObject** is pointed to by the **screenObject** variable, which itself contains a **shape3d** object, which in turn contains a list of vertices that are soon to be drawn on the screen.

```
viewModelMatrix->multiply(viewMatrix, modelMatrix);
theModel->screenObject->currentShape->transformAndProject(viewModelMatrix);
```

At this point we have applied the desired graphic transformations to the boundary points of the current model. We are now ready to draw the points on the screen. Before proceeding, we need to check for the presence of a backdrop image. If the current model meets the backdrop image criteria (described earlier), the backdrop image is opened and displayed in the client window area using the function **memImage::display2**. We first need to obtain the device context of the client window prior to calling the display function and then release it after we are finished. If the current model is not a backdrop image, we then call the **screenObject**'s member function **drawStill**, which calls the appropriate Windows GDI functions to draw the current model vertices on the display screen. Functions **display2** and **drawStill** are described further in later sections of this chapter.

```
if(modelCounter == 1 && the Model->warpIndicator == 0 &&
theModel->blendIndicator == 0) {
  HDC theDC = GetDC(theWindow);
  backdropImage->display2(theDC, outputColumns, outputRows);
  ReleaseDC(theWindow, theDC);
  eraseOldBoundary = FALSE;
}
else {
  theModel->screenObject->drawStill(theWindow, theModel->modelName,
  (float)xOffset, (float)yOffset, eraseOldBoundary, outputRows);
}
```

Finally, the last step is to increment the model pointer to point to the next model in the scene list:

```
theModel = theModel->nextentry;
```

Here is a complete listing of the function **previewStill**:

```
short sceneList::previewStill(HWND theWindow, tMatrix
*modelMatrix,
  tMatrix *viewMatrix){
  const float DTR = 3.1415926 / 180.0;
  short myStatus = 0;
  char sceneName[MAXPATH], msgText[MAXPATH];
  short effectType, colorMode;
  int outputRows, outputColumns;
  int firstFrame, lastFrame, frameCounter;
  short modelCounter;
  short eraseOldBoundary;
  scene *theScene;
  sceneElement *theModel;
  motionNode *aMotion = new motionNode;
      // current model location, orientation
      // if moving
  bundle *xfrm = new bundle(); // create a bundle of transforms;
  tMatrix *viewModelMatrix = new tMatrix();
  getSceneInfo(sceneName, &effectType,   &colorMode,
    &outputRows, &outputColumns);
//
//  Preview the scene Models
  theScene = sceneListHead;
  theScene = theScene->nextEntry;  //Skip over the list header
  if the Scene == 0{
    StatusPrint("previewStill: the scene list is empty");
    delete aMotion;
    delete xfrm;
    delete viewModelMatrix;
    return NULL;
}
  firstFrame = lastFrame = 0;
  if(effectType == SEQUENCE)
    theScene->sensorMotion->getFirstLastFrame(&firstFrame, &lastFrame);
  eraseOldboundary = TRUE;

  for(frameCounter = firstFrame; frameCounter <=lastFrame; frameCounter++){
    theModel = theScene->head;  //point to the first model
    if(effectType == SEQUENCE)getViewMatrix(viewMatrix, frameCounter,
      theScene);
    modelCounter = 0;
```

```
while (theModel != 0){
// if the renderObject has not been created, create it
modelCounter++;
if(theModel->screenObject == 0){
  theModel->statusIndicator = 0;
  theModel->screenObject = new renderObject(theModel->fileName,
  theModel->modelType);
  if (!theModel->screenObject->isValid()) {
    theModel->statusIndicator = 1;
    sprintf(msgText, "Preview: Could not create renderObject: %s\0",
    theModel->modelName);
    StatusPrint(msgText);
    delete aMotion;
    delete xfrm;
    delete viewModelMatrix;
    return -1;
  }
}
// setup the scene's backdrop image if needed
if(modelCounter == 1 && theModel->warpIndicator == 0 &&
 theModel->blendIndicator == 0) {
   if(backdropImage == 0)
     backdropImage = new memImage(
       theModel->fileName,0,0,RANDOM,'R',GREENCOLOR);
   }

  if(theModel->statusIndicator == 0){
   modelMatrix->setIdentity();
   long xOffset = 0;
   long yOffset = 0;


  // compose the model transforms
  if(effectType == SEQUENCE && theModel->modelMotion >NULL)
    theModel->modelMotion->getNode(frameCounter, aMotion);
  copyTransforms(effectType, theModel, aMotion, xfrm);


  modelMatrix->scale(xfrm->sx, xfrm->sy, xfrm->sz);
  float xRadians = xfrm->rx * DTR;
  float yRadians = xfrm->ry * DTR;
  float zRadians = xfrm->rz * DTR;


  modelMatrix->rotate(xRadians, yRadians, zRadians);
  modelMatrix->translate(xfrm->tx, xfrm->ty, xfrm->tz);
  //
  // Combine the model matrix with the view Matrix
  viewModelMatrix->multiply(viewMatrix, modelMatrix);
  //
  // apply the matrix
  theModel->screenObject->currentShape->transformAndProject(viewModelMatrix);
```

```
      // if this is a backdrop image, blt it to the screen
      if(modelCounter == 1 && theModel->warpIndicator == 0 &&
        theModel->blendIndicator == 0) {
          HDC theDC = GetDC(theWindow);
          backdropImage->display2(theDC, outputColumns, outputRows);
          ReleaseDC(theWindow, theDC);
          eraseOldBoundary = FALSE;
      }
      else {
        // draw the object
        theModel->screenObject->drawStill(theWindow, theModel->modelName,
        (float)xOffset, (float)yOffset, eraseOldBoundary, outputRows);
      }
      } // end if valid screen object
      theModel = theModel->nextentry;
    }
  } //end of a single frame calculation
  delete viewModelMatrix;
  delete xfrm;
  delete aMotion;
  return myStatus;
}
```

13.5 *Displaying a Backdrop Image*

In this section we describe a function that displays a `memImage` object to a user-supplied screen device context, which is often abbreviated *dc*. The dimensions of the rectangular area into which the image is to be displayed are supplied by two of the function's arguments, `outWidth` and `outHeight`. If the dimensions of the image object are larger than the indicated rectangular area, then `outWidth` by `outHeight` pixels of the image are selected beginning with the lower-left corner of the image and displayed on the screen.

The function **display2** first creates a device-independent bitmap object (DIB) and then copies the `memImage` pixels into the DIB object. In order to create the DIB, a monochrome color palette is also created along with the requisite header information describing the DIB. Once these steps have been taken, the DIB is created with the Windows GDI function **CreateDIBitmap**:

```
hBitmap = CreateDIBitmap(dc, (BITMAPINFOHEADER FAR*) pbmi, CBM_INIT,
  bytes, pbmi, DIB_RGB_COLORS);
```

where **hBitmap** is a handle to the newly created DIB. Next a device-compatible memory *dc* is created with the statement:

```
newdc = CreateCompatibleDC(dc);
```

The variable **newdc** is a handle to an off-screen memory area that, in our case, contains the **memImage** image pixels to be displayed. The DIB object is next selected into the memory device context using the statement:

```
holdBitmap=(HBITMAP)SelectObject(newdc,hBitmap);
```

This step assigns the pixels from the **memImage** object to the memory device context. Next, calculations are performed that determine the portion of the image to be displayed if the image is larger than the desired rectangular area in the screen device context. Once this rectangular area has been determined, the appropriate rectangular area of the image in the memory device context is transferred to the screen using the Windows GDI function **BitBlt**:

```
BitBlt(dc, 0, 0, localWidth, localHeight, newdc, 0, yDelta, SRCCOPY);
```

The name **BitBlt** is an abbreviation of the term *bit-block-transfer*. Function **BitBlt** transfers all of the pixels from the desired rectangular area of the off-screen bitmap onto the screen in what seems like an instantaneous single step. We make more use of this technique in section 13.7, which describes the sequence preview tool.

Windows GDI functions such as **BitBlt**, **CreateCompatibleDC**, **Select-Object**, **and CreateDIBitmap** are described in greater detail in sources such as [PETZ92].

Finally, after transferring the image to the screen, the DIB is selected out of the memory device context and the memory device context itself is deleted, completing the display task. These steps must be followed in the indicated order if the corresponding GDI memory resources are to be properly released back to Windows. Here is a listing of function **Display2**:

```
void memImage::display2(HDC dc, short outWidth, short outHeight){
  HBITMAP hBitmap,holdBitmap;
  HDC newdc;
  HANDLE hloc;
  PBITMAPINFO pbmi;
  HBITMAP hbm;
  RGBQUAD pal[256];
  hloc = LocalAlloc(LMEM_ZEROINIT | LMEM_MOVEABLE,
    sizeof(BITMAPINFOHEADER) + (sizeof(RGBQUAD) * 256));
  pbmi = (PBITMAPINFO) LocalLock(hloc);
  for(short a = 0; a < 256; a++){
   pal[a].rgbRed=a;
   pal[a].rgbGreen=a;
   pal[a].rgbBlue=a;
   pal[a].rgbReserved=0;
  }
```

```
pbmi->bmiHeader.biSize = sizeof(BITMAPINFOHEADER);
pbmi->bmiHeader.biWidth = imageWidth;
pbmi->bmiHeader.biHeight = imageHeight;
pbmi->bmiHeader.biPlanes = 1;
pbmi->bmiHeader.biBitCount = 8;
pbmi->bmiHeader.biCompression = BI_RGB;
memcpy(pbmi->bmiColors, pal, sizeof(RGBQUAD) * 256);
//create a bitmap data structure containing the memimage bits
hBitmap = CreateDIBitmap(dc, (BITMAPINFOHEADER FAR*) pbmi, CBM_INIT,
    bytes, pbmi, DIB_RGB_COLORS);
LocalFree(hloc);
// create a memory DC
  newdc=CreateCompatibleDC(dc);
// select the bitmap into the memory DC
  holdBitmap=(HBITMAP)SelectObject(newdc,hBitmap);
  int localHeight = imageHeight;
  int localWidth = imageWidth;
  if (localHeight > outHeight) localHeight = outHeight;
  if (localWidth > outWidth) localWidth = outWidth;
  int yDelta = imageHeight - localHeight;
  int xDelta = imageWidth - localWidth;
  if(yDelta < 0) yDelta = 0;
  if(xDelta < 0) xDelta = 0;
  BitBlt(dc,0,0,localWidth,localHeight,newdc,0,yDelta,SRCCO PY);
    SelectObject(newdc,holdBitmap);
    DeleteObject(hBitmap);
    DeleteDC(newdc);
}
```

13.6 Drawing Models

In this section we describe the function **drawStill**, which draws each model on the Windows display screen. Here is the **drawStill** function prototype:

```
void renderObject::drawStill(HWND theWindow, char *modelName,
  float xOff, float yOff, short eraseOldBoundary, short screenHeight);
```

The function **drawStill** takes as its arguments a handle to the window on which to display, the name of the model to display, an *x* and *y* screen offset by which to offset the drawing if desired, the flag **eraseOldBoundary**, and finally the screen height in pixels. As mentioned earlier, the function **drawStill** encapsulates all the specific information needed to draw lines on the Windows display screen. A related function, **drawSequence**, is used by the sequence preview tool.

Skipping back for a moment to the listing of function **previewStill** in section 13.4, it is important to notice the use of function **SetMapMode**:

```
SetMapMode(theDC, MM_TEXT);
```

The function **SetMapMode** sets the screen mapping mode to that indicated by Windows constant MM_TEXT. This mode sets the logical screen coordinate mapping function equal to the physical coordinate mapping. The effect of using this function is that the coordinates used in subsequent calls to Windows GDI functions such as **MoveToEx** and **LineTo** will be interpreted by Windows as physical screen pixel units.

Returning now to our discussion of function **drawStill**, as was mentioned earlier, ICT operates in the right-handed Cartesian coordinate system. When operating the scene preview tool, it can be observed that the models move about on the screen as one would expect them to move in a right-handed coordinate system. In reality, the default Windows display coordinate system is inverted with respect to the Y-axis of the right-handed Cartesian coordinate system. In other words, the origin of the default Windows screen coordinate system is located in the upper-left corner of the display, not the lower-left corner as is the origin of the right-handed Cartesian coordinate system. Furthermore, the positive Y axis of the screen coordinate system points downward from the origin, not upward from the origin as does the *Y* axis of the right-handed Cartesian system. We have accounted for this discrepancy in coordinate systems by incorporating the appropriate conversions in the drawing operations used in function **drawStill**. The coordinate conversions applied in function **drawStill** assume that the shape objects used during screen preview contain right-handed Cartesian coordinates. As described in Chapter 8, the Windows screen *Y* coordinates of a shape object produced as result of the cutout creation process are inverted, thus converting them from Windows screen coordinates into right-handed Cartesian coordinates. The result of the coordinate conversions performed in function **drawStill** is that models are drawn during scene preview as they would appear moving around in the right-handed Cartesian coordinate system.

Function **drawStill** sets the Windows GDI drawing mode so that the model/boundaries are always visible, regardless of the backdrop image which may be present. This is accomplished by using the GDI functions: **GetROP2** and **SetROP2**. Function **drawStill** operates in one of two possible modes: In the first mode, the **renderObject** object remembers the last boundary used to preview this model as well as the current boundary. In this mode, the variable **eraseOldBoundary** is equal to TRUE and the model's previous projected boundary is erased first by drawing the previous shape with a white pen. This erasing action is based on an assumption that is obviously valid only if a backdrop image is not being used. If the variable **eraseOld-Boundary** is FALSE, then only the new boundary is drawn using a black pen. The scene preview tool currently operates in the second mode, which sets the **eraseOldBoundary** flag to FALSE. In this mode, the entire client window area is erased and redrawn with the receipt of each Windows WM_PAINT message. The drawing operation itself consists of an initial call to the GDI function **MoveToEx**, which positions the selected pen to the first screen location indicated by the current shape object's first vertex. Then the Windows GDI **LineTo** function is called for each vertex contained in the shape object. A final call to function **LineTo** is made to draw a line connecting the last vertex with the first.

After the model's boundary has been drawn, the centroid of the screen object is calculated and the GDI function **TextOut** is called to annotate each model boundary with its name. Finally, the device context is released and the Windows pen objects are deleted. The last step is to transfer the current set of screen vertices into the shape3d object named **last-Shape**. This step prepares this **renderObject** should the control flag **eraseOldBoundary** be set to TRUE on the next call to **drawStill**. Note that the *Y* coordinates used in all calls to the functions **MoveToEx** or **LineTo** are inverted using the equation:

$$Y = \text{screenHeight} - y$$

where *Y* is the Windows *Y*-axis coordinate and *y* is the right-handed Cartesian coordinate.

Here is a listing of function **drawStill**:

```
void renderObject::drawStill(HWND theWindow, char *modelName,
  float xOff, float yOff, short eraseOldBoundary, short screenHeight){
  HDC theDC = GetDC(theWindow);
  int nDrawMode = GetROP2(theDC);
  HPEN hBlackPen, hWhitePen;
  SetMapMode(theDC, MM_TEXT); //Logical units = physical units = pixel
  currentShape->initCurrentVertex();
  if(currentShape->getNumVertices() == 0) return;
  lastShape->initCurrentVertex();
  hWhitePen = CreatePen(PS_SOLID, 1, RGB(255, 255, 255));
  SelectObject(theDC, hWhitePen);
  short xOffset = (short) xOff + 0.5;
  short yOffset = (short) yOff + 0.5;
  //
  // Erase the old border
  int index;
  float ax, ay;
  int firstx, firsty;
  if(eraseOldBoundary){
    firstx = lastShape->currentVertex->sx;
    firsty = screenHeight - lastShape->currentVertex->sy;
```

```
    MoveToEx(theDC, firstx + xOffset, firsty - yOffset, OL);
    for (index = 1; index < lastShape->getNumVertices(); index++){
      lastShape->currentVertex++;
      LineTo(theDC,lastShape->currentVertex->sx + xOffset,
      screenHeight - lastShape->currentVertex->sy - yOffset);
    }
    LineTo(theDC,firstx + xOffset, firsty - yOffset);

    ax = lastShape->averageX() + lastShape->minX;
    ay = screenHeight - (lastShape->averageY() + lastShape->minY);
    SetTextColor(theDC,RGB(255,255,255));
    TextOut(theDC,(int) ax + xOffset, (int) ay - yOffset,
    modelName,strlen(modelName));
}
//
// Draw the new border
if(!eraseOld Boundary)SetROP2(theDC, R2_NOT);  // Draw the inverse of the
                                               // background color.
hBlackPen = CreatePen(PS_SOLID, 1, RGB(0, 0, 0));
SelectObject(theDC, hBlackPen);
firstx = currentShape->currentVertex->sx;
firsty = screenHeight - currentShape->currentVertex->sy;
MoveToEx(theDC,firstx + xOffset, firsty - yOffset, OL);
for (index = 1; index < currentShape->getNumVertices(); index++){
  currentShape->currentVertex++;
  LineTo(theDC,current Shape->currentVertex->sx + xOffset,
  screenHeight - currentShape->currentVertex->sy - yOffset);
  }
LineTo(theDC,firstx + xOffset,firsty - yOffset);

ax = currentShape->averageX() + currentShape->minX;
ay = screenHeight - (currentShape->averageY() + currentShape->minY);
SetTextColor(theDC,RGB(255,0,0)); // red
TextOut(theDC,(int)ax + xOffset, (int)ay - yOffset,
modelName, strlen(modelName));

ReleaseDC(theWindow,theDC);
DeleteObject(hBlackPen);
DeleteObject(hWhitePen);

// Make the current shape the old shape
currentShape->initCurrentVertex();
lastShape->initCurrentVertex();

for (index = 0; index < currentShape->getNumVertices(); index++){
  lastShape->currentVertex->sx = currentShape->currentVertex->sx;
  lastShape->currentVertex->sy = currentShape->currentVertex->sy;
  currentShape->currentVertex++;
  lastShape->currentVertex++;
}
```

```
    lastShape->setNumVertices(currentShape->getNumVertices());
    SetROP2(theDC,nDrawMode);   //Return the draw mode to its initial state
}
```

13.7   *Previewing a Sequence*

In this section we describe the approach taken to produce smooth animation that serves to preview a visual effect sequence. The **sceneList** member
function **previewSequence** essentially follows the same set of steps as that
described in detail for **previewStill**. The major difference between these
two functions is that in function **previewSequence**, the models in the effect
are drawn first to an off-screen bitmap image. After all the models have
been drawn onto the off-screen bitmap, the off-screen image is transferred
to the display screen in a single step using the Windows GDI function **Bit-
Blt**. The result is a smooth animation. If you wish, an experiment can be
performed by using the **previewStill** drawing technique to preview a
sequence instead of a still image. To perform the experiment, simply replace
the contents of the ICT client window **Paint** function described earlier in
this chapter to:

```
if(previewingSequence){
    status = mySceneList->previewSequence(HWindow, modelMatrix, viewMatrix);
    if(status != 0) exit;
}
```

to:

```
if(previewingSequence){
    status = mySceneList->previewStill(HWindow, modelMatrix, viewMatrix);
    if(status != 0) exit;
}
```

and recompile. Now try previewing the sequence defined in the scene file
motion1.scn found on the accompanying diskette. To preview the sequence,
select the **Tools|Read Scene File...** menu item, enter the scene filename,
and then select the **Preview|Sequence** menu item. As the sequence is pre-
viewed, you will notice the screen flash slightly. What is happening is that
the *integration* or *dwell time* of the human eye is short enough to detect the
flash of white created momentarily when the screen is erased at the beginning of the drawing operation for each frame in the sequence. If you replace
the code as it appeared originally, rebuild ICT, and again preview the
sequence motion1.scn, no such flash appears. This is because the **preview-
Sequence** animation technique performs all erase and draw operations in

memory (out of sight from the viewer). Only completed frames are transferred to the screen, with the result that the perception of a flash vanishes. The function **previewSequence** uses a slight variation of the **renderObject drawStill** member function called **drawSequence**. This member function is identical to **drawStill** except that the off-screen bitmap is used instead of an on-screen device context (the frame counter is also displayed on the screen). Here is the complete listing of function **previewSequence**:

```
short sceneList::previewSequence(HWND theWindow, tMatrix *modelMatrix,
  tMatrix *viewMatrix){
  const float DTR = 3.1415926 / 180.0;
  short myStatus = 0;
  char sceneName[MAXPATH], msgText[MAXPATH];
  short effectType, colorMode;
  int outputRows, outputColumns;
  int firstFrame, lastFrame, frameCounter;
  motionNode *aMotion = new motionNode;
  bundle *xfrm = new bundle();
  tMatrix *viewModelMatrix = new tMatrix();

  getSceneInfo(sceneName, &effectType, &colorMode,
  &outputRows, &outputColumns);
  //
  //  Setup for smooth animation.  Create a memory DC
  HBITMAP hBitmap, hOldBitmap;
  HDC memoryDC, dc;
  dc = GetDC(theWindow);
  memImage *tempImage = new memImage(outputRows, outputColumns);
  hBitmap = CreateBitmap((int)outputColumns, (int)outputRows, (UINT)1,
  (UINT)1, (const void HUGE *)tempImage->getBytes());
  if(hBitmap == 0){
    StatusPrint("SceneList::Preview. Unable to create internal bitmap");
    return -1;
  }
  memoryDC = CreateCompatibleDC(dc);
  hOldBitmap = (HBITMAP)SelectObject(memoryDC, hBitmap);
  // Clear the memoryDC by drawing a filled white rectangle
  RECT myRect;
  SetRect(&myRect, 0, 0, outputColumns, outputRows);
  FillRect(memoryDC, &myRect, (HBRUSH)GetStockObject(WHITE_BRUSH));
  //
  // Preview the scene Models
  scene *theScene = sceneListHead;
  theScene = theScene->nextEntry; // Skip over the list header
  if the Scene == 0{
    StatusPrint("previewSequence: the scene list is empty");
    delete aMotion;
    delete xfrm;
    delete viewModelMatrix;
```

```
      delete tempImage;
      return NULL;
}
  firstFrame = lastFrame = 0;
  if(effectType == SEQUENCE)
    theScene->sensorMotion->getFirstLastFrame(&firstFrame, &lastFrame);
  short modelCounter, eraseOldBoundary;

  for(frameCounter = firstFrame; frameCounter <=lastFrame; frameCounter++){
    sceneElement *theModel = theScene->head;
    modelCounter = 0;
    eraseOldBoundary = TRUE;
    if(effectType == SEQUENCE)
      getViewMatrix(viewMatrix, frameCounter, theScene);
    while (theModel != 0){
    //
    // if the renderObject has not been created, create it
    modelCounter++;
    if(theModel->screenObject == 0){
      theModel->statusIndicator = 0;
      sprintf(msgText,"Creating RenderObject: %s",theModel->modelName);
      StatusPrint(msgText);
      theModel->screenObject = new renderObject(theModel->fileName,
        theModel->modelType);
      if (!theModel->screenObject->isValid()) {
        theModel->statusIndicator = 1;  // this object could not be opened
        sprintf(msgText, "Preview: Couldn't create renderObject: %s",
        theModel->modelName);
        StatusPrint(msgText);
        return -1;
      }
      // Get the scene's backdrop image if needed
      if(modelCounter == 1 && theModel->warpIndicator == 0 &&
        theModel->blendIndicator == 0) {
          if(backdropImage == 0)
            backdropImage = new memImage(
          theModel->fileName,0,0,RANDOM,'R',GREENCOLOR);
      }
    }
    if(theModel->statusIndicator == 0){  // if this is a valid model...
      modelMatrix->setIdentity();
      long xOffset = 0, yOffset = 0;
      //
      // compose the model transforms
      if(effectType == SEQUENCE && theModel->modelMotion > NULL)
        theModel->modelMotion->getNode(frameCounter, aMotion);
      copyTransforms(effectType, theModel, aMotion, xfrm);
      modelMatrix->scale(xfrm->sx, xfrm->sy, xfrm->sz);
      float xRadians = xfrm->rx * DTR;
      float yRadians = xfrm->ry * DTR;
```

```
        float zRadians = xfrm->rz * DTR;
        modelMatrix->rotate(xRadians, yRadians, zRadians);
        modelMatrix->translate(xfrm->tx, xfrm->ty, xfrm->tz);
        //
        // Combine the model matrix with the view Matrix
        viewModelMatrix->multiply(viewMatrix, modelMatrix);
        //
        // apply the matrix
        theModel->screenObject->currentShape->transformAndProject
          (viewModelMatrix);
        //
        // if this is a backdrop image, blt it to the screen
          if(modelCounter == 1 && theModel->warpIndicator == 0 &&
          theModel->blendIndicator == 0) {
          HDC theDC = GetDC(theWindow);
          backdropImage->display2(theDC, outputColumns, outputRows);
          // backdropImage->display2(memoryDC, outputColumns, outputRows);
          ReleaseDC(theWindow, theDC);
          eraseOldBoundary = FALSE;
          }
        else {
          //
          // draw the object
          theModel->screenObject->drawSequence(memoryDC, theModel->modelName,
            (float)xOffset, (float)yOffset, eraseOldBoundary, outputRows,
             frameCounter);
          }
      } // end if valid screen object
      theModel = theModel->nextentry;
      BitBlt(dc, 0, 0, outputColumns, outputRows, memoryDC, 0, 0, SRCCOPY);
      }
  } // end of a single frame calculation
  delete viewModelMatrix;
  delete xfrm;
  delete aMotion;
  // clean up the memoryDC
  SelectObject(memoryDC, hOldBitmap);
  DeleteDC(memoryDC);
  ReleaseDC(theWindow, dc);
  DeleteObject(hBitmap);
  delete tempImage;
  return myStatus;
}
```

13.8   *Rendering Scenes and Sequences*

In this section we describe the scene list member function **render**, which produces the photo-based output images for visual effects that are either a single (still) image or a sequence of images. The general flow of the **sceneList::render** function resembles that of **sceneList::preview** in that all of the models in the scene are traversed in the process of producing the output image. Despite the similarity, this render function is quite different from the preview functions since a model is processed by warping and/or compositing its image. Consequently, many additional class member functions are described here for the first time.

Since the initial setup portion of function **sceneList::Render** is identical to that described for **sceneList::Preview**, we will not repeat a description of the setup steps here. Instead, we begin the description of this function with the **for** loop, which iterates over each frame in the sequence:

```
for(frameCounter = firstFrame; frameCounter <= lastFrame;
frameCounter++){
```

The first step is to depth sort the models appearing in the scene:

```
depthSort(models, distances, &numModels, depthSortingEnabled);
```

The steps taken by function **depthSort** depend on the value of the control flag **depthSortingEnabled**. By default, this control flag is set to TRUE. Its value can be toggled by checking or unchecking the **Render|Depth Sorting** menu item. The first argument of function **depthSort** is an array of pointers to the models defined in the scene list. The second argument is an array of corresponding three-dimensional distances between the viewpoint and each model. The third argument is returned by function **depthSort** and is equal to the number of model pointers and their distances, which were stored in the arrays **models** and **distances**. The fourth argument is the control flag **depthSortingEnabled**, which should be set to TRUE if the array of model pointers and their distances are to be sorted by distance in descending order. If **depthSortingEnabled** is FALSE, then the arrays of model pointers and distances are populated by the **depthSort** function; however they are not sorted.

Next, the viewpoint transformation matrix **viewMatrix** is recalculated if the effect type is a sequence. In the case of a sequence, the viewpoint transformations are retrieved from the **motionPath** node associated with the scene object of the sceneList.

Next, an additional loop is initiated for the color processing. If the effect is to be generated in monochrome, the green channel of the true color images is used. If the effect is to be generated in true color, the color loop will execute three times, processing the red component of the model images first, then the green, then the blue.

```
if(effectType == SEQUENCE)
    getViewMatrix(viewMatrix, frameCounter, theScene);
    //
```

```
//  Setup the Color Mode
short firstColor = GREEN;
short lastColor = GREEN;
if (colorMode == COLOR) {
  firstColor = RED;
  lastColor = BLUE;
}


for (short theColor = firstColor; theColor <= lastColor; theColor++){
```

Now the output image is opened. If the image could not be opened, an error message would be posted to the process log.

```
memImage *outputImage = new memImage(outputRows, outputColumns);
    if (outputImage == 0) {
      sprintf(msgText, "Not enough memory to open output image");
      StatusPrint(msgText);
      delete aMotion;
      delete xfrm;
      return -1;
    }
```

Now we begin the inner loop, which appropriately renders each model in the scene. A pointer to the current model **theModel** is assigned. The remaining steps in this inner loop are applied only to models that are image based and whose status indicator indicates a clean bill of health:

```
for(short currentModel = 0; currentModel <= numModels-1; currentModel++){
  theModel = models[currentModel];
  // Only render objects of type IMAGE
  if (theModel->modelType == IMAGE && theModel->statusIndicator == 0){
```

Next, the current model image is opened. The alpha image is also opened based on whether the scene file specified a particular alpha image. If no alpha image is specified and the model is to be blended, then the model is assumed to be a cutout and the name of the alpha image is determined by substituting the last letter of the cutout image filename (before the suffix) with the letter *a*. For example, if the model image name is "photolc.bmp," then the alpha image name derived from it would be "photola.bmp." Alpha images are always assumed to be 8-bit monochrome images.

```
if(strcmpi(theModel->alphaPath, "NONE") != 0)
  strcpy(alphaName, theModel->alphaPath);
else
  getMaskName(theModel->fileName, alphaName);
  alphaImage = new memImage(alphaName, 0, 0, RANDOM, 'R',
    EIGHTBITMONOCHROME);
```

If the model is moving, the set of graphic transforms is retrieved from the model's **motionPath** object. If the model is not moving, the transforms are retrieved from the model's scene list node. As in the case of the scene preview function, the transforms are copied to a **bundle** object in order to simplify the remaining code that must further process the transforms.

```
if(effectType == SEQUENCE && theModel->modelMotion > NULL)
  theModel->modelMotion->getNode(frameCounter, aMotion);
copyTransforms(effectType, theModel, aMotion, xfrm);
```

At this point we pass the input, output, and alpha image pointers along with the nine graphic transformations, the viewpoint transformation matrix, the warp and blend indicators, and the alpha scale factor to function **iRender**. Function **iRender** in turn calls the appropriate functions that warp and/or blend the model image, compositing it into the output image. We discuss function **iRender** in the next section of this chapter.

```
myStatus = iRender(outputImage, alphaImage, inputImage,
xfrm->rx,xfrm->ry,xfrm->rz, xfrm->sx,xfrm->sy,xfrm->sz,
xfrm->tx,xfrm->ty,xfrm->tz, viewMatrix,
theModel->warpIndicator, theModel->blendIndicator, xfrm->alpha);
```

The reason the nine model graphic transformations are passed separately into **iRender** instead of being passed as a **TMatrix** object is that the function **iRender** needs to process some of the graphic transformation factors individually, before they are combined with the view matrix.

After the processed model image has been composited into the output scene by function **iRender**, the client window device context is obtained and the output scene is transferred to the screen using the **memImage** display function **display2**. Note that this step is not actually necessary. All of the image compositing operations are occurring in memory image objects that are independent of display resources. We add this step because it provides great feedback on the progress of the scene generator as it builds the effect images one model at a time. After the output image is displayed, the device context is released and the input image object is destroyed. If this model utilized an alpha image, the alpha image is also destroyed at this point.

```
HDC theDC = GetDC(displayWindow);
outputImage->display2(theDC, outputColumns, outputRows);
ReleaseDC(displayWindow, theDC);
delete inputImage;
if(alphaImage != NULL) delete alphaImage;
```

13.9 *Creating True Color Images*

Now we move forward in the process to the point where all of the models have been processed for one of the color images produced in a color visual effect. The filename of the output image file for the current color is determined by function **getFileName**. The output image filename returned by this function consists of the first four characters of the scene name followed by three zero-filled digits indicating the frame number in the sequence. Thus the maximum number of frames that can be produced in a sequence is 1,000. If the visual effect is a still image, the three digits are "000." The eighth character of the filename is either the letter *g* for monochrome effects (the letter *g* indicates the green color channel was used to produce the output) or the letter *c* for true color effects. Finally, the output image is saved as a windows bitmap image file using the function **writeBMP**.

```
getFileName(outputFileName, theScene->sceneName, frameCounter, theColor);
if (theColor == RED) strcpy (redFileName, outputFileName);
if (theColor == GREEN) strcpy (greenFileName, outputFileName);
if (theColor == BLUE) strcpy (blueFileName, outputFileName);
outputImage->writeBMP(outputFileName);
```

Finally, if the effect is being rendered in color, after each of the red, green, and blue color images have been produced, the function **makeRGBimage** is called, which combines the red, green, and blue .bmp formatted image files together into a single true color .bmp image file. The final true color output image is stored in the directory specified by the ICT preference object. The default location for this directory is x:\ict\output. After the component color image files have been combined, they are deleted from the file system in order to conserve storage resources.

```
makeRGBimage(redFileName, greenFileName, blueFileName, RGBPath);
```

A listing of the function **makeRGBimage** is provided in section 13.11, later in this chapter.

Here is a listing of function of the **sceneList** member function **render**:

```
int sceneList::render(HWND displayWindow,tMatrix *viewMatrix,
  short depthSortingEnabled){

char msgText[MAXPATH],outputFileName[MAXPATH],
sceneName[MAXPATH];
char redFileName[MAXPATH], greenFileName[MAXPATH],
blueFileName[MAXPATH],
```

```
      RGBFileName[MAXPATH],currentColor[32];
      short effectType, colorMode;
      int outputRows, outputColumns;
      int firstFrame, lastFrame, frameCounter;
      motionNode *aMotion = new motionNode;
      bundle *xfrm = new bundle();
      getSceneInfo(sceneName, &effectType, &colorMode,
        &outputRows, &outputColumns);
      scene *theScene = sceneListHead;
      theScene = theScene->nextEntry;
      if theScene == 0{
      StatusPrint("render: the scene list is empty");
      delete aMotion;
      delete xfrm;
      return NULL;
}

      sceneElement *theModel = theScene->head;
      sceneElement *models[MAXMODELS];
      float distances[MAXMODELS];
      short numModels, myStatus;
      firstFrame = lastFrame = 0;

      if(effectType == SEQUENCE)
        theScene->sensorMotion->getFirstLastFrame(&firstFrame, &lastFrame);

      for(frameCounter = firstFrame; frameCounter <= lastFrame;
      frameCounter++){
        depthSort(models, distances, &numModels, depthSortingEnabled);
        if(effectType == SEQUENCE)
          getViewMatrix(viewMatrix, frameCounter, theScene);
        //
        //  Setup the Color Mode
        short firstColor = GREEN;
        short lastColor = GREEN;
        if (colorMode == COLOR) {
          firstColor = RED;
          lastColor = BLUE;
        }

        for (short theColor = firstColor; theColor <= lastColor; theColor++){
        memImage *outputImage = new memImage(outputRows, outputColumns);
        if (outputImage == 0) {
          sprintf(msgText, "Not enough memory to open output image");
          StatusPrint(msgText);
          delete aMotion;
          delete xfrm;
          return -1;
        }

       for(short currentModel = 0; currentModel <= numModels-1; currentModel++){
        theModel = models[currentModel];
```

```
        // Only render objects of type IMAGE
        if (theModel->modelType == IMAGE && theModel->statusIndicator == 0){
  if(theModel->screenObject == NULL){
    sprintf(msgText, "RenderObject Not Defined. Skipping Image: %s",
    theModel->modelName);
    StatusPrint(msgText);
    break;
  }


  if(theColor == RED) strcpy(currentColor, "Red");
  if(theColor == GREEN) strcpy(currentColor, "Green");
  if(theColor == BLUE) strcpy(currentColor, "Blue");
  sprintf(msgText, "Color: %s Processing: %s",
  currentColor, theModel->modelName);
  StatusPrint(msgText);
  short RGorB = theColor;
  //
  // Open the images
  memImage *inputImage = new memImage(theModel->fileName, 0, 0, RANDOM, 'R',
    RGorB);
  if (inputImage->isValid() == 0){
    sprintf(msgText, "sceneList.Render: Can't open image: %s",
      theModel->fileName);
    StatusPrint(msgText);
    delete aMotion;
    delete xfrm;
    return -1;
  }


  memImage *alphaImage;
  if(theModel->blendIndicator){
    char alphaName[MAXPATH];
    if(strcmpi(theModel->alphaPath, "NONE") != 0)
      strcpy(alphaName, theModel->alphaPath);
    else
      getMaskName(theModel->fileName, alphaName);

    alphaImage = new memImage(alphaName, 0, 0, RANDOM, 'R',
      EIGHTBITMONOCHROME);
    if (alphaImage->isValid() == 0) {
      sprintf(msgText, "sceneList.Render: Can't open alpha image: %s",
        alphaName);
      StatusPrint(msgText);
      delete aMotion;
      delete xfrm;
      return -1;
    }
  }
  else
    alphaImage = NULL;
```

```
   //
   // Get the desired transforms from either the model or the motion file
      // copy them to the xfrm object
      //
      if(effectType == SEQUENCE && theModel->modelMotion > NULL)
        theModel->modelMotion->getNode(frameCounter, aMotion);
      copyTransforms(effectType, theModel, aMotion, xfrm);
      //
      //  Properly render the image, based on desired options
      myStatus = iRender(outputImage, alphaImage, inputImage,
        xfrm->rx,xfrm->ry,xfrm->rz, xfrm->sx,xfrm->sy,xfrm->sz,
        xfrm->tx,xfrm->ty,xfrm->tz, viewMatrix,
        theModel->warpIndicator, theModel->blendIndicator, xfrm->alpha);

    HDC theDC = GetDC(displayWindow);
    outputImage->display2(theDC, outputColumns, outputRows);
    ReleaseDC(displayWindow, theDC);
    delete inputImage;
    if(alphaImage != NULL) delete alphaImage;
    }
  }
  //
  // One color channel of the scene is complete! Save it
  getFileName(outputFileName, theScene->sceneName, frameCounter, theColor);
  if (theColor == RED) strcpy (redFileName, outputFileName);
  if (theColor == GREEN) strcpy (greenFileName, outputFileName);
  if (theColor == BLUE) strcpy (blueFileName, outputFileName);
  sprintf(msgText, "Writing image: %s",outputFileName);
  StatusPrint(msgText);
  outputImage->writeBMP(outputFileName);
  delete outputImage;
  }  //end of color loop

  //
  //  Combine the color channels together
  myStatus = 0;
  if(colorMode == COLOR){
    sprintf(msgText, "Render: Creating RGB image from R, G, and B images");
    StatusPrint(msgText);
    //  Prepare a pathname to the standard output image location
    getFileName(RGBFileName, theScene->sceneName, frameCounter, 0);
    char RGBPath[MAXPATH], *RGBDir;
    RGBDir = ictPreference->getPath(OutputImageDirectory);
    sprintf(RGBPath, "%s%s", RGBDir, RGBFileName);
    myStatus =
    makeRGBimage(redFileName, greenFileName, blueFileName, RGBPath);
    }
  }  // End of Sequence Loop
  delete xfrm;
  delete aMotion;
```

```
    sprintf(msgText, "Scene Generation has Completed");
    StatusPrint(msgText);
    return myStatus;
}
```

13.10   *Function iRender*

This section describes function **iRender**, which applies the inverse warping and blending functions described in Chapters 9 and 10 respectively to each model as an output scene is being generated. The first step is to initialize the **xOffset** and **yOffset** variables to zero if neither warp nor blend options have been selected for the current model.

```
if(!(warpIndicator || blendIndicator)){
    xOffset = 0;
    yOffset = 0;
}
```

If the model is to be warped, then the **warpIndicator** will be equal to TRUE. An intermediate image object is created and the model image is warped by function **iwarp**, which is described in detail in Chapter 9. Recall that function **iwarp** always centers the warped image in the supplied output image object. The reason for this should become clear in a moment. In addition, function **iwarp** passes back the offsets (**imXOffset**, **imYOffset**) that it used to center the warped image in the output image. The approach of centering the warped output image in the supplied output image accommodates the use of **iwarp** as an interactive warp tool used in the ICT **Tools** menu, and it also permits a convenient application of the blend tool to an already warped image. We will see more specifically how this works in a moment.

```
if(warpIndicator){
  midImage = new memImage(outputRows, outputCols);
  iwarp(inImage, midImage, rx, ry, rz, sx, sy, sz, tx, ty, tz,
    viewMatrix, &imXOffset, &imYOffset);
}
```

If both **warpIndicator** and **blendIndicator** are TRUE, then the alpha image also needs to be warped. An intermediate **memImage** object is created into which the warped alpha image is placed.

```
if(warpIndicator && blendIndicator){
  midMaskImage = new memImage(outputRows, outputCols);
  iwarp(maskImage, midMaskImage, rx, ry, rz, sx, sy, sz, tx, ty, tz,
    viewMatrix, &msXOffset, &msYOffset);
}
```

If only the blend indicator is TRUE, then the **blend** function is called using the *x* and *y* offsets derived from the *x* and *y* translations passed into function **iRender**. This action permits models that are only blended to be translated in the plane of the screen if desired. In the case where both **blendIndicator** and **warpIndicator** are TRUE, then the **blend** function is called using the warped model and alpha images and the negative *x* and *y* offsets returned by function **iWarp** during the previous image warping operation. Using the negative offsets will cause the warped image and alpha image to be composited into the correct location in the output image. After the blend operation is complete, one or both of the intermediate images are destroyed.

```
if(blendIndicator){
  if(!warpIndicator)
    myStatus =
      blend(inImage, maskImage, outImage, alphaScale, xOffset, yOffset);
  else {
    myStatus =
      blend(midImage, midMaskImage, outImage, alphaScale, -imXOffset,
        -imYOffset);
    delete midImage;
    delete midMaskImage;
  }
}
```

We have only two remaining cases. In the case where only **warpIndicator** is TRUE, the warped image is copied into the output image using the negative offsets returned by function **iWarp**. If neither **warpIndicator** nor **blendindicator** are TRUE, then the image is simply copied into the output image.

```
else
  if(warpIndicator){ // copy warped image to output
    midImage->copy(outImage, -imXOffset, -imYOffset);
    delete midImage;
  }
else                 // copy input image to output
  inImage->copy(outImage, xOffset, yOffset);
return myStatus;
```

Here is the listing of function **iRender**:

```
short iRender(memImage *outImage, memImage *maskImage,
memImage *inImage,
  float rx, float ry, float rz, float sx, float sy, float sz,
  float tx, float ty, float tz, tMatrix *viewMatrix,
  short warpIndicator, short blendIndicator, float alphaScale){
```

```
char msgText[MAXPATH];
int outputRows = outImage->getHeight();
int outputCols = outImage->getWidth();
memImage *midImage, *midMaskImage;
long xOffset = tx; // Set these for the blend nowarp case
long yOffset = ty;
long imXOffset, imYOffset, msXOffset, msYOffset;


if(!(warpIndicator || blendIndicator)){
  xOffset = 0;
  yOffset = 0;
}


if(warpIndicator){
  midImage = new memImage(outputRows, outputCols);
  if (!midImage->isValid()){
    sprintf(msgText,"Unable to open intermediate warp image");
    StatusPrint(msgText);
    return -1;
  }
  iwarp(inImage, midImage, rx, ry, rz, sx, sy, sz, tx, ty, tz,
    viewMatrix, &imXOffset, &imYOffset);
}
if(warpIndicator && blendIndicator){
  //
  // Open intermediate mask image
  midMaskImage = new memImage(outputRows, outputCols);
  if (!midMaskImage->isValid()){
    sprintf(msgText,"Unable to open intermediate warp mask image");
    StatusPrint(msgText);
    delete midImage;
    return -1;
  }
  iwarp(maskImage, midMaskImage, rx, ry, rz, sx, sy, sz, tx, ty, tz,
    viewMatrix, &msXOffset, &msYOffset);
}
//
// Composite the cutout image into the output scene
short myStatus;
if(blendIndicator){
  if(!warpIndicator)
    myStatus =
    blend(inImage, maskImage, outImage, alphaScale, xOffset, yOffset);
  else {
    myStatus =
    blend(midImage, midMaskImage, outImage, alphaScale, -imXOffset,
      -imYOffset);
    delete midImage;
    delete midMaskImage;
```

```
    }
  }
  else
    if(warpIndicator){ // copy warped image to output
      midImage->copy(outImage, -imXOffset, -imYOffset);
    delete midImage;
    }
  else                    // copy input image to output
    inImage->copy(outImage, xOffset, yOffset);
  return myStatus;
}
```

13.11   Function makeRGBImage

As noted in section 13.8, a function is provided during the scene render process that creates a 24-bit (true color) image from three monochrome images, where each monochrome image contains the red, green, and blue color channels respectively of the true color image to be created. The function is called **makeRGBimage**. Function **makeRGBimage** is not a member function of any class because it can be applied generically to any set of three **memImage** image objects. The function **makeRGBimage** is largely an application of **memImage** class member functions, described in Chapter 5. Since no new concepts are introduced in this function, the listing is provided here without additional comment:

```
short makeRGBimage(char *redImage, char *greenImage, char *blueImage,
  char *outFileName){
  char msgBuffer[MAXPATH];
  //
  //  Combine separate color channels into one RGB BMP
  short rHeight, rWidth, gHeight, gWidth, bHeight, bWidth;

  memImage *theRed = new memImage(redImage, 0, 0,
    SEQUENTIAL, 'R', REDCOLOR);
  if (!theRed->isValid()) {
    sprintf(msgBuffer,"makeRGBImage: Unable to open Red image: %s",
      redImage);
    StatusPrint(msgBuffer);
    return 1;
  }
  memImage *theGreen = new memImage(greenImage, 0, 0, SEQUENTIAL,'R',
    GREENCOLOR);
  if (!theGreen->isValid()) {
    sprintf(msgBuffer,"makeRGBImage: Unable to open Green image: %s",
      greenImage);
    StatusPrint(msgBuffer);
```

```
      return 1;
    }
  memImage *theBlue = new memImage(blueImage, 0, 0, SEQUENTIAL,'R',
    BLUECOLOR);
  if (!theBlue->isValid()) {
    sprintf(msgBuffer,"makeRGBImage: Unable to open Blue image: %s",
  blueImage);
    StatusPrint(msgBuffer);
    return 1;
  }
  rHeight = theRed->getHeight();
  rWidth = theRed->getWidth();
  gHeight = theGreen->getHeight();
  gWidth = theGreen->getWidth();
  bHeight = theBlue->getHeight();
  bWidth = theBlue->getWidth();

  if (!(rWidth == gWidth && gWidth == bWidth && rWidth == bWidth)) {
    sprintf(msgBuffer,
      "makeRGBImage: R,G, and B image widths are not equal.");
    StatusPrint(msgBuffer);
    return 1;
  }
  if (!(rHeight == gHeight && gHeight == bHeight && rHeight == bHeight)) {
    sprintf(msgBuffer,
      "makeRGBImage: R,G, and B image heights are not equal.");
    StatusPrint(msgBuffer);
    return 1;
  }
  memImage *theRGB = new memImage (outFileName, gHeight, gWidth,
    SEQUENTIAL, 'W', RGBCOLOR);
  if (!theRGB->isValid()) {
    sprintf(msgBuffer,"makeRGBImage: Unable to open RGB image.");
    StatusPrint(msgBuffer);
    theRed->close();
    theGreen->close();
    theBlue->close();
    return 1;
  }

  BYTE HUGE *redPixel, HUGE *greenPixel, HUGE *bluePixel, HUGE *rgbPixel;
  short rStatus, gStatus, bStatus;

  for (int y = 1; y <= gHeight; y++){
    rStatus = theRed->readNextRow();
    if (rStatus != 0){
      sprintf(msgBuffer,"makeRGBImage: red readNextRow error.");
      StatusPrint(msgBuffer);
      theRed->close();
      theGreen->close();
```

```
        theBlue->close();
        return 1;
    }
    gStatus = theGreen->readNextRow();
    if (gStatus != 0){
      sprintf(msgBuffer,"makeRGBImage: green readNextRow error.");
      StatusPrint(msgBuffer);
      theRed->close();
      theGreen->close();
      theBlue->close();
      return 1;
    }
    bStatus = theBlue->readNextRow();
    if (bStatus != 0){
      sprintf(msgBuffer,"makeRGBImage: blue readNextRow error.");
      StatusPrint(msgBuffer);
      theRed->close();
      theGreen->close();
      theBlue->close();
      return 1;
    }

    redPixel = theRed->getBytes();
    greenPixel = theGreen->getBytes();
    bluePixel = theBlue->getBytes();
    rgbPixel = theRGB->getBytes();
    for (int x = 1; x <= gWidth; x++){
      *rgbPixel = *bluePixel;
      rgbPixel++;
      *rgbPixel =*greenPixel;
      rgbPixel++;
      *rgbPixel = *redPixel;
      rgbPixel++;
      redPixel++;
      greenPixel++;
      bluePixel++;
    }
    //
    // Write the output
    theRGB->writeNextRow();
  }
  //
  // Close the files and destroy the objects
  theRed->close();
  theGreen->close();
  theBlue->close();
  theRGB->close();
  delete theRed;
  delete theGreen;
  delete theBlue;
```

```
    delete theRGB;
    remove(redImage);     // To conserve disk space, remove the
    remove(greenImage);   // input files
    remove(blueImage);
    return 0;
}
```

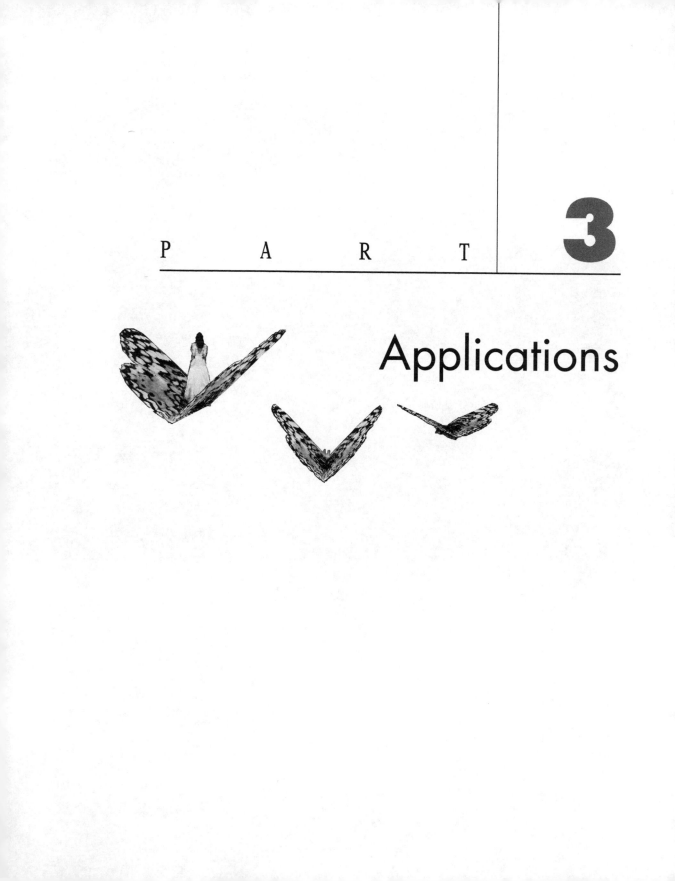

P A R T **3**

Applications

14

Morphing and Other Applications

In this chapter our perspective shifts to that of user/visual effect artist. Now that all of the technical aspects of ICT have been described, we explore a few examples of some of the types of effects that are possible by applying compositing techniques and a little creativity. All examples in this chapter were created on a 66 MHz 80486 DX2 PC with 20 megabytes of memory, and local bus video. The operating system was Windows 95 beta 3.

14.1 UFOs Spotted in the Evening Sky

Having been somewhat fascinated in the past by pictures of UFOs in the media; this seems like an appropriate time to try creating an effect like this of our own. This first example shows how a visual effect can be created from layers of composited images. In this example, we first create a spaceship from two cutouts and then composite the result several times into a final scene to create an effect of a small fleet of spacecraft hovering in an evening sky. Figure 14.1 shows a building from the grounds of a venerable university that just

Figure 14.1 A venerable institution with an attractive dome.

happens to have a rather attractive dome for our purposes. Figure 14.1 was purposefully cropped so that the university's identity is not immediately obvious. Figure 14.2 shows a stormy sky near sunset. Each of these images was scanned on a Hewlett-Packard Scanjet IIcx at a resolution of 150 dpi.

The first step is to make a cutout of the dome itself, which is shown in Figure 14.3*a*. Since the viewpoint of the final scene will be one of looking up into the sky, we would like to darken the bottom side of the dome cutout in order to simulate the effect of a shadow. A shadow is created by making another cutout of the part of the dome that will become the bottom side of the spacecraft, as shown in Figure 14.3*b*. The alpha image of this cutout is shown in Figure 14.3*c*. The shadow cutout is composited onto the dome

Figure 14.2 A sunset sky.

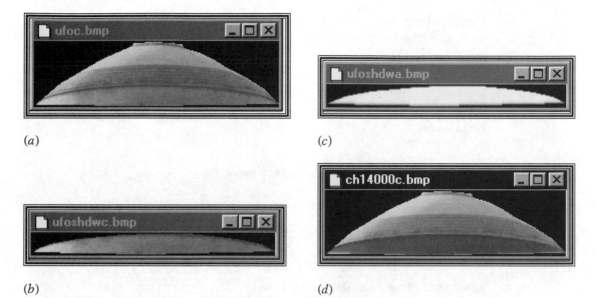

Figure 14.3 The UFO cutout image and its shadow.

cutout (Figure 14.3*a*) using a negative alpha scale factor to obtain the resulting spacecraft model shown in Figure 14.3*d*. The scene file for this step is:

```
scene ch14_1 Still 63,235 Color
Rotation 0,0,0
Translation 0,0,0
MotionPath None

Model ufo NoBlend NoWarp AlphaScale 1 Image
FileName D:\ICT\CUTOUT\UFOC.BMP
MotionPath None
AlphaImagePath Default
Rotation 0,0,0
Scale 1,1,1
Translation 0,0,0
Model shadow Blend Warp AlphaScale -0.4 Image
FileName D:\ICT\CUTOUT\UFOSHDWC.BMP
MotionPath None
AlphaImagePath Default
Rotation 0,0,0
Scale 1,1,1
Translation -3,0,0
```

The last step is to composite the spacecraft created in the previous step into the evening sky. The name of the spacecraft image produced in the previous step is used: CH14000C.BMP. A second scene file is created featuring the sky1.bmp image as a backdrop image and three copies of the spacecraft model. Scene preview is then used to position and orient the three spacecraft, as shown in Figure 14.4. The resulting scene file created during this step is:

```
scene c14b Still 320,295 Color
Rotation 0,0,0
Translation 0,0,0
MotionPath None

Model sky NoBlend NoWarp AlphaScale 1 Image
FileName D:\ICT\GALLERY\SKY1.BMP
MotionPath None
AlphaImagePath Default
Rotation 0,0,0
Scale 1,1,1
Translation 0,0,0

Model ufo1 Blend Warp AlphaScale 1 Image
FileName D:\ICT\OUTPUT\CH14000C.BMP
MotionPath None
AlphaImagePath D:\ICT\CUTOUT\UFOA.BMP
```

Figure 14.4 UFO preview.

```
Rotation 0,0,12
Scale 0.2,0.2,1
Translation -22,220,0
Model ufo2 Blend Warp AlphaScale 1 Image
FileName D:\ICT\OUTPUT\CH14000C.BMP
MotionPath None
AlphaImagePath D:\ICT\CUTOUT\UFOA.BMP
Rotation 0,0,6
Scale 0.3,0.3,1
Translation 110,110,0

Model ufo3 Blend Warp AlphaScale 1 Image
FileName D:\ICT\OUTPUT\CH14000C.BMP
MotionPath None
AlphaImagePath D:\ICT\CUTOUT\UFOA.BMP
Rotation 0,0,0
Scale 0.4,0.4,1
Translation -3,30,0
```

The effect is rendered in color and shown in Figure 14.5. The Win16 version of ICT created the effect in 22 seconds. The Win32 version of ICT created the effect in 10 seconds.

Figure 14.5 UFOs at sunset.

14.2 Morphing

A popular technique called morphing is explored in this section. The term *morphing* is short for morphological transformation. The morphing technique usually involves the creation of a visual effect sequence in which an image of some physical object is transformed into another object. This technique has many forms. There are two- and three-dimensional forms of morphing. The ICT is capable of creating two-dimensional morphing sequences, called *morphs,* which are consistent with the definition of morphing taken from [WOLB94], which defines a morph as a cross-dissolve between two image sequences. In this form of morphing, a sequence is created in which two photo-based models are superimposed. As the sequence progresses, the opaqueness of one model is varied from one to just greater than zero (recall that setting the alpha scale to exactly zero will erase the model). Simultaneously, the opaqueness of the other model is varied from just greater than zero to one. Using the ICT we can also simultaneously warp either of the models to vary their shape as the morph sequence proceeds. This type of morphing has been used in the movies for many years to create effects such as the transformation of ordinary humans into creatures and monsters of various kinds.

Another variation of morphing is to use what is called a mesh warp in conjunction with the cross-dissolve. The mesh warp begins by labeling a set of vertices in the first image. An equal number of vertices is defined for the second image such that the ith point in the vertex list of the first image corresponds to the ith point of the vertex list of the second image. A mesh of splines is then formed from the two lists of vertices. The splines are used to vary the contents of each image over a series of frames. As the cross-dissolve proceeds, the first image is gradually transformed into the second image.

A Simple Morphing Example

Figure 14.6 shows two images from which a morph sequence will be created. The morph sequence will create the effect of changing the face carved in stone, whom we affectionately refer to as Rocky, shown on the right side of Figure 14.6, into the face of the baby, whom we call John, shown on the left side of Figure 14.6. Each of these images were scanned on a Hewlett-Packard Scanjet IIcx at a resolution of 200 dpi.

We first observe that the image of John is rotated with respect to, and is slightly larger than, the image of Rocky. We need to adjust John's face so that its orientation and size matches as closely as possible the orientation of Rocky's face. The first step is to create a cutout each of John's and Rocky's face. Next, a scene file is created for a single-image effect that contains the original Rocky image (which serves as a backdrop) and the two cutouts created in the previous step. Now a scene list is created from the new scene file

Figure 14.6 Candidates for a morph sequence.

by using the `Tools|Create Scene List...` menu item. The scene preview tool is used to adjust the location, orientation, and size of the John and Rocky cutouts so that they are oriented as closely as possible over the original rock face. When the cutouts are positioned as desired, the changes are saved in the scene file. The resulting scene file is shown here:

```
scene morph1 Still 518,361 Monochrome
Rotation 0,0,0
Translation 0,0,0
MotionPath None

Model backdrop NoBlend NoWarp AlphaScale 1 Image
FileName c:\deskscan\rockface.BMP
MotionPath None
AlphaImagePath Default
Rotation 0,0,0
Scale 1,1,1
Translation 0,0,0

Model rocky Blend Warp AlphaScale 1 Image
FileName D:\ict\CUTOUT\rockC.BMP
MotionPath None
AlphaImagePath Default
Rotation 0,0,0
```

```
Scale 1,1,1
Translation 65,98,0


Model john Blend Warp AlphaScale 1 Image
FileName D:\ict\cutout\johnc.BMP
MotionPath None
AlphaImagePath Default
Rotation 0,0,14
Scale 1.03,1.02,1
Translation 57,93,0
```

Having positioned each of the cutouts as desired, we now create a second scene file for the morph sequence itself. Since we are creating a sequence, we need three motion path files. The first motion path file is associated with the scene node in the scene list object and it indicates to ICT the length of the sequence in terms of the number of frames. The second and third motion path files describe the change in opaqueness of each of the cutouts as the sequence proceeds. Since location, orientation, and size information are taken from motion path files when a model is changing in a sequence, we need to transfer the location and orientation information for the John and Rocky cutouts collected from the scene preview step into the appropriate motion path files. The resulting scene file and motion path files are listed here:

```
// Morph1.scn
scene morph1 Sequence 518,361 Monochrome
Rotation 0,0,0
Translation 0,0,0
MotionPath d:\ict\scene\seq7.pth


Model backdrop NoBlend NoWarp AlphaScale 1 Image
FileName c:\deskscan\rockface.BMP
MotionPath NONE
AlphaImagePath NONE
Rotation 0,0,0
Scale 1,1,1
Translation 0,0,0
Model matt Blend Warp AlphaScale 0 Image
FileName D:\ict\CUTOUT\rocka.BMP
MotionPath None
AlphaImagePath Default
Rotation 0,0,0
Scale 1,1,1
Translation 65,98,0


Model rocky Blend Warp AlphaScale 1 Image
FileName D:\ict\CUTOUT\rockC.BMP
MotionPath d:\ict\scene\rocky.pth
```

```
AlphaImagePath Default
Rotation 0,0,0
Scale 1,1,1
Translation 65,98,0

Model john Blend Warp AlphaScale 1 Image
FileName D:\ict\cutout\johnc.BMP
MotionPath d:\ict\scene\john.pth
AlphaImagePath Default
Rotation 0,0,14
Scale 1.03,1.02,1
Translation 57,93,0

// seq7.pth
// frame rx ry rz sx sy sz tx ty tz alpha
1 0 0 0 1 1 1 0 0 0 1
7 0 0 0 1 1 1 0 0 0 1

// John.pth
// frame rx ry rz sx sy sz tx ty tz alpha
1 0 0 14 1.03 1.02 1 57 93 0 .1
7 0 0 14 1.03 1.02 1 57 93 0 1

// Rocky.pth
// frame rx ry rz sx sy sz tx ty tz alpha
1 0 0 0 1 1 1 65 98 0 1
7 0 0 0 1 1 1 65 98 0 .1
```

You will notice an extra model in this scene file that has the name of "matt" and an alpha scale factor of zero. The purpose of the matt model is to first erase the area of the backdrop image in which the morphing will occur. With each successive frame in the morph sequence, we want to gradually reduce the contribution made by the backdrop image in the morphing area. If the matt model is not used, then the backdrop image will contribute fully in all frames of the sequence since the alpha-blending tool always includes the contribution of the output image as part of its result at each pixel. By using the matt to erase the backdrop image area first, we can now use the models labeled Rocky and John to create a morph effect that is purely a weighted sum of these two models. Now we are ready: First, the depth-sorting option is turned off by unchecking the **Render|Depth Sorting** option. The models will now be rendered in the order in which they appear in the scene file. The sequence is now rendered in monochrome and seven images are produced in the x:\ict\output\directory. The image names are morp00xg.bmp, where *x* ranges between one and seven. Figures 14.7 through 14.10 are samples taken from the morph sequence. The Win16 version of ICT generated a single color frame in the sequence in 150 seconds. The Win32 version of ICT generated the same frame in 58 seconds.

Figure 14.7 A cross-dissolve morph sequence.

Figure 14.8 A cross-dissolve morph sequence.

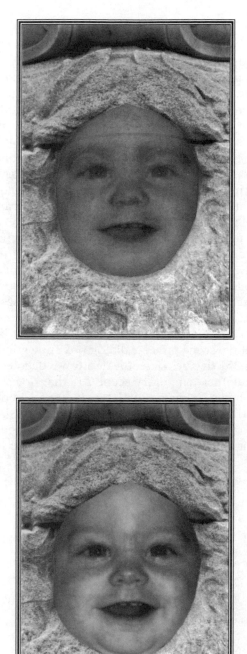

Figure 14.9 A cross-dissolve morph sequence.

Figure 14.10 A cross-dissolve morph sequence.

14.3 *Take These Broken Wings and Learn to Fly . . .*

In this section we develop an example that emphasizes the three-dimensional nature of the ICT. The butterfly wing images shown (in Appendix B) are used to create a single-image effect that depicts a collection of butterflies flying together into a city. To create a Disneyesque atmosphere, we add the image of a princess who will ride one of the butterflies. A photograph of a European city was scanned at a resolution of 200 dpi and is shown in Figure 14.11. The butterfly image is taken from a royalty-free CD-ROM sampler and is shown in Figure 14.12. The princess image, shown in Figure 14.13, was also scanned from a photographic print. The first step is to create the left and right butterfly wings. We want to cut the wings out precisely so that they can later be juxtaposed against each other perfectly. From Figure 14.12 we observe that the butterfly is rotated about the Z axis. Removing this rotation first will make subsequent steps less complicated. To do this we need to first determine the angle of rotation. A convenient means of doing this is to first cut out the entire butterfly as a single model. The second step is to rotate the resulting butterfly model interactively in scene preview until the angle that causes the butterfly to be perfectly aligned is known. The result of this alignment process is shown in Figure 14.14. The final Z rotation angle appears in the text box located in the lower-left portion of the scene preview dialog box shown in Figure 14.14. The Z rotation angle is 351 degrees or, equivalently, −9 degrees. We use this information to create another temporary scene file that does nothing more than rotate the image shown in Figure 14.12 by −9 degrees about the Z axis. The left and right butterfly wings are then created as cutouts using the rotated image. Figure 14.15 shows the resulting left and right wing models (labeled *lf* and *rt*) as they appear juxtaposed relative to each other in the scene preview

Figure 14.11 Backdrop image.

Figure 14.12 Original butterfly image.

tool. Note that the common boundary between the left and right wing models is perfectly straight. This relatively high degree of precision will enhance the level of smoothness with which the warped butterfly wings are blended together in the output scene. Now that the butterfly wings have been prepared, we produce a three-dimensional butterfly by creating a scene file containing only the left and right wing models. We begin by rotating the left and

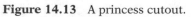

Figure 14.13 A princess cutout.

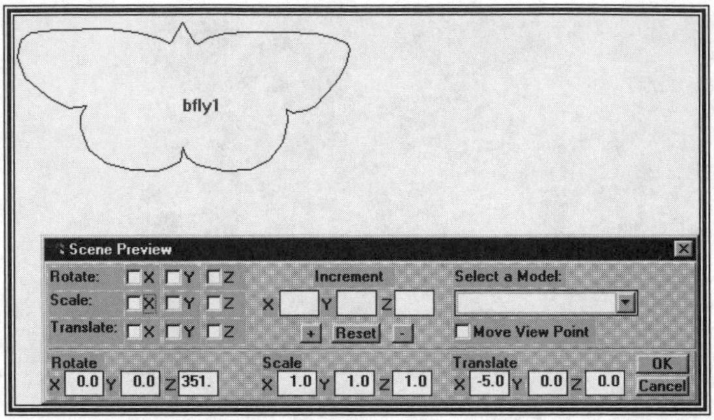

Figure 14.14 Butterfly with rotation removed.

right wings each –90 degrees about the *Y* axis. This transformation places both wings in the direction facing forward, into the city image. We now rotate the left wing –45 degrees about the *Z* axis and the right wing 45 degrees about the *Z* axis. This further transformation rotates the wings properly; however, a gap exists at the location where the two wing models should be joined together. This situation is caused by the nature of the rotation transformation itself: ICT always rotates a model about its centerpoint. The effect we wish to achieve requires that we rotate each model about the edge surface that is shared by the juxtaposed left and right wing models. To compensate, we

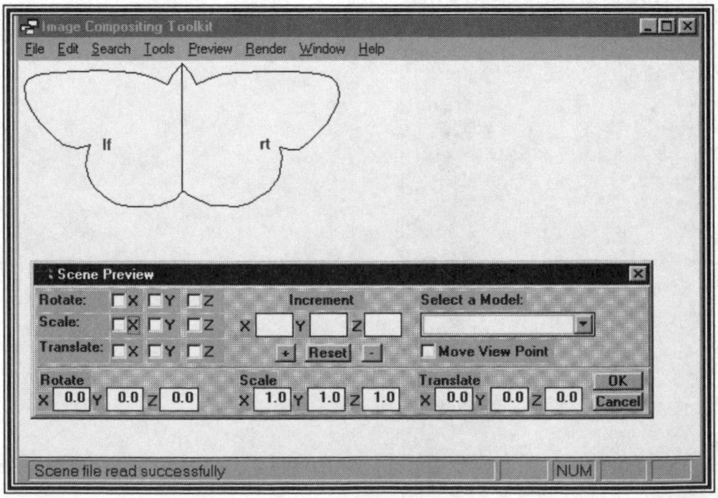

Figure 14.15 Two butterfly wings.

rotate each wing about its centerpoint then translate one or both wing models until the interior wing edges meet. After applying this approach to several instances of the left and wing models and varying the wing Z angles of each butterfly, the scene preview appears as shown in Figure 14.16. The princess model is added to one of the butterflies to give the appearance that she is riding into the city, accompanied by a band of loyal consorts. You will notice from the scale factors in the scene file that the princess was slimmed down slightly for her appearance in this effect. Now the backdrop image is added and the effect is rendered in color. The rendered scene appears in Figure 14.17. The Win16 version of ICT generated this color effect in 140 seconds. The Win32 version of ICT generated the same image in 55 seconds. The completed scene file for this effect is listed here:

```
scene prin Still 431,626 Color
Rotation 5,0,0
Translation 0,0,-130
MotionPath None


Model backdrop noBlend noWarp AlphaScale 1 Image
FileName c:\deskscan\heidl200.BMP
MotionPath None
AlphaImagePath DEFAULT
```

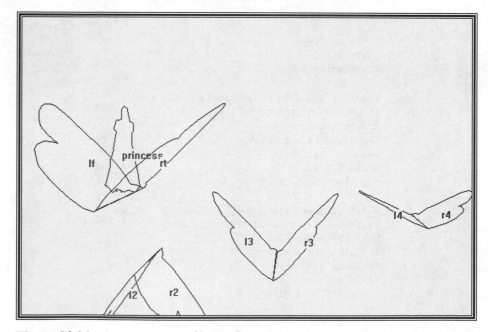

Figure 14.16 Scene preview of butterfly consort.

Figure 14.17 Butterfly consort in flight.

```
Rotation 0,0,0
Scale 1,1,1
Translation 0,0,0

Model lf Blend Warp AlphaScale 1 Image
FileName D:\ict\cutout\bfleftc.BMP
MotionPath None
AlphaImagePath DEFAULT
Rotation 270,0,315
Scale 1,1,1
Translation 68,180,0

Model princess Blend Warp AlphaScale 1 Image
FileName D:\ICT\CUTOUT\PRINCESC.BMP
MotionPath None
AlphaImagePath DEFAULT
Rotation 0,0,0
Scale 0.13,0.18,1
Translation 74,51,0

Model rt Blend Warp AlphaScale 1 Image
FileName D:\ict\cutout\bfrightc.BMP
```

```
MotionPath None
AlphaImagePath DEFAULT
Rotation 270,0,45
Scale 1,1,1
Translation 166,180,0


Model 12 Blend Warp AlphaScale 1 Image
FileName D:\ict\cutout\bfleftc.BMP
MotionPath None
AlphaImagePath DEFAULT
Rotation 270,0,45
Scale 1,1,1
Translation -63,-38,-200


Model r2 Blend Warp AlphaScale 1 Image
FileName D:\ict\cutout\bfrightc.BMP
MotionPath None
AlphaImagePath DEFAULT
Rotation 270,0,315
Scale 1,1,1
Translation 29,-38,-200


Model 13 Blend Warp AlphaScale 1 Image
FileName D:\ict\cutout\bfleftc.BMP
MotionPath None
AlphaImagePath DEFAULT
Rotation 270,0,315
Scale 0.6,0.6,1
Translation 268,100,0


Model r3 Blend Warp AlphaScale 1 Image
FileName D:\ict\cutout\bfrightc.BMP
MotionPath None
AlphaImagePath DEFAULT
Rotation 270,0,45
Scale 0.6,0.6,1
Translation 327,100,0


Model 14 Blend Warp AlphaScale 1 Image
FileName D:\ict\cutout\bfleftc.BMP
MotionPath None
AlphaImagePath DEFAULT
Rotation 270,0,335
Scale 0.6,0.6,1
Translation 454,100,-100


Model r4 Blend Warp AlphaScale 1 Image
FileName D:\ict\cutout\bfrightc.BMP
MotionPath None
```

```
AlphaImagePath DEFAULT
Rotation 270,0,25
Scale 0.6,0.6,1
Translation 527,100,-100
```

14.4 Heightening Realism: Paying Attention to Visual Cues

Thus far, we have covered many of the technical aspects of the digital image compositing techniques used to create visual effects. There are a number of additional generally nontechnical guidelines that, if followed, will result in more realistic and compelling visual effects. Here is a list of some of the most important considerations:

- The lighting conditions in composited cutouts should match as closely as possible the lighting conditions of the scene into which the cutout is being composited. As you will notice if you experiment with the ICT, the human eye is quite sensitive to lighting-related irregularities such as variations in the angles by which shadows are cast.

- The viewpoint from which the subject in a cutout image appears should match the viewpoint of the scene into which the cutout is being composited.

- The farther a model is located from the viewpoint, the more the color spectrum of the model shifts toward the blue frequencies. This phenomenon is caused in the real world by the color-absorptive properties of the atmosphere. Mountains, for example, when viewed from great distances tend to exhibit predominantly blue color tones.

- In order to appear anchored to the ground, a model composited into a background image generally needs to be accompanied by a shadow or other dark object. Without a shadow, the model will appear float in mid-air.

- The spatial resolution of the cutout image should match the spatial resolution of the area of the background image into which it is being composited. In other words, the composited model should appear in proper scale relative to the scene into which it is being composited. Also, the degree of sharpness of the cutout image should match the degree of sharpness of the image into which the cutout is being composited.

Appendices

ICT Setup

A.1 ICT Files and Directories

The Image Composition Toolkit (ICT) operates under the assumption that a certain directory structure is in place. Figure A.1 illustrates the subdirectories under the ICT directory. The ICT installation procedure sets up this directory structure automatically. All files needed to produce the executable ICT are stored in the ICT directory. Table A.1 describes the support data file types stored in each of the subdirectories as well as the suffixes used to denote each file type. All of the support data file types are ASCII text files and can be viewed and modified using the ICT menu selection **File | Open Scene File...** or any word processor.

A.2 Setup

The following is a list of Minimum Recommended Hardware:

> 486 DX 33 MHz computer
>
> 8 MB memory
>
> 15 MB Disk on hard drive C

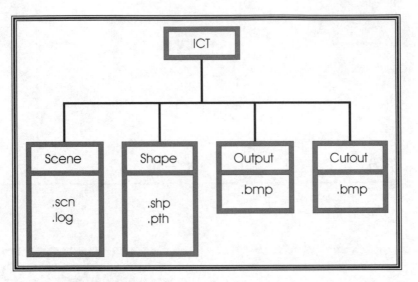

Figure A.1 ICT directory structure.

1. Turn on your computer and start Windows.

2. Select the Windows Setup icon from the Control Panel and set your video card to High Color Resolution (65,536 colors) by selecting or installing the proper video driver. A screen resolution of 800×600 pixels is recommended.

3. Place the ICT diskette into your floppy disk drive and select the File|Run menu item. Type x:\setup (where x is the drive letter of your floppy drive). The setup procedure creates the directory ICT on the root of volume of hard drive C:. Under this directory the following subdirectories are created: \cutout, \gallery, \output, \shape, \scene, \sfm, and \starter. The setup script then decompresses the ICT files and copies them into the appropriate subdirectory of directory c:\ICT.

4. If you install the software on a hard drive other than C:, the following steps are recommended:

   4.1. Make the following modification to one of the source files:

   4.1.1 Start a text editor and open the file childwn.cpp. This file is found in directory x:\ICT\ where x is the new hard drive letter. Locate the following lines in the file:

```
preference::preference(){
  strcpy(processLogPath, "c:\\ict\\process.log");
  strcpy(shapeFileDir, "c:\\ict\\shape\\");
```

Table A.1   ICT Directory Summary

Directory	*File Type(s)*	*Suffix*	*Description*
SFM	NA	NA	Scene File Maker. Contains the Visual basic files needed to create the scene file maker utility sfm.exe.
Shape	shape files	.shp	Each shape file describes a 3D *n*-sided polygon.
	path files	.pth	Each path file describes a 3D motion path.
Output	image files	.bmp	Contains the results of ICT processing. Both single-image effects and sequences are stored here.
Scene	scene file	.scn	Each scene file describes an individual visual effect to be created.
Gallery	image files	.bmp	Contains unprocessed images used in the visual effect examples.
Cutout	cutout images	.bmp	Filename convention: *c.bmp.
	alpha images	.bmp	Filename convention: *a.bmp.
Starter	NA	NA	Contains the ICT starter application.
ICT	ICT log file	.log	In addition to containing all files needed to support creation of ICT itself, the ICT directory contains the ICT process log file: ict.log.

```
    strcpy(sequenceFileDir, "c:\\ict\\shape\\");
    strcpy(outputImageDir, "c:\\ict\\output\\");
    strcpy(inputImageDir, "c:\\ict\\cutout\\");
    strcpy(maskDir, "c:\\ict\\cutout\\");
    strcpy(warpTestPath, "c:\\ict\\gallery\\ericGlas.bmp");
}
```

4.1.2 Change all of the drive letters in these pathnames to the desired drive letter. For example, if your desired drive letter is d: The edited source code would look like this:

```
preference::preference(){
    strcpy(processLogPath, "d:\\ict\\process.log");
    strcpy(shapeFileDir, "d:\\ict\\shape\\");
    strcpy(sequenceFileDir, "d:\\ict\\shape\\");
    strcpy(outputImageDir, "d:\\ict\\output\\");
    strcpy(inputImageDir, "d:\\ict\\cutout\\");
    strcpy(maskDir, "d:\\ict\\cutout\\");
    strcpy(warpTestPath, "d:\\ict\\gallery\\ericGlas.bmp");
}
```

4.1.3 Close the text editor and proceed with the software installation.

5. Start the Borland C++ compiler and select Project|Open Project menu item and select the ict.ide project file located in the X:\ICT directory that was created by the install program.

6. Change the directories section under Project|Options to point to the location of your Borland libraries and include files.

7. Build the ICT project. This project has been compiled successfully using the Borland C++ version 4.5 16- and 32-bit compilers running on a 486 DX2 with 8MB of memory. The code has been tested in Windows 3.1, Win32s, and Windows 95 environments.

8. If the project compiles and links successfully you are ready to try the example files described in Appendix B.

9. You may wish to use the program manager to create a program group labeled ICT and create an icon for the ICT application and Scene File Maker (SFM) utility. You will need bwcc.dll and bc402rtl.dll (which are supplied with the Borland compiler) to operate ICT. You will also need to copy vbrun300.dll from the diskette to c:\Windows\system in order to operate the scene file maker utility.

Windows 3.1 vs Windows 95

ICT operates in both Windows 3.1 and Win32 target environments. If you are going to build versions of ICT for both target environments it is recommended that separate directories be used for each version. If you do decide to use the same project directory when rebuilding ICT in a new target environment, here is a point to remember: All object files (*.obj) and the ictapp.res file need to be deleted before rebuilding. If this step is not taken the linker will try to incorporate both 16- and 32-bit components into the new application, which will result in errors.

B

ICT User Guide

The Image Composition Toolkit (ICT) contains a variety of tools for experimenting and learning about the fascinating topic of digital image compositing technology. This technology is a combination of image processing, three-dimensional graphics and, of course, a bit of creative handiwork on the part of the investigator. This guide uses a series of examples that take you on a quick tour of the topics covered in more detail in the accompanying text.

B.1 Warping the ICT Test Image

Let's begin our tour by looking at one of the major tools in the ICT. The warp tool is interesting because it can perform graphic operations on an image instead of a polygon. For example, the warp tool can rotate an image a certain number of degrees or it can shrink or expand an image using a scale factor.

Let's try using the warp tool now. Start ICT and select the `Warp Image . . .` option from the ICT tools menu. The warp tool dialog box shown in Figure B.1 appears. From this dialog box we may enter any combination of angles and scale factors and the warp tool will create a test

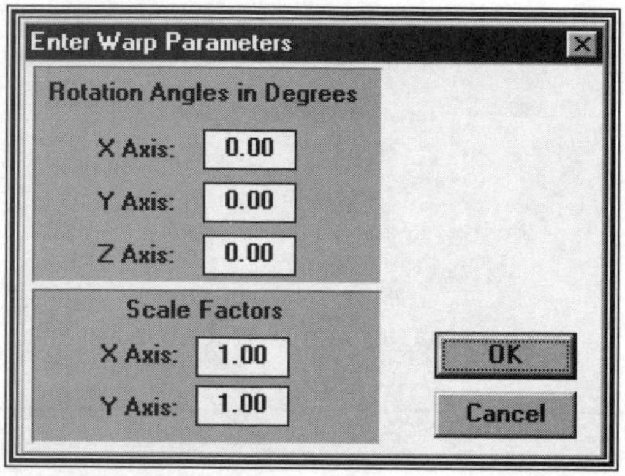

Figure B.1 The warp parameter dialog box.

image that appears as though it has been rotated and or scaled in the way we have specified. Let's try rotating the test image 45 degrees about the Y axis. Type "45" into the text box labeled **Y Axis** as shown in Figure B.2. Click the **OK** button. After a few seconds you should see two images: the original test image and the same image rotated 45 degrees in the counterclockwise direction, as shown in Figure B.3.

B.2 Three-Dimensional Coordinate System

In order to become more familiar with the three-dimensional world in which the warp tool operates, the left panel of Figure B.4 shows the right-handed coordinate system that is used to specify angles and directions. As you may observe from the right panel of Figure B.4, your right hand is a

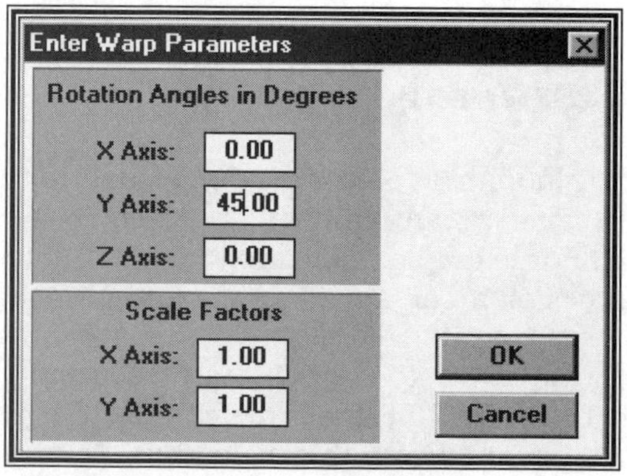

Figure B.2 Warp parameter dialog box.

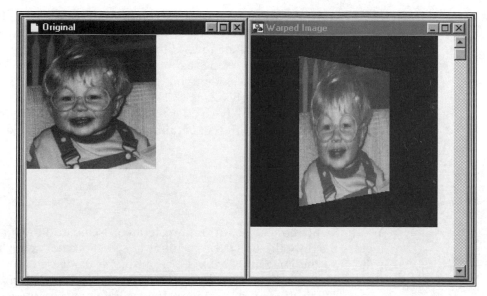

Figure B.3 A rotated image.

handy visual aid that can be used to remember how the X, Y, and Z axes are oriented relative to each other. Let's take another look at the situation. Imagine you are sitting in front of your computer screen. The origin of the right-handed coordinate system shown in Figure B.4 is located on the lower-left corner of your computer screen. The positive Y axis starts at the origin and is aligned with the left vertical side of your screen, the positive X axis starts at the origin and is aligned with the bottom horizontal side of your screen. The positive Z axis can be visualized by imagining a line that

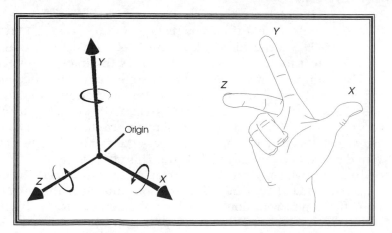

Figure B.4 The right-handed cartesian coordinate system.

begins at the origin and points back toward you. Positive angles will cause a rotation in the counterclockwise direction when viewed from a location on any positive axis looking toward the origin. In this sense, negative angles rotate an image in the clockwise direction. It is important to know that the warp tool always assumes that you, the viewer, are located 512 units from the origin on the positive Z axis. The right-handed coordinate system is described in more detail in Chapter 6. You may wish to experiment with the warp tool by entering different combinations of angles to get a sense of how the tool behaves.

B.3 Scaling

You probably noticed that the warp tool can scale an image as well. Scale factors magnify the image or shrink it in size. A scale factor less than one will cause the image to shrink. For example, if 0.5 were entered in each of the *x* and *y* scale factor text boxes, the sides of the warped image would be one-half their original dimensions. If a scale factor is greater than one, the image will be magnified. For example, a scale factor of 1.5 will cause the sides of the warped model to be one and a half times larger than the original image. You will notice that larger scale factors, for example, three or four, will cause the image to become blocky looking. This is a normal artifact of processing, called *aliasing*. This topic is discussed further in Chapter 10. You may wish to experiment further with the warp tool by entering combinations of rotation angles and scale factors.

B.4 Image Display

The ICT creates visual effects by reading and processing a text file, called a *scene file*. The scene file contains a set of instructions that describe the desired effect to be produced. ICT creates the intended effect by warping and blending a set of *models* that are visible from a specified viewpoint. The viewpoint as well as each model's location and orientation are described in the scene file using the coordinate system shown in Figure B.4. For now, let's think of each model as a digital photograph. We will now create a simple visual effect by having ICT process the scene file bfly3D.scn, which is found on the accompanying diskette. This effect is created from two images of butterfly wings. First, let's look at these two images from within ICT. Select the **File|OpenImage...** option and open the images bflylc.bmp and bflyrc.bmp. You should now have a screen that looks like the one shown in Figure B.5. We are going to warp these images so they look like a three-dimensional butterfly.

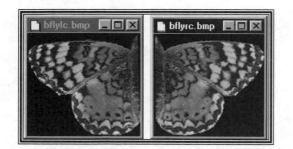

Figure B.5   Butterfly wings.

Example 1: A True Color Butterfly

Close the images bflylc.bmp and bflyrc.bmp by clicking the small close box located in the upper-left corner of each of the image windows. Now select the **Tools|Read Scene File....** menu item. Use the file browser to select the file x:\ict\scene\bfly3D.scn where x is the drive letter of your hard drive. Click the **OK** button. The status bar should display the message Scene File Read Successfully.

B.5   Using Scene Preview

Now select the **Preview | Scene** menu item. You should see the outline of a three-dimensional butterfly on the screen as shown in Figure B.6. Let's try moving around the butterfly by changing our viewpoint. Check the checkbox labeled **Move View Point.** Check the **Rotate Y** checkbox on the left side of the dialog box, enter the number 5 in to the text box marked **Y** as shown in Figure B.7, and then click the small button labeled with the plus sign (+) located in the center of the dialog box. The butterfly outline rotates five degrees in the counterclockwise direction about the *Y* axis. If you click the minus button, the butterfly rotates five degrees in the opposite direction. If you enter larger or smaller numbers in the increment text boxes, larger or smaller rotations will be made each time the plus or minus button is pressed. There is a lot more to investigate on this dialog box, but for now let's continue with the example. We will return to this dialog box in the next example to use more of its capabilities.

This visual effect contains two models: one model for each butterfly wing. The name of each model is displayed in the center of the model boundary. Now let's render the butterfly. Click the **OK** button. A dialog box appears asking if you wish to save the changes you have made. If you click the **NO** button, the changes will not be saved; however, the settings you have made are still active in memory and will be used if you now subsequently

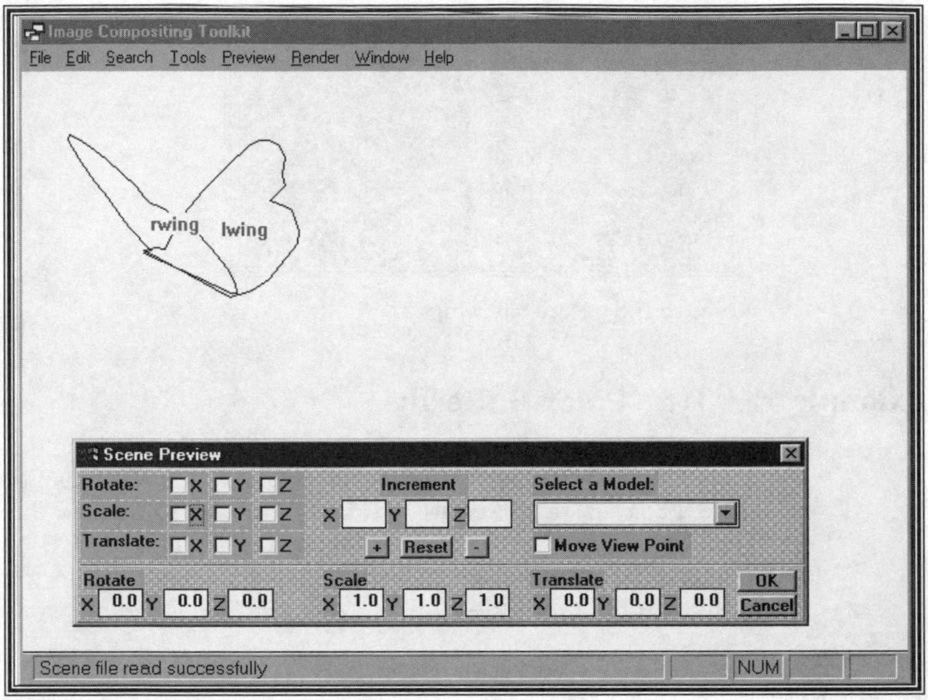

Figure B.6 Previewing a three-dimensional butterfly.

choose to render the effect scene. Let's not save the changes. Click the **NO** button to return to the main menu.

B.6 *Rendering the Scene*

Now select the Render menu and make certain that the **Depth Sorting** menu item is not checked. Select the **Render | Scene** option. ICT now creates the scene by warping each of the butterfly wing images as we specified in the scene file. Since this effect is rendered in color, three different versions of the scene are actually created: one version for each of the red, green, and blue colors. The three resulting finished versions of the scene are then combined to produce the final true color result. As the scene is being rendered the status bar indicates which color and model are currently being processed. When ICT has finished rendering the scene the status bar contains the message Scene Generation is Complete. At this point the result image has been saved in a .bmp file in the directory x:\ict\output. The name of the output file was determined from the first four letters of the name of the scene specified in the scene file. For details see Chapter 13. Select the

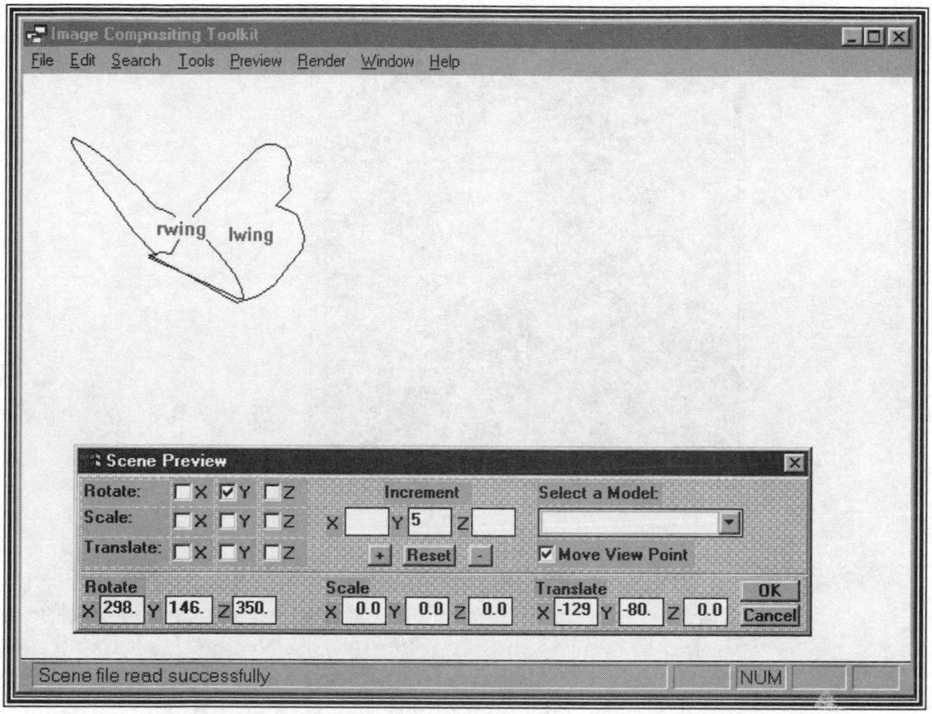

Figure B.7 Changing the observer viewpoint.

File|Open Image.. menu item and use the file browser to open the file bfly000c.bmp. A true color butterfly similar to that shown in Figure B.8 should appear on the screen.

Example 2: Blending

The ICT blending tool implements an image compositing technique discussed in Chapter 10. The blending tool combines the pixels in a model image with corresponding pixels in the output effect image. A third image, called an *alpha image,* is actually used to determine the percentages of pixels from each image to mix together. The blending tool has many applications. It is used here to smooth the edges of models as they are composited into the output scene. Blending is also used to vary the opaqueness of a model. In the following example, we will create an effect using several models based on the same image. By varying the blending technique used with each model you will get a glimpse of the versatility of this tool. We also introduce a *backdrop image* to more fully show the blending tool in action. The models in this example are purposefully magnified to show the blending effects more clearly.

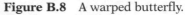

Figure B.8 A warped butterfly.

Open the scene file: x:\ict\scene\jenna3.scn using the **Tools|Read Scene File** menu item. Select the menu item **Preview|Scene.** Your screen should appear as shown in Figure B.9. Notice the four models and their similar names. The backdrop image appears in monochrome. Now let's explore some additional capabilities of the scene preview dialog box. Using the combo box on the right side of the dialog box, select the model labeled jenna1. Let's move the model jenna1 to the right several screen units. Type a "5" in the Increment text box labeled **x**. Check the **Translate X** check box. Click the **+** button. The jenna1 shape now moves five screen units to the right. We have already set the dialog box for a five-unit translation along the *X* axis. We will now select another model and apply the transformation in the opposite direction. Select the model jenna3 from the model combo box. Click the – button. The model jenna3 now moves five screen units to the left. Click the **OK** button and elect not to save the changes to the scene file. Having returned to the main menu, now select the **Render|Scene** menu item. ICT renders the image using the instructions we have just created. This example scene file creates a black-and-white output image that can now be displayed by opening the file x:\ict\output\jenn000g.bmp. The image should appear similar to that shown in Figure B.10.

B.7 What Is a Backdrop Image?

In this visual effect, we wanted to blend our models onto an existing image that is copied into the output image as the first step in the creation of the

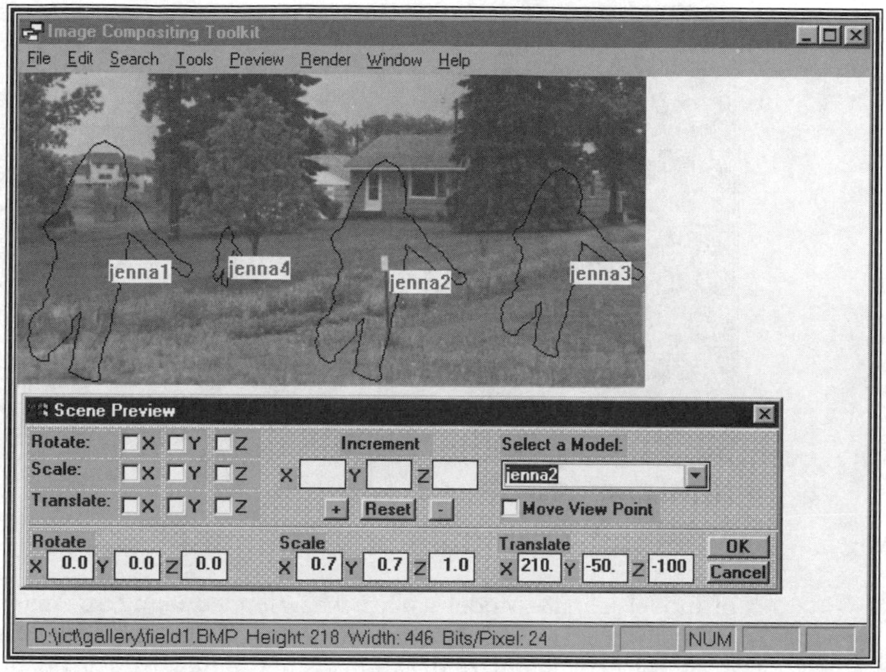

Figure B.9 Preview of a blending example.

effect. To do this, a backdrop image is defined in the scene file. A backdrop image is defined if the first model in the scene file is not blended or warped. If such a model exists in the scene file ICT copies the backdrop image into the output image before processing any other models. A backdrop image is displayed in monochrome during the scene preview step so that the other models in the scene can be positioned with reference to it. Now let's examine the effects produced by the remaining models.

All of the models in this example are actually based on the same image. The image used here is an example of a cutout image that can be created with ICT using the cutout tool described in Chapter 8. When the cutout is created, an additional image, called an *alpha image,* is also created that smooths the edges of the cutout image when it is blended with the output image. Models jenna2 and jenna4 were blended using the alpha image automatically created when the cutout image was made. In the case of models jenna1 and jenna3, the automatically produced alpha images were substituted with different alpha images to produce the effects you see in Figure B.10. Model jenna1 was blended using an image of a checkerboard. You may wish to display the image x:\ict\gallery\check8.bmp. A different effect was produced in the case

Figure B.10   Examples of alpha-blending.

of model jenna3. Model jenna3 was blended using an image containing an intensity wedge. The image can be found in x:\ict\gallery\wedge.bmp. We cover the explanation of these effects in Chapter 10. The opaqueness of model jenna3 was adjusted further using the alphaScale factor of 0.7. More uses of this powerful tool are discussed in Chapter 10.

Example 3: Creating a Sequence

The ICT can create another class of visual effect called a *sequence*. As the name implies, a sequence is a series of images in which the viewpoint and/or one or more models in the scene move. We will again explore this capability by look-ing at an example. Open the scene file x:\ict\scene\motion1.scn using the **Tools|Read Scene File** menu item. Now select the **Preview|Sequence** menu item. Each of the models in the scene moves along a predetermined path. You can play the animation again by pressing the plus button. If you now select the **Render|Sequence** menu item, ICT will produce one image for each frame in the sequence. Don't select this option unless you are certain you wish to proceed. As with still-image effects, sequences can be generated either in black-and-white or true color. So far we have seen that a sequence of images can be previewed and the corresponding frames of imagery generated. Now for some sobering news: A means is not available in this book to play back the image sequences produced by ICT in the form of a movie. This is because the most convenient way to do this is to obtain a product such as Microsoft Video for Windows and use the video editor to create an .avi file from the sequence of .bmp images produced by ICT. This process is considered outside the scope of this book.

B.8 What Is a Scene File?

We have now looked at many of the capabilities of the ICT. In each example above, the scene file contained the instructions to produce each of the effects. Let's look at the format of the file itself.

The generic scene file format is:

```
scene sceneName [Sequence|Still] outHeight,outWidth [Color|Monochrome]
Rotation Rx,Ry,Rz
Translation Tx,Ty,Tz
MotionPath [None|PathName]


Model modelName [Blend|NoBlend] [Warp|NoWarp] AlphaScale a [Image|Shape]
FileName pathName
MotionPath [None|pathName]
AlphaImagePath [Default|pathName] (optional)
Rotation rx,ry,rz
Scale sx,sy,sz
Translation tx,ty,tz
```

where **[x|y]** indicates that either **x** or **y** must be specified and the **a** in **AlphaScale a** is a floating point opaqueness value with 0.01 indicating transparency and one indicating complete opaqueness. The scene file format is discussed in detail in Chapter 3.

Listed below are the scene files used in each of the three examples mentioned in this user guide.

Example 1 Scene File

```
//
// A warping Example. True Color Butterfly
scene bfly3d Still 256,256 Color
Rotation 310,60,0
Translation -30,0,0
MotionPath None


Model lwing NoBlend Warp AlphaScale 1 Image
FileName D:\ict\cutout\bflylc.BMP
MotionPath None
Rotation 0,315,0
Scale 1,1,1
Translation 0,50,0


Model rwing NoBlend Warp AlphaScale 1 Image
FileName D:\ict\cutout\bflyrc.BMP
MotionPath None
Rotation 0,45,0
```

```
Scale 1,1,1
Translation 95,50,0
```

Example 2 Scene File

```
//
// A blending Example
scene jenna3 Still 218,446 monochrome
Rotation 0,0,0
Translation 0,0,0
MotionPath none

Model field NoBlend NoWarp AlphaScale 1 Image
FileName D:\book\gallery\field1.bmp
MotionPath none
AlphaImagePath Default
Rotation 0,0,0
Scale 1,1,1
Translation 0,0,0

Model jenna1 Blend Warp AlphaScale 1 Image
FileName D:\ict\cutout\jenna4c.bmp
MotionPath none
AlphaImagePath D:\ict\gallery\check8.bmp
Rotation 0,0,0
Scale 0.75,0.75,1
Translation -25,-40,-50

Model jenna2 Blend Warp AlphaScale 1 Image
FileName D:\ict\cutout\jenna4c.bmp
MotionPath none
AlphaImagePath Default
Rotation 0,0,0
Scale 0.75,0.75,1
Translation 210,-50,-100

Model jenna3 Blend Warp AlphaScale 0.7 Image
FileName D:\ict\cutout\jenna4c.bmp
MotionPath none
AlphaImagePath D:\ict\gallery\wedge.bmp
Rotation 0,315,0
Scale 0.75,0.75,1
Translation 420,-50,-200

Model jenna4 Blend Warp AlphaScale 1 Image
FileName D:\ict\cutout\jenna4c.bmp
MotionPath none
Rotation 0,315,0
Scale 0.3,0.3,1
Translation 110,-60,-400
```

Example 3 Scene File

```
//
// An Example Sequence
scene seq1 Sequence 400,400 Color
Rotation 0,0,0
Translation 0,0,0
MotionPath d:\ict\scene\seq60.pth

Model leaf NoBlend Warp AlphaScale 1 Image
FileName D:\ict\cutout\mpleafc.bmp
MotionPath d:\ict\scene\leaf.pth
Rotation 0,0,0
Scale 0.5,0.5,1
Translation 0,0,-500

Model jenna Blend Warp AlphaScale 1 Image
FileName D:\ict\cutout\jenna3c.bmp
MotionPath d:\ict\scene\jenna.pth
Rotation 0,0,0
Scale 0.5,0.5,1
Translation 220,0,-500

Model berry Blend Warp AlphaScale 1 Image
FileName D:\ict\cutout\strbrryc.bmp
MotionPath d:\ict\scene\berry.pth
Rotation 0,0,0
Scale 1,1,1
Translation 150,250,-500
```

B.9   What Is a Motion File?

A motion file is a shorthand method for specifying how a model or the scene viewpoint is to move through the frames in a sequence. An example motion file is shown below. The motion file format is described in detail in Chapter 12.

```
// leaf.pth
// frame rx ry rz sx sy sz tx ty tz alpha
1 0 0 0 0.5 0.5 1 0 0 -500 1
60 180 0 0 0.5 0.5 1 0 0 0 1
```

B.10   Using the Scene File Maker Utility

As you may have noticed, the syntax of the scene file is rather involved. In order to reduce the amount of time required to produce a syntactically correct scene file, a scene file maker utility program is provided that will walk you through each step, and then create the appropriate scene file. In this section we describe how to use this utility. The scene file maker (SFM) utility is written in Visual Basic. The source code is supplied on the accompanying diskette in the directory x:\ict\sfm. The executable program is also supplied on the diskette. Other SFM setup considerations are covered in Appendix A.

Introduction

The idea behind SFM is that it provides a convenient means of setting up the initial scene file for a visual effect you are considering. The numerous file locator dialog boxes let you find the files that need to be associated together with a minimum of effort. There is no capability within SFM to position the models; that step must be performed with the scene preview option as described in the examples earlier in this appendix. The basic flow is to first define the desired overall characteristics of the effect, then define the characteristics of each model that appears in the effect.

The first SFM screen is shown in Figure B.11. The name of the scene file to be created is entered in the textbox on the right. The directory to which the completed scene file will be written is shown on the left side of the screen. The directory textbox is not editable by default in order to avoid accidental entry of the filename that is entered in the textbox at the right. To change the default scene file directory, click the **Change Directory** button. This step permits the directory textbox to be edited. Your change is saved when the **next** button is clicked. After you have entered the name of the

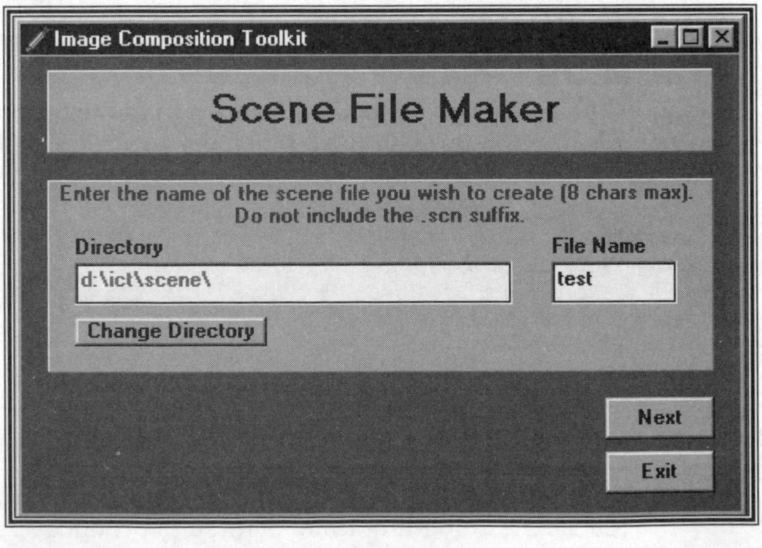

Figure B.11 Scene file maker utility.

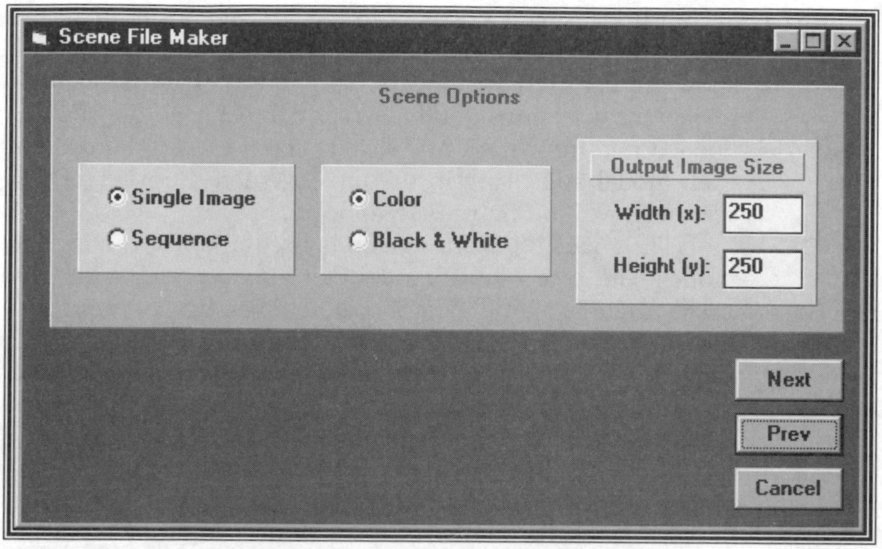

Figure B.12   Setting visual effect options.

scene file you wish to create in the textbox on the right side of the screen, click the **next** button. The screen shown in Figure B.12 appears. This screen is where the scene options are selected. Here you select whether the desired visual effect is a single (still) image or a sequence and whether the effect will be rendered in color or black and white. The size of the output image or images can also be selected. Having made the appropriate selections, press the **next** button. If you are creating a sequence, the screen shown in Figure B.13 appears, asking for the name of the motion file that describes how the viewpoint moves during the sequence. This motion file must be supplied,

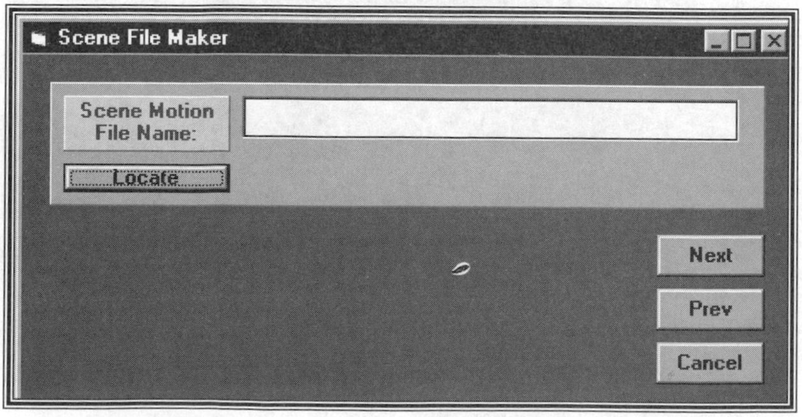

Figure B.13   Defining a moving viewpoint.

even if the viewpoint does not move during the sequence (this is explained further in Chapter 12). If you defined a single image effect, the screen shown in Figure B.14 appears. This screen essentially gives you a chance to review the selections you have made thus far before the output scene file is opened and information is saved. The next step is to define attributes for each model appearing in the effect. When the **next** button is clicked, the screen shown in Figure B.15 appears.

The **Model Options** screen is used to enter the name of an individual model. The type of the model can also be selected. If the model type is **Image**, the File Name locator will help you find an appropriate .bmp image file. If the model type is **Shape**, the File Name locator will help you locate a .shp file. In either case, each model must have an associated filename. The processing options panel located in the center of the screen is used to indicate whether a model of type image is to be warped and/or blended into the final scene. An opaqueness value may also be entered. This value will usually be equal to one. A value of one indicates total opaqueness; a value of 0.01 indicates the model is transparent. An opaqueness value of 0 will cause a matt to be created in the output image. Small negative opaqueness values are also allowed. See Chapter 10 for details. If the model is of type **image**, then the option to change the alpha image is available on the bottom of the screen. This option is not activated for models of type **shape**. The default alpha-image option assumes the model is a cutout image and that you wish to use the alpha-image created by ICT. If you wish to use an image other than the one created by ICT, then you may enter it using the file locator. When all of the appropriate selections have been made, click the **next** button. The screen shown in Figure B.16 appears. If you have defined an effect

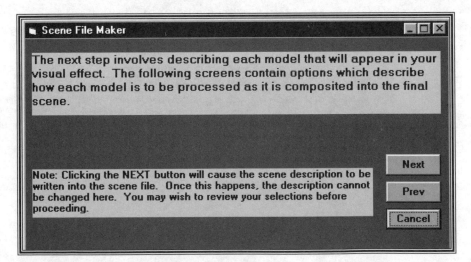

Figure B.14 Getting another chance.

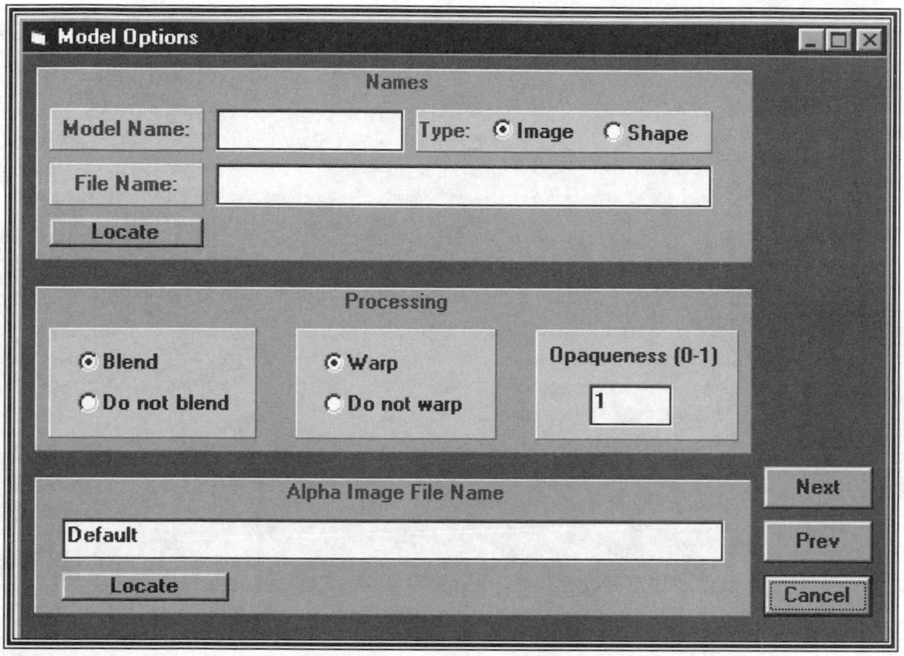

Figure B.15 Setting model options.

that is a sequence, then the option to associate a motion file with the current model is activated. If this particular model is moving in the sequence, use the file locator to find the appropriate motion path file. If the desired effect is a single image, the motion file option is not activated. You may review your selections by pressing the **prev** button. If all is in order, and you wish to enter more model information, press the **New Model** button and you will be returned to the model option screen (Figure B.15) to enter a new model.

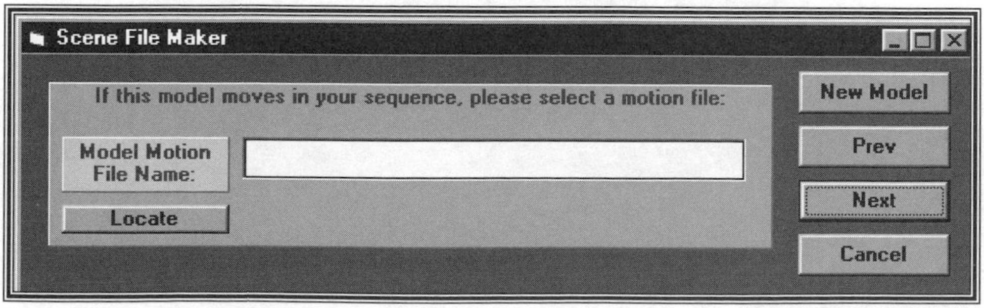

Figure B.16 Defining a moving model.

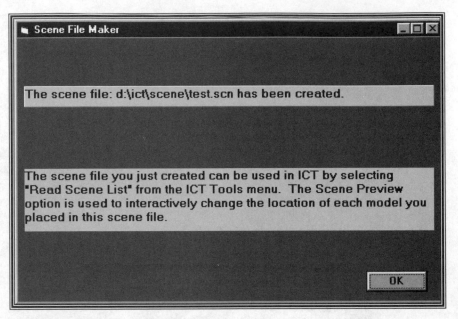

Figure B.17 Creating the scene file.

You can continue entering models in this way until all models have been entered. At this point you should be on the screen shown in Figure B.16. Press the **Next** button. The screen shown in Figure B.17 appears. At this point, the scene file created by SFM from the selections you have made is saved. The full pathname of the created scene file is displayed as well as an informative message indicating how the scene file can be used by ICT.

Visual C++ Notes

A version of the ICT compatible with Visual C++ version 2.1 or greater is available on the diskette accompanying this text. This version of ICT was tested on the Windows 95 final beta (M8). The porting strategy was to recreate the ICT starter application developed in Chapter 2 using the Visual C++ code generator. All of the ICT classes and functions which are independent of the graphical user interface (for example, memImage, warp, blend, scene generation) are essentially identical in both versions of ICT.

However, it was necessary to recreate all ICT menus and dialog boxes using the Visual C++ resource editor. It was also necessary to rewrite the **imageWindow** class to utilize MFC classes and the Document/View metaphor. The **ClientWindow** class has been replaced with a **mainFrame** window class which contains an application shell based on MFC instead of OWL. Because the Visual C++ 2.0 code generator automatically generates document/view classes, two MDI document templates were created manually and added to the code generated by Visual C++. The first MDI document template class is based on the MFC class **CEditView** which enables text files (scene file, ict log, motion files) to be opened and edited. A second MDI document template was created from the **imageView** and **imageDoc** classes previously mentioned. The **imageView** class is a descendant of the MFC class **CScrollView**. In order to be able to change the caption of image document windows in this version of ICT an additional step needed to be taken:

Setting Captions

Here is a tale of a seemingly minor porting task which turned into more than one would have expected. It turns out that MFC MDI child windows are not permitted by default to have changeable captions. Notice that the ICT interactive warp tool displays two windows, each with a customized caption ("Original Image", "Warped Image"). In order to permit these captions to be changed, the MFC **MDIChildWnd** class was overridden. The descendant class, called **ICTMDIChildWnd**, contains a member function named **PreCreateWindow** which sets a private base class data member in order to enable the caption to be modified. A second member function named **SetCaption** can be used to alter the new window's caption. In order to make use of this new **ICTMDIChildWnd** class, the creation of the image document template includes a reference to the **ICTMDIChildWnd** class. This procedure is described in more detail in Microsoft Product Support Services document number Q99182 available on any recent Developer Network CD-ROM.

The code for each dialog box class is found in separate files. This came about because the Visual C++ code generator places code for separate classes in separate files. Table C.1 shows the correspondence between source code files for the window classes found in each version of ICT. Table C.1 should enable you to relate the discussions in the book with the proper classes and files found in the Visual C++ version of ICT.

Table C.1   Correspondence Between Microsoft and Borland Compatible Versions of ICT

Borland Compatible ICT Class	*Visual C++ Compatible ICT Class and Source File Name*
imageWindow	imageDoc, imageView; imageDoc.cpp, imageVew.cpp
TEditFile	ictDoc, ictView; ictDoc.cpp,ictVew.cpp
ictMDIClient	mainFrame; mainfrm.cpp
nameDialog	CNameDialog; nameDlg.cpp
warpDialog	CWarpParamDlg; WarpParm.cpp
scenePreviewDialog	CScenePreviewDlg; scnPrevw.cpp

D

ICT Source Code Index

Appendix D lists each ICT function alphabetically as well as the source code file in which the function resides. If the function is a member function, the class to which the function belongs is provided.

CLASS	FUNCTION	FILE
imageWindow	~bmpWindow	imageWn.cpp
ictMDIChild	~ictMDIChild	ChildWn.cpp
ictMDIClient	~ictMDIClient	clientWn.cpp
memImage	~memImage	memImage.cpp
motionPath	~motionPath	motion.cpp
preference	~preference	ChildWn.cpp
renderObject	~renderObject	render.cpp
sceneElement	~sceneElement	model.cpp
sceneList	~sceneList	sceneLst.cpp
scenePreviewDialog	~scenePreviewDialog	ctdialog.cpp
shape3d	~shape3d	shape3d.cpp

CLASS	FUNCTION	FILE
tMatrix	~tMatrix	tMatrix.cpp
warpDialog	~warpDialog	ctdialog.cpp
sceneList	addScene	model.cpp
sceneList	addSceneElement	model.cpp
shape3d	addWorldVertex	shape3d.cpp
imageWindow	adjustScroller	imageWn.cpp
memImage	allocate	memImage.cpp
	appendFileName	sceneLst.cpp
shape3d	averageX	shape3d.cpp
shape3d	averageY	shape3d.cpp
	blend	blend.cpp
imageWindow	bmpWindow	imageWn.cpp
scenePreviewDialog	cancel	mydialog.cpp
ictMDIClient	ceCreateCutout	clientWn.cpp
ictMDIClient	cePreviewScene	clientWn.cpp
ictMDIClient	cePreviewSequence	clientWn.cpp
ictMDIClient	ceRenderScene	clientWn.cpp
ictMDIClient	ceRenderSequence	clientWn.cpp
scenePreviewDialog	chooseModel	mydialog.cpp
sceneList	clear	model.cpp
memImage	clear	memImage.cpp
motionNode	clear	motion.cpp
warpDialog	clickFinish	ctdialog.cpp
scenePreviewDialog	clickFinish	mydialog.cpp
memImage	close	memImage.cpp
imageWindow	cmFileOpen	imageWn.cpp
imageWindow	cmFileRead	imageWn.cpp
ictApp	CmHelpAbout	ictApp.cpp
memImage	copy	memImage.cpp
motionNode	copy	motion.cpp
	createCutout	blend.cpp
memImage	createMask	blend.cpp

CLASS	FUNCTION	FILE
	createMask	render.cpp
scenePreviewDialog	decrement	mydialog.cpp
shape3d	deleteLastWorldVertex	shape3d.cpp
sceneList	depthSort	depthsrt.cpp
sceneList	display	model.cpp
tMatrix	display	tMatrix.cpp
memImage	display2	memImage.cpp
memImage	drawMask	memImage.cpp
renderObject	drawSequence	render.cpp
renderObject	drawStill	render.cpp
ictMDIClient	evBuildSceneList	clientWn.cpp
ictMDIClient	evFileNew	clientWn.cpp
ictMDIClient	evFileOpen	clientWn.cpp
ictMDIClient	evHardware	clientWn.cpp
imageWindow	evLButtonDblClk	imageWn.cpp
imageWindow	evLButtonDown	imageWn.cpp
imageWindow	evLButtonUp	imageWn.cpp
ictMDIClient	evMakeAlpha	clientWn.cpp
ictMDIClient	evOpenImage	clientWn.cpp
ictMDIClient	evPreviewScene	clientWn.cpp
ictMDIClient	evPreviewSequence	clientWn.cpp
imageWindow	evRButtonDblClk	imageWn.cpp
imageWindow	evRButtonDown	imageWn.cpp
imageWindow	evRButtonUp	imageWn.cpp
ictMDIClient	evRenderScene	clientWn.cpp
ictMDIClient	evRenderSequence	clientWn.cpp
imageWindow	evSetFocus	imageWn.cpp
imageWindow	evPaletteChanged	imageWn.cpp
ictMDIClient	evWarpParams	clientWn.cpp
imageWindow	fileNew	imageWn.cpp
	fPolar	mydialog.cpp
sceneElement	fshowlist	model.cpp

CLASS	FUNCTION	FILE
memImage	getAccessMode	memImage.cpp
	getAlphaName	sceneLst.cpp
memImage	getBmp	memImage.cpp
memImage	getBytes	memImage.cpp
memImage	getColorSpec	memImage.cpp
sceneList	getCurrentModel-Transform	sceneLst.cpp
	getDistance	depthsrt.cpp
	getFileName	sceneLst.cpp
memImage	getHeight	memImage.cpp
	getIntervals	iwarp.cpp
shape3d	getLastWorldVertex	shape3d.cpp
	getLineEquation	iwarp.cpp
memImage	getMPixel(long, long)	memImage.cpp
memImage	getMPixel(long, long, char)	memImage.cpp
	getNextLine	shape3d.cpp
	getNextMotionDelim	motion.cpp
motionPath	getNode	motion.cpp
shape3d	getNumVertices	shape3d.cpp
preference	getPath	ChildWn.cpp
shape3d	getPreviousWorldVertex	shape3d.cpp
sceneList	getSceneInfo	sceneLst.cpp
sceneList	getSceneOutImageSize	sceneLst.cpp
	getShapePath	shape3d.cpp
renderObject	GetSizes	render.cpp
shape3d	getTCentroid	depthsrt.cpp
ictMDIClient	getViewMatrix	clientWn.cpp
sceneList	getViewPoint	sceneLst.cpp
shape3d	getWCentroid	shape3d.cpp
memImage	getWidth	memImage.cpp
ictMDIChild	ictMDIChild	ChildWn.cpp

CLASS	FUNCTION	FILE
ictMDIClient	ictMDIClient	clientWn.cpp
scenePreviewDialog	increment	mydialog.cpp
shape3d	initCurrentVertex	shape3d.cpp
ictApp	InitMainWindow	ictApp.cpp
	insertionSort	iwarp.cpp
	insertionSort(short, short[])	render.cpp
	insertionSort2	depthsrt.cpp
tMatrix	invertg	tMatrix.cpp
shape3d	invertY	shape3d.cpp
	iRender	iwarp.cpp
memImage	isValid	memImage.cpp
renderObject	isValid	render.cpp
shape3d	isValid	shape3d.cpp
scene	isValid	sceneLst.cpp
sceneElement	isValid	sceneLst.cpp
	iwarp	iwarp.cpp
sceneList	listLength	sceneLst.cpp
imageWindow	loadBitmapFile	imageWn.cpp
	makeRGBImage	memImage.cpp
	mapBitsPerPixelTo-ColorSpec	memImage.cpp
	mapColorSpecTo-BitsPerPixel	memImage.cpp
	matcopy	tMatrix.cpp
	matmult	tMatrix.cpp
memImage	memImage(char *, short, short, short, char, short)	memImage.cpp
memImage	memImage(memImage *)	memImage.cpp
memImage	memImage(short, short)	memImage.cpp
motionPath	motionPath	motion.cpp
tMatrix	multiply	tMatrix.cpp

CLASS	FUNCTION	FILE
nameDialog	nameDialog	ctDialog.cpp
ictMDIClient	OpenFile	clientWn.cpp
ictMDIClient	OpenImageFile	clientWn.cpp
shape3d	originalBoundingBox	shape3d.cpp
	OwlMain	ictApp.cpp
ictMDIClient	Paint	clientWn.cpp
imageWindow	Paint	imageWn.cpp
preference	preference	ChildWn.cpp
	prepareCutout	render.cpp
sceneList	previewSequence	sceneLst.cpp
sceneList	previewStill	sceneLst.cpp
shape3d	printShape	shape3d.cpp
motionNode	read	motion.cpp
motionPath	read	motion.cpp
memImage	readBMP	memImage.cpp
shape3d	readBMPFile	shape3d.cpp
memImage	readBMPHeader	memImage.cpp
sceneList	readList	sceneLst.cpp
memImage	readNextRow	memImage.cpp
shape3d	readShape	shape3d.cpp
	removeDuplicates	render.cpp
sceneList	render	sceneLst.cpp
renderObject	renderObject(point3d *, point3d *, point3d *, point3d *)	render.cpp
renderObject	renderObject(short, char *, short)	render.cpp
scenePreviewDialog	reset	mydialog.cpp
tMatrix	rotate	tMatrix.cpp
tMatrix	scale	tMatrix.cpp
scene	scene	model.cpp
sceneElement	sceneElement	model.cpp

CLASS	FUNCTION	FILE
sceneList	sceneList	sceneLst.cpp
scenePreviewDialog	scenePreviewDialog	ctdialog.cpp
shape3d	screenBoundingBox	shape3d.cpp
imageWindow	setCaption	imageWn.cpp
sceneList	setCurrentModel	sceneLst.cpp
sceneList	setCurrentModel-Transform	sceneLst.cpp
tMatrix	setIdentity	tMatrix.cpp
memImage	setMPixel	memImage.cpp
shape3d	setNumVertices	shape3d.cpp
	setPalette	render.cpp
preference	setPath	ChildWn.cpp
scenePreviewDialog	setTextBoxesWith-ModelTransform	mydialog.cpp
scenePreviewDialog	setTextBoxesWith-ViewTransform	mydialog.cpp
ictMDIClient	SetupWindow	clientWn.cpp
warpDialog	SetupWindow	ctdialog.cpp
scenePreviewDialog	SetupWindow	ctdialog.cpp
sceneList	setViewPoint	sceneLst.cpp
scenePreviewDialog	setViewPoint	mydialog.cpp
shape3d	shape3d(char *)	shape3d.cpp
shape3d	shape3d(int)	shape3d.cpp
shape3d	shape3d(point3d *, point3d *, point3d *, point3d *)	shape3d.cpp
shape3d	shape3d(shape3d *)	shape3d.cpp
shape3d	shape3d(short *, char *, short)	shape3d.cpp
sceneList	showModels	sceneLst.cpp
memImage	smoothX3NN	memImage.cpp
memImage	smoothY3NN	memImage.cpp
	StatusPrint	ictApp.cpp

CLASS	FUNCTION	FILE
	Stripes	clientWn.cpp
tMatrix	tMatrix()	tMatrix.cpp
tMatrix	tMatrix(tMatrix *)	tMatrix.cpp
shape3d	transformAndProject	shape3d.cpp
shape3d	transformBoundingBox	shape3d.cpp
tMatrix	transformPoint	tMatrix.cpp
tMatrix	translate	tMatrix.cpp
shape3d	translateS	shape3d.cpp
shape3d	translateT	shape3d.cpp
shape3d	translateW	shape3d.cpp
tMatrix	transpose	tMatrix.cpp
memImage	unPack	blend.cpp
imageWindow	updatePalette	imageWn.cpp
warpDialog	warpDialog	ctdialog.cpp
ictMDIClient	warpImage	clientWn.cpp
memImage	writeBMP	memImage.cpp
sceneElement	writeFile	model.cpp
scene	writeFile	model.cpp
sceneList	writeList	sceneLst.cpp
memImage	writeNextRow	memImage.cpp
shape3d	writeShape	shape3d.cpp

E

Glossary

aliasing.   Simply stated, aliasing occurs in many forms and is a common artifact of image processing that introduces a blocky or stairstepped appearance into the processed image.

anti-aliasing.   An approach used to combat a form of aliasing.

binary image.   An image whose pixels are allowed to have only two values. Some definitions require that these two values be zero and one.

CASE Tool.   Computer Aided Software Engineering. A tool that helps document the requirements in terms of a process model, data model, or both.

color plane, color channel, component color.   A component color is one of the component colors that make up a true color; thus, there are only three component colors: red, green, and blue. A true color image can be said to consist of three component images: red, green, and blue. The terms *color channel* and *color plane* are synonymous with the term *component image*.

coordinate.   A location in a coordinate system indicated by stating a distance from the origin to that location along each axis in coordinate system.

data member.   A variable associated with a C++ class definition. An object's properties are instances of the corresponding C++ class data members.

image.   A digitized photograph consisting of a rectangular array of pixels.

interpolation.   Calculation of an intermediate quantity based on a known proportion. (Described further in section 12.2.)

location.   Shorthand for the set of three translations: tx, ty, tz. A location is also a coordinate, since every coordinate is in fact a set of translations from the origin.

MDI.   Multi-Document Interface. A style of Windows interface in which one or more MDI child windows can be managed simultaneously within the visual area of an MDI parent window.

MDI client window.   Although technically not the same as the MDI parent window, it can be thought of as referring to the MDI parent window.

member function.   A function associated with a C++ class definition. A member function acts on the object with which it is associated.

monochrome.   Technically, the term means "single color." Any of the color channels in a true color image are actually monochrome images.

orientation.   Shorthand for the set of three rotation angles: rx, ry, rz.

origin.   The location in the coordinate system where all the axes intersect. By definition, the location (0,0,0).

pixel.   A picture element. A 1-byte quantity (8 bits) indicating the intensity of an image at a certain location.

point.   See *coordinate* or *vertex*.

scan line.   A horizontal row of pixels in an image

special effect.   A reference to the wide range of effects produced for the movie and television industries.

true color.   A representation of color in which each color value consists of a set of three component values. Each component value represents the amount of red, green, and blue color present in the true color value. True color is implemented in many computer systems as a 24-bit value with 8 bits allocated for each component color.

vertex.   A 2D or 3D coordinate.

viewpoint.   A location and orientation from which a scene is viewed.

visual effect.   In this text, any output of the software program ICT.

world coordinate system.   Synonymous with the right-handed Cartesian coordinate system. A world coordinate always has three dimensions.

A P P E N D I X F

References

[BOOC91] G. Booch, *Object-Oriented Design with Applications*, Redwood City, CA, Benjamin/Cummings, 1991.

[CATM80] E. Catmull and A. R. Smith, "3-D Transformations of Images in Scanline Order," *SIGGRAPH* 80, 279–285.

[COAD90] P. Coad and E. Yourdon, *Object-Oriented Analysis*, Englewood Cliffs, NJ, Prentice-Hall, 1990.

[FOLE90] J. Foley, A. vanDam, S. Feiner, and J. Hughes, *Computer Graphics, Principles and Applications*, second edition, Reading, MA, Addison-Wesley, 1990.

[HEAR86] D. Hearn and M. P. Baker, *Computer Graphics*, Englewood Cliffs, NJ, Prentice-Hall, 1986.

[HOFF92] J. D. Hoffman, *Numerical Methods for Scientists and Engineers*, Berkeley, CA, McGraw-Hill, 1992.

[PETZ92] C. Petzold, *Programming Windows 3.1*, third edition, Redmond, WA, Microsoft Press, 1992.

[PORT84] T. Porter, and T. Duff, "Compositing Digital Images," *SIGGRAPH* 84, 253–259.

[PRES92] W. H. Press, S. A. Teukolsky, W. T. Vetterling, and B. P. Flannery, *Numerical Recipes in C: The Art of Scientific Computing*, second edition, New York, NY, Cambridge University Press, 1992.

[SEDG84] R. Sedgewick, *Algorithms*, Reading, MA, Addison-Wesley, 1984.

[SHAW84] M. Shaw, "Abstraction Techniques in Modern Programming Languages," *IEEE Software*, October 1984, vol. 1(4), p. 10.

[WOLB94] G. Wolberg, *Digital Image Warping*, Los Alamitos, CA, IEEE Computer Society Press, 1994.

I N D E X